VALLEY QUEST
DISCOVER OUR SPECIAL PLACES

89 Treasure Hunts in the Upper Valley

A project of:

VITAL COMMUNITIES
104 Railroad Row
White River Junction, VT 05001
Phone: (802) 291-9100
E-mail: info@vitalcommunities.org
Website: www.vitalcommunities.org

Second printing, July 2002
Published by Vital Communities, White River Junction, VT 05001
©2001 by Vital Communities
All rights reserved.
This book, or parts thereof, may not be reproduced in any form without permission from the publisher.

Printed in Canada

Stamp art, maps, map and stampbook extracts by Valley Quest children, parents, and teachers
Regional map design by Geographic Data Technology, Inc.
Photo on page iii courtesy of Peter Stettenheim
Photos on page 25 courtesy of the Fairlee Historical Society
Book design and illustration by Suzanne Church / Blue Door Communications

While students, teachers, land owners, the editor, and the publisher have tried to make the information presented in this book as accurate as possible, they accept no responsibility for loss, injury, or inconvenience sustained by any person using this book.

VALLEY QUEST is a trade name of Vital Communities and Antioch New England Institute.

VITAL COMMUNITIES works to engage citizens in community life and to foster the long-term balance of cultural, economic, environmental and social well being in our region. For more information, please contact Vital Communities at: (802) 291-9100.

VITAL COMMUNITIES STAFF:
Leonard Cadwallader, Executive Director
Steven Glazer, Valley Quest / Development Coordinator
Lisa Johnson, Valley VitalSigns Coordinator
Beckley Wooster, Office Manager

VITAL COMMUNITIES BOARD OF DIRECTORS:
Alexander Daniell, Charlotte Faulkner, Eugenia Hamilton, Peter Mallary, Norm Marshall, Jane Kitchel McLaughlin, Walter Paine, Betty Porter, Sylvia Provost, Bruce Schwaegler, Anne Silberfarb, Stuart V. Smith, Jr., Peter Stein, and Frederic Thomas

ISBN 0-9708460-0-2

Dedicated to the life and memory of
Linny Levin
1951–2000
Who taught and shared
The magic and wildness
Of this special place.

CONTENTS

xi   Introduction to Questing
xiii   Valley Quest Code
xiv   Regional Maps

THE QUESTS

Quests are arranged alphabetically by town name; also included here are brief descriptions, and an estimation of how long it takes to complete the Quest.

BELLOWS FALLS, VERMONT

1   **1 /** Bellows Falls History Quest, created by the Compass School's 7th and 8th grade. *Explores the rich history of Bellows Falls.* (1 hour)

CORNISH, NEW HAMPSHIRE

4   **2 /** Blacksmith Covered Bridge Quest, created by the Cornish Elementary School Valley Quest Exploratory. *Discover this historic bridge, built by James F. Tasker in the nineteenth century.* (20 minutes)

6   **3 /** Blow Me Down Mill Quest, created by Linda Fuerst's 4th grade. *View an historic mill near Saint Gaudens National Monument.* (20 minutes)

8   **4 /** Trinity Church Quest, created by Ros Siedel's 4th grade. *Visit the gracious old Trinity Church—and the graves of many of Cornish's first settlers.* (15 minutes)

10   **5 /** Jonathan Wyman Sawmill Quest, created by the Cornish Elementary School Valley Quest Exploratory. *A journey through Cornish history, including an old stone bridge and mill site.* (20 minutes)

CROYDON, NEW HAMPSHIRE

12   **6 /** Croydon Schoolhouse Quest, created by Judy Hatch's 1st–3rd grade. *A fun walk around Croydon's one-room schoolhouse.* (10 minutes)

14   **7 /** Croydon's Past Quest, created by Judy Hatch's 1st–3rd grade. *Stroll up an old logging road with foundations and artifacts from Croydon's early history.* (1.5 hours). Bring a mountain bike if you prefer.

16   **8 /** Four Corners Cemetery Quest, created by Judy Hatch's 1st–3rd grade. *Find an unusual gravestone in a peaceful setting with towering trees.* (15 minutes)

ENFIELD, NEW HAMPSHIRE

18   9 / Enfield Rail Trail Quest, created by the homeschooling family of Dale Shields, John Auble, and their kids Cecilia, Nathan, and Devin. *An easy hike or bike along the rail trail in Enfield to the banks of Lake Mascoma.* (1.5 hours)

20   10 / Shaker Village Ceremonial Site Quest, created by Mary Ellen Burrit's Girl Scout troop. *Travel up a wooded lane to discover an unusual Shaker ceremonial site from the 1800s.* (45 minutes)

FAIRLEE, VERMONT

22   11 / Fairlee Depot Quest, created by Rebecca Bailey's 3rd and 4th grade. *Examines this historic structure, and the transportation history of Fairlee.* (20 minutes)

24   12 / Fairlee Glen Falls Quest, created by Linny Levin's 5th and 6th grade. *This short ramble leads from Lake Morey up to a beautiful waterfall.* (30 minutes)

26   13 / Miraculous Tree Quest, created by Ted Levin and Steven Glazer. *Discover the trees of the northern forest—and meet a surprising survivor.* (45 minutes) Please bring a measuring tape!

28   14 / Palisades Quest, created by Joyce Berube's Girl Scout troop. *A steep, uphill hike, towards an ancestral nesting site for peregrine falcons— and a great view.* (1 hour)

GRAFTON, VERMONT

30   15 / Grafton Ponds Quest, created by students at the Compass School. *This Quest along Grafton trails can be walked, biked, or skied.* (time varies)

33   16 / Grafton Town—The Cave Quest, created by Nate Hutchins and Kyle Haseltine. *Meanders through beautiful Grafton village and into a lovely town park.* (1 hour)

GRANTHAM, NEW HAMPSHIRE

36   17 / Dunbar Hill Cemetery Quest, created by Nan Parsons' 4th and 5th grade. *A walk through the village up to an old cemetery.* (1.25 hours)

HANOVER, NEW HAMPSHIRE

38   18 / Amphitheater Quest, created by Lynn Ujlaky's 2nd and 4th grade reading buddies. *Moves from the bustle of the Dartmouth green to a place of quiet beauty.* (20 minutes)

40   19 / Balch Hill Quest, created by Cathy MacDonald and Pam Graham's Girl Scout troop. *A delightful hike up hill to grand old trees and a view.* (1 hour)

42   20 / Libraries of Hanover Quest, created as part of the Howe Library Centennial Celebration. *Explores the history of Hanover's libraries—and mysterious moving buildings!* (45 minutes)

44   21 / Mink Brook Quest, created by Ginger Wallis and Linny Levin with Jay Davis. *A naturalists' exploration of one of Hanover's most beautiful places.* (1 hour)

HANOVER, NEW HAMPSHIRE, CONTINUED

46   22 / Moose Mountain Quest, created by Marjorie Rose and Betsy Davis' Hanover Brownie troop. *Big hike up to a big view.* (2+ hours)

48   23 / Velvet Rocks Quest, created by Mitsu Chobanian's Girl Scout troop. *An uphill climb through a forest over mossy rocks.* (1.5 hours)

HARTFORD, VERMONT

50   24 / Hartford Historical Museum Quest, created by Pat Stark. *An indoor journey through the historical society collection.* (1.75 hours.) Please note: This Quest can only be completed when the historical society is open, the first Tuesday of any month, from 6:00 to 8:00 p.m., or the first Sunday of any month, 1:30 to 4:00 p.m., or by appointment.

53   25 / Hartford Recycling Quest, created by Victoria Davis. *Come and see the most fascinating recycling center on Earth!* (30 minutes.) Please note: This Quest can only be completed when the recycling center is open, Monday through Saturday from 8:00 a.m. to 4:00 p.m.

HARTLAND, VERMONT

56   26 / Hartland Three Corners Quest *Stroll through Hartland Three Corners, to seek its mysteries and learn some history.* (45 minutes)

LEBANON, NEW HAMPSHIRE

58   27 / Colburn Park Quest, created by Jill Janas and Marilyn Mock's 5th grade. *A winding walk around downtown Lebanon.* (45 minutes.) Please note: this Quest box is only accessible weekdays from 9:00 a.m. to 4:00 p.m.

60   28 / Runnemede School Quest, created by the Runnemede School. *An architectural walking tour of Lebanon.* (45 minutes)

LYME, NEW HAMPSHIRE

62   29 / Pinnacle Hill Quest, created by Lynn Bischoff's 4th grade. *Climb up logging roads to a ridge with views overlooking the Connecticut River Valley.* (1 hour)

64   30 / Lyme Sheep Quest, created by Steven Dayno's and Sara Goodman's 4th grade classes. *A great hike from an old orchard and tavern to an abandoned hill farm.* (1 hour)

NEWBURY, NEW HAMPSHIRE

66   31 / Hay Refuge Quest, created by Maggie Stier and Loa Winter. *A walk along historic, cultivated gardens and woodlands to a house built by John Hay.* (45 minutes)

NEW LONDON, NEW HAMPSHIRE

68   32 / Sargent/Hayes Farm Quest, created by Meredith Bird Miller. *Dedicated to the spirit of Linny Levin, this Quest explores scenic Great Brook.* (1.25 hours)

71   33 / Wolf Tree Quest, created by Meredith Bird Miller. *A steep climb to a historic homestead and lovely orchard.* (1.25 hours)

NORWICH, VERMONT

74 34 / The Elm Street Loop Quest, created by T. J. Grossman, Ryan McCabe, and Elaine Warshell. *A 1.5 mile walk along paved roads with views, waterfalls, and a lot of history.* (45 minutes)

76 35 / Gile Mountain Hawk and Haiku Quest, created by Steven Glazer and Ginger Wallis. *Climb up to views of seasonal hawk migration.* (1.5 hours)

78 36 / Grand Canyon of Norwich Quest, created by Ginger Wallis and Linny Levin. *This beautiful hike focuses on learning to "read" the forest.* (45 minutes)

80 37 / Montshire Quest, created Amy Vanderkooi. *Wander the scenic grounds of Norwich's Montshire Museum of Science.* (30 minutes)

ORFORD, NEW HAMPSHIRE

82 38 / Boat Landing Quest, created by Sue Kling's 2nd grade. *Meander to a scenic spot down by the river.* (25 minutes)

84 39 / Orford Brick Quest, created by Gary Barton's 4th grade students. *This walk through Orford focuses on town and architectural history.* (30 minutes)

86 40 / Flat Rock Quest, created by Sue Kling's 2nd grade. *Welcome to a favorite swimming hole and fishing spot. Bring a pole—or swimsuit.* (15 minutes)

88 41 / Indian Pond Quest, created by Sue Kling's 2nd grade. *A short walk along the edge of a remote pond. Bring binoculars, canoe, or swimsuit!* (15 minutes)

PLAINFIELD, NEW HAMPSHIRE

90 42 / French's Ledges Quest, created by Betsy Rybeck Lynd's 2nd grade class. *A panoramic view awaits you after an uphill journey through the northern forest.* (1 hour)

92 43 / Plainfield Village Quest, created by Mindy (Longacre) Taber's 3rd grade class. *A historic walking tour of Plainfield Village.* (45 minutes)

QUECHEE, VERMONT

94 44 / Old Quechee Cemetery Quest, created by Amy Kinder's 5th grade. *This village walk ends at a neat old cemetery.* (30 minutes)

96 45 / Ottauquechee Quest, created by Sarah Rhoades and Ellen Bantin's 5th grade class. *Explores the interesting details of another local cemetery.* (45 minutes)

98 46 / Quechee Gorge Quest, created by Cathie Ely's 5th grade. *Hike off the beaten path into a deep ravine.* (50 minutes)

100 47 / Quechee Library Quest, created by Amy Kinder's 5th grade. *Stroll through the historic village of Quechee.* (20 minutes)

102 48 / Simon Pearce Waterfall Quest, created by Amy Kinder's 5th grade. *This casual walk features an impressive waterfall.* (30 minutes)

ROCKINGHAM, VERMONT

104   **49** / Rockingham Meeting House Quest, created by the Compass School 7th and 8th grade. *Have fun while exploring a lovely and historic setting.* (25 minutes)

SPRINGFIELD, NEW HAMPSHIRE

106   **50** / Kidder Brook Quest, created by Philip Major's class at Kearsarge Regional Elementary School. *A fabulous hike incorporating ancient and modern water-use structures.* (1.75 hours)

108   **51** / McDaniel's Marsh Quest, created by Steve Pruyne. *A pristine wilderness area—rich with plants and animals. Bring a canoe and binoculars for further exploration.* (15 minutes)

SPRINGFIELD, VERMONT

110   **52** / North Springfield Bog Quest, created by Marita Johnson's 7th grade. *A unique wetland environment with a boardwalk. Save time to explore the bog!* (20 minutes)

112   **53** / Springweather Quest A, created by students of Marita Johnson and Mike Frank. *This woodland walk leads to a fine spot for viewing great blue herons.* (40 minutes)

114   **54** / Springweather Quest B, created by students of Marita Johnson and Mike Frank. *Travel through mixed forest to an excellent view.* (40 minutes)

SUNAPEE, NEW HAMPSHIRE

116   **55** / Sunapee Harbor Quest, created by Meredith Bird Miller. *A gentle stroll around Sunapee Harbor with historic and natural features.* (20 minutes)

THETFORD, VERMONT

118   **56** / Houghton Hill Quest, created by Linny Levin and Ginger Wallis with Jay Davis. *A close look at the natural history of a scenic hilltop—with views of two states.* (45 minutes)

121   **57** / Lonesome Pine Quest, created by Bill Shepard. *A country walk to a scenic wetland—and premiere birding site.* (45 minutes)

124   **58** / Moving Houses Quest, created by Joe Deffner's 7th grade. *This Quest explores the "hidden past" on Thetford Hill.* (15 minutes)

126   **59** / Peabody Library Quest, created by the children of the After School Program. *Explore the details of an historic, one-room library in Post Mills.* (15 minutes.) Please note: the Peabody Library is only open Tuesdays from 5:00 to 8:00 p.m. and Wednesdays from 2:00 to 8:00 p.m.

128   **60** / Thetford Canoe Quest, created by Kristin Brown and Stuart Close. *A 1.5-mile-long canoe trip on the Connecticut River.* (1.5 hours)

130   **61** / Union Village Quest, created by Bill Shepard. *A naturalist reveals a hidden jewel in Union Village.* (25 minutes)

VERSHIRE, VERMONT

132   **62** / Copperfield Town Quest, created by Barbara Griffin's 2nd and 3rd grade. *Discover an abandoned town site—once home to over one thousand people.* (45 minutes)

134   **63** / Vershire Village Quest, created by Becky French's 5th grade. *Starts in the village center and ends with a steep climb to a nice view.* (1 hour)

WALPOLE, NEW HAMPSHIRE

136   **64** / Fall Mountain Quest, created by students at the Compass School. *Ascend Fall Mountain to spectacular views.* (1.5 hours)

WARREN, NEW HAMPSHIRE

138   **65** / The Moosilauke Historical Quest, created by Sue Kirincich and Chuck Wooster. *A story of the human and forest history related to Moosilauke.* (1 hour)

WEATHERSFIELD, VERMONT

146   **66** / Crystal Cascade Quest, created by Wendy Smith. *Hike up Mt. Ascutney to the second highest waterfall in Vermont.* (2 hours)

WEST FAIRLEE, VERMONT

148   **67** / Linny's Loop Bicycle Quest, created by Steven Glazer and Ted Levin. *A 9-mile bicycle loop circuiting the scenic Middle Brook and Blood Brook valleys.* (2 hours)

WEST LEBANON, NEW HAMPSHIRE

150   **68** / Boston Lot Quest, created by Phyllis Wolford's 5th grade. *Ascend an old logging road to a beautiful upland lake.* (45 minutes)

152   **69** / Dana House Quest, created by Rickey Poor's 1st grade. *This historic site in West Lebanon dates to the mid-1700s.* (15 minutes)

WHEREVER YOU WISH, VERMONT OR NEW HAMPSHIRE

154   **70** / The Fall Cider Quest, created by YOU. *Find the wild apples in your neighborhood—and make cider.* (All day)

WHITE RIVER JUNCTION, VERMONT

156   **71** / By the Numbers Quest, created by Steven Glazer, Byron Hathorn, and David Briggs. *This walk around the downtown focuses on buildings.* (20 minutes)

158   **72** / The Junction Quest, created by Linny Levin, Sue Kirincich, and Marty Layman-Mendonca. *A historic walk through town and along the river bank.* (30 minutes)

160   **73** / Lyman Point Quest, created by Linny Levin and Sue Kirincich. *Explores the confluence of the White and Connecticut rivers.* (25 minutes)

WINDSOR, VERMONT

162   74 / Constitution House Quest, created by Karen Hull's 4th grade. *Features historic Windsor and the Runnemede Pond.* (1 hour)

164   75 / Historic Windsor Quest, created by Tim Ives' 4th grade. *Discover Windsor's industrial past—and a very special bridge.* (1.25 hours)

166   76 / North Main Street Quest, created by Linda Parker's 4th grade. *A stroll through Windsor's downtown.* (1 hour)

168   77 / Paradise Park Quest, created by Barbara Rhoad. *A walk along wooded trails to a scenic pond.* (1 hour)

WOODSTOCK, VERMONT

170   78 / Woodstock CWM Quest, created by John Souter's 4th grade. *A cultural and historical exploration of the town center.* (30 minutes)

172   79 / The George, Frederick, & Laurance Quest, created by Woodstock Elementary School 4th grade. *Examine some of the details of scenic Woodstock.* (45 minutes)

174   80 / GPM Quest, created by John Souter's 4th grade. *Quest through Woodstock's business district and residential area.* (25 minutes)

176   81 / Mount Tom Quest, created by Steve Pruyne and Jamie MacDonald. *A gradual hike to the summit of Mount Tom where the quest begins.* (1 hour)

178   82 / Room with a View Quest, created by Ms. Bahlenhorst's 4th grade. *A naturalist's dream—bring along a field guide!* (1 hour)

180   83 / RSC Quest, created by John Souter's 4th grade. *Stroll through a peaceful area of Woodstock.* (25 minutes)

182   84 / Village Green Quest A, created by John Souter's and Kathy Sehnal's 4th grades. *A pleasant walk in a residential area of Woodstock.* (40 minutes)

184   85 / Village Green Quest B, created by John Souter's and Shirley Burrough's 4th grades. *A historical journey along Woodstock sidewalks and paths.* (30 minutes)

186   86 / Village Green Quest C, created by John Souter's 4th and Richard Burrough's 6th grades. *A walk through the Village, with views of the Ottauquechee River.* (30 minutes)

188   87 / Village Green Quest D, created by John Souter's 4th and Cindy Siegler's 3rd grades. *A gentle stroll through Woodstock's historic business district.* (40 minutes)

190   88 / Village Green Quest E, created by John Souter's 4th and Jill Holran's 3rd grades. *An exploration of one of Woodstock's historic manufacturing sites.* (40 minutes)

192   89 / Vermont Institute of Natural Science Quest, created by 1997 Student Naturalist Program. *Wander through the woods of a wildlife refuge.* (50 minutes)

194   Quest Directory
197   How to Make a Quest
199   New Quest Submission Form
200   Acknowledgments

INTRODUCTION TO QUESTING

WHAT IS IT?

Valley Quest is a series of eighty-nine treasure hunts stretching across thirty-one towns in the Connecticut River Valley of Vermont and New Hampshire. Quests, making use of hand-drawn maps and riddle-like clues, lead to hidden special places, such as remote lakes, old cellar holes, favorite trees, and forgotten cemeteries. Quests are exciting adventures that gently share and teach the natural and cultural history of the region. They are the perfect way to spend a day with family or friends.

OLD ROOTS

Valley Quest was born out of a 150-year-old tradition in the region surrounding Dartmoor National Park in southwest England. Antioch New England Graduate School faculty member David Sobel observed this tradition while on a sabbatical. In this region of England, people—from toddlers and teens to parents and pensioners—don their Wellington boots, and following maps and rhyming riddles, traipse the moors in search of hidden boxes. "Letterboxing," as this tradition is called, has become a hugely popular pastime, with thousands of boxes hidden in both natural and cultural locations. This tradition helps connect people to their ancestry and heritage as well as providing a fun reason to go out for a walk!

NEW LEAVES

Vital Communities built upon this tradition on this side of the Atlantic by developing the Valley Quest program. Our eighty-nine treasure hunts, or Quests as we prefer to call them, are the outcomes of an educational program whose goal is to foster place-based education and stewardship. The Quests contained in this book were created between 1996 and 2000. More than 1,000 children, adults, families, scouts, students, and historical society members contributed to the creation of these Quests and this book. Out Questing, you will help to celebrate and strengthen community life—and forge lifelong connections to the landscape and culture of our region.

HOW TO QUEST

Look through the table of contents, flip through the book, or review the Quest directory in the back of the book. Find the Quest that excites you most. Note that in many cases, several Quests are clustered in the same town—so go on a few! Then use the regional maps (located up front) and the location directions (located on the Quest page) to find your Quest's starting point. Note that every Quest has a number, and each number matches with a star on one of the regional maps. Once you have found your starting point, use the Quest map, clues, and your own intuition to solve the Quest.

TREASURE BOXES

Each Quest ends with a treasure box, hidden out of view somewhere at the Quest site. Treasure boxes are never buried, so you will not have to dig underground to find them. You may have to look in a secluded cranny, or see through a clever disguise, however. Inside the treasure box, you will discover information about the site, a rubber stamp, a sign-in field journal, and a pencil. Sign your name in the book, adding a few notes or a sketch from your walk, and collect an impression of the stamp as a momento of your journey. Then, carefully re-hide the box exactly where you found it. Remember to save time to explore the Quest site!

PASSPORT BOOKS AND STAMPS

If you plan to go on more than one Quest, you will probably want to create your own "passport book" or field journal into which you can imprint the stamp collected at each treasure box. Or you may choose to record the stamps on the blank page at the back of this book. You may also want to create or buy your own personal stamp so that you can leave your mark in each Quest's log book, along with your name. This book is filled with the imprints of stamps left by children and adults in our treasure boxes. It's fun to see the stamps and read the notes left by other Questers.

VALLEY QUEST PATCH

When you have solved twenty or more Quests, you can send in a copy of the stamp imprints you've collected to Valley Quest at Vital Communities, 104 Railroad Row, White River Junction, VT 05001. We will send you a Valley Quest certificate and a beautiful embroidered Valley Quest patch, which shows our valleys and hills covered in bright autumn foliage.

BOX MONITORS

Each Quest treasure box is checked on a regular basis during the Questing season by a local volunteer box monitor. These generous and fun-loving people help keep the Valley Quest program alive and running smoothly. If you have a problem with a Quest box, please contact the Valley Quest office at 802-291-9100 or info@vitalcommunities.org and we'll pass the word along to the appropriate monitor. If you are interested in being a box monitor for a Quest in your town, please let us know!

PROBLEMS OR QUESTIONS

If you have any trouble finding the site or the box, or have any news to report to us, please contact the Valley Quest office at 802-291-9100, or e-mail us at info@vitalcommunities.org or check our website at www.vitalcommunities.org for the latest changes/information.

WHAT TO BRING

Just like any outdoor activity, be prepared for changes in the weather! It is also important to bring a good map—the DeLorme Atlas and Gazetteers for Vermont and New Hampshire are fine. Also bring a compass, a water bottle, snacks, and wear comfortable shoes. It is always a good idea to carry a first aid kit if you will be out in the woods. And do consider bringing along a field guide to local plants and animals, binoculars, a hand lens for magnification—as well as your passport book/field journal and personal stamp.

NEW QUESTS

If you would like to make a Quest in your community, please refer to the information about making Quests located at the back of this book. Or call us, and we'll help you get started! When we have enough new Quests, we'll publish Volume II!

VALLEY QUEST CODE

1. Allow yourself plenty of time.
2. Be prepared for weather.
3. Keep to established paths.
4. Avoid damaging fences and stone walls.
5. Do not disturb or remove cultural or historical artifacts.
6. There's no need to dig—none of our Quest boxes are buried underground.
7. Respect the "treasure" box as the private property of the host group.
8. Don't reveal the location of the hidden boxes.
9. Re-hide the box carefully where you found it.
10. Keep pets under control.
11. Observe wildlife from a distance.
12. Please do not feed wild animals.
13. Don't litter—pack it in and pack it out!
14. No fires.
15. Carry sufficient drinking water.
16. Respect wildlife, plants, and trees.
17. Be especially careful in wet areas, on steeper slopes, and in sensitive wildlife habitat.
18. Keep eyes, ears, and heart wide open.
19. Look and listen and learn from the world.
20. Always follow the Valley Quest Code. Don't risk getting lost. Have a good map and compass whenever you go into an unfamiliar area—as well as a field guide and first aid kit. Be respectful of other beings and the land, and have a wonderful time Questing!

REGIONAL MAPS

xv	Vital Communities Region
xvi	Vermont Northern Region detail
xvii	New Hampshire Northern Region detail
xviii	Vermont Central Region detail
xix	New Hampshire Central Region detail
xx	Vermont Southern Region detail
xxi	New Hampshire Southern Region detail

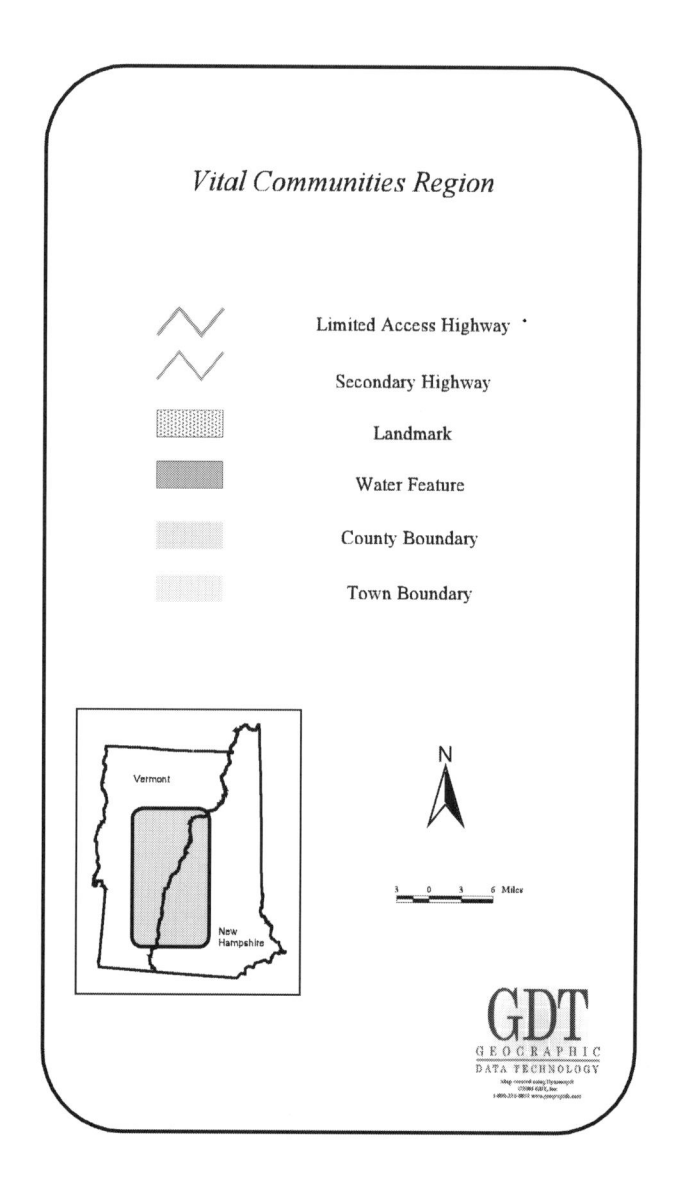

Vital Communities Region

Limited Access Highway
Secondary Highway
Landmark
Water Feature
County Boundary
Town Boundary

Vermont
New Hampshire

N

3 0 3 6 Miles

GDT
GEOGRAPHIC
DATA TECHNOLOGY

VITAL COMMUNITIES REGION

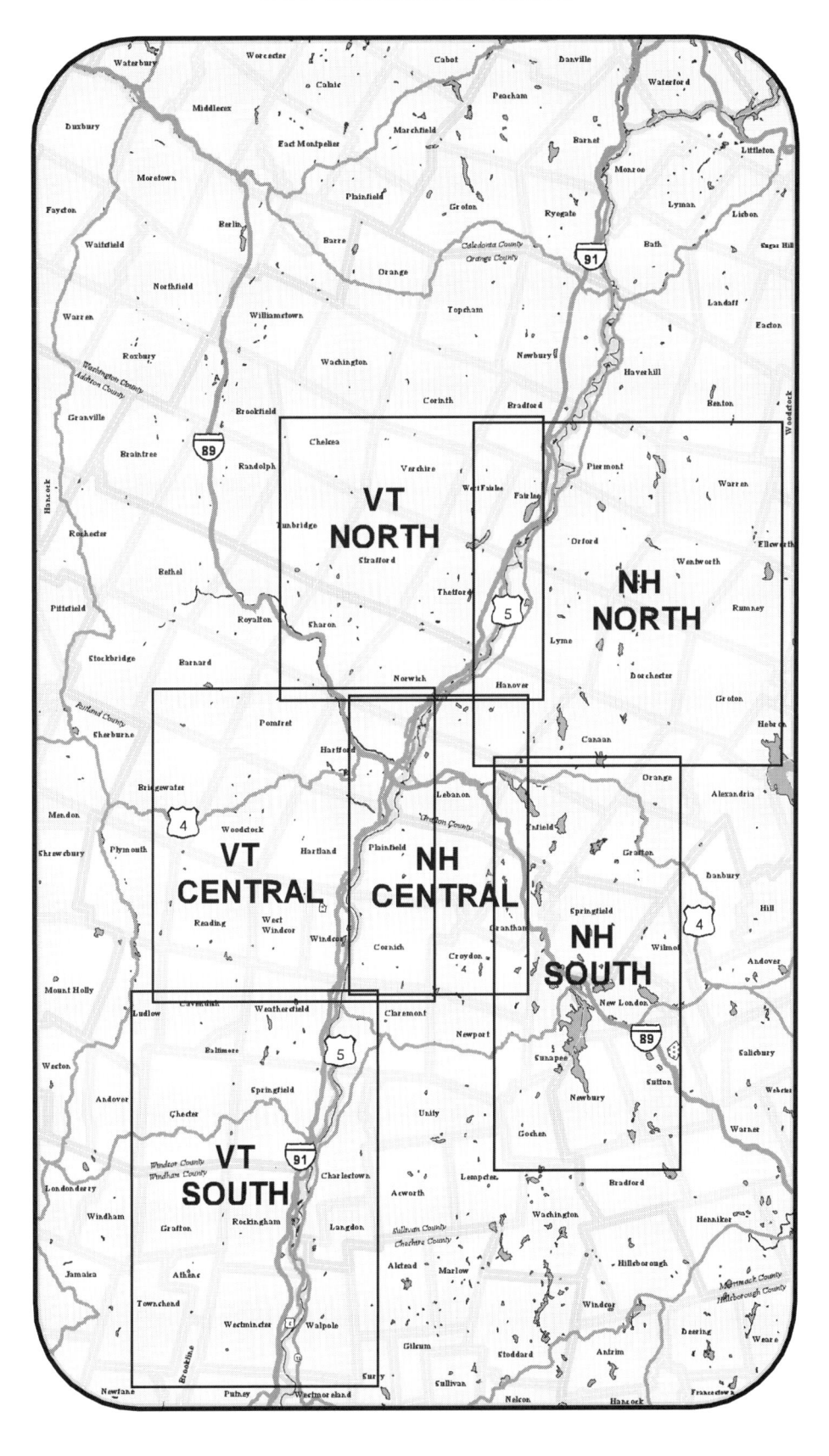

REGIONAL MAPS

VERMONT NORTHERN REGION

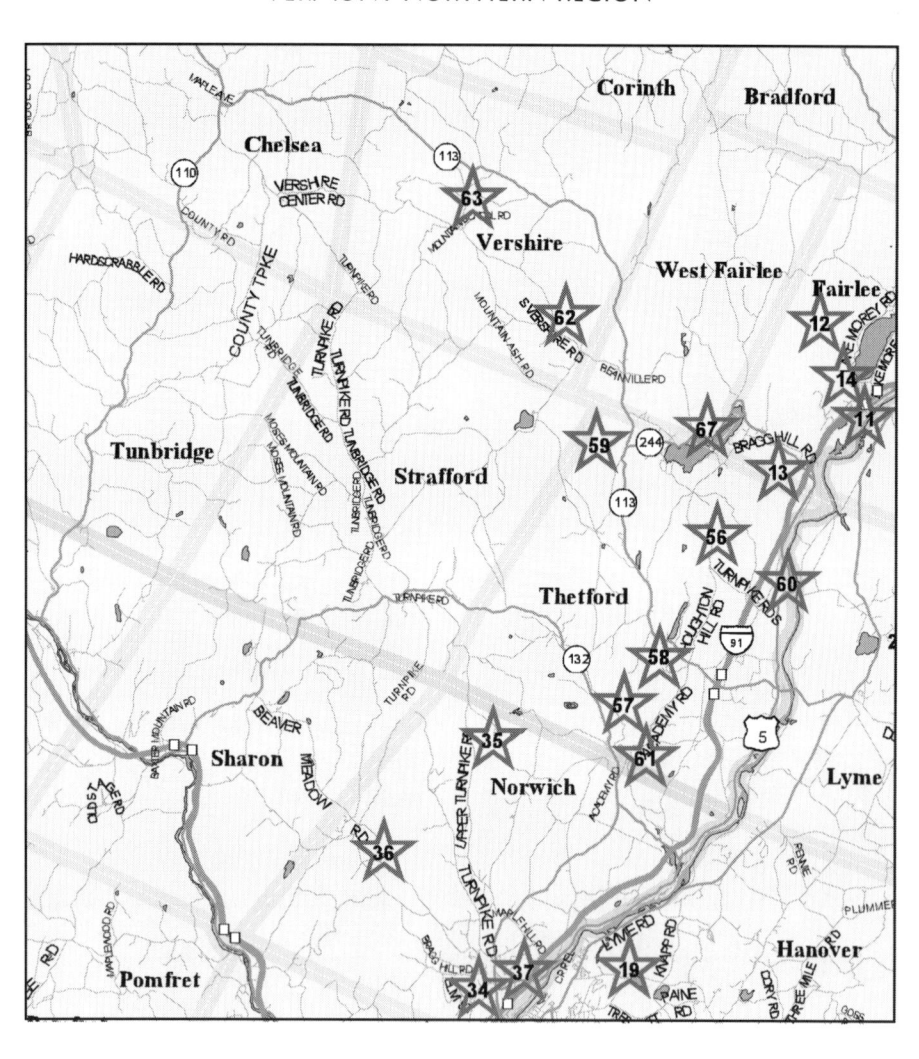

NEW HAMPSHIRE NORTHERN REGION

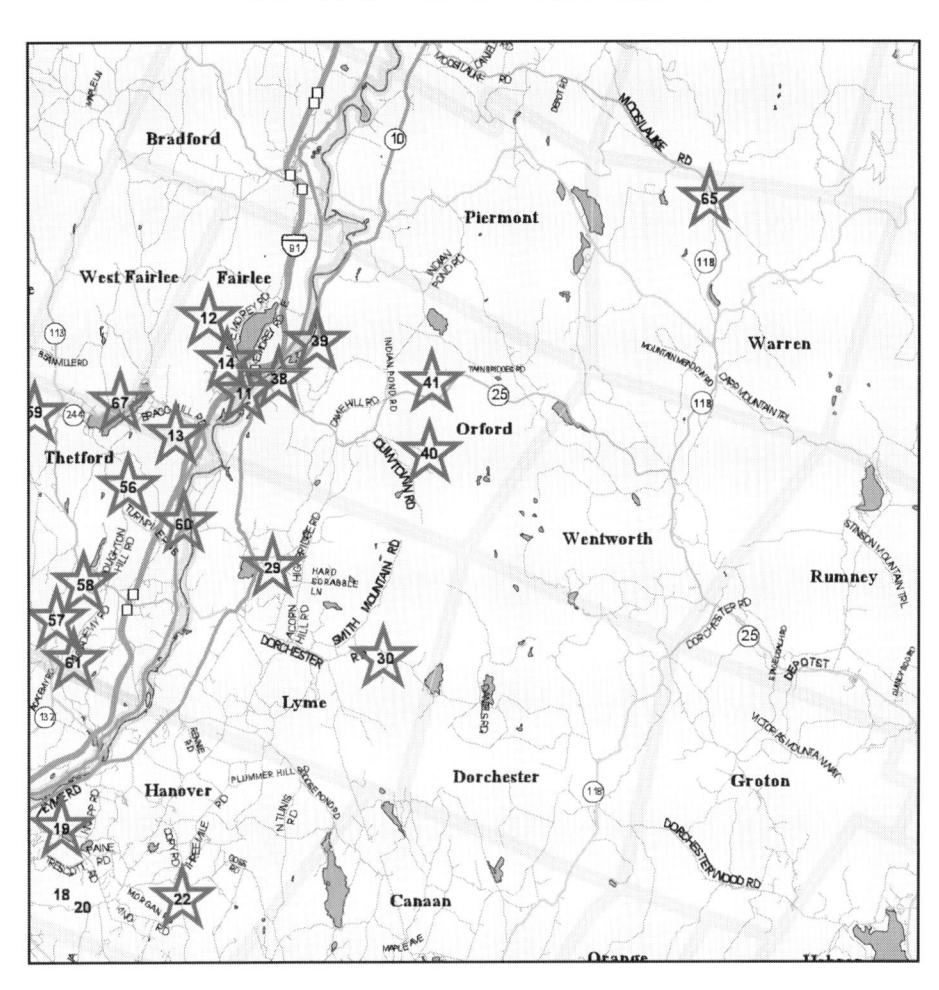

∿	Limited Access Highway	☆		▬	Water Feature
∿	Secondary Highway				County Boundary
∿	Local Thoroughfare		Quests		Town Boundary
∿	Local Street			▭	Landmark

REGIONAL MAPS   xvii

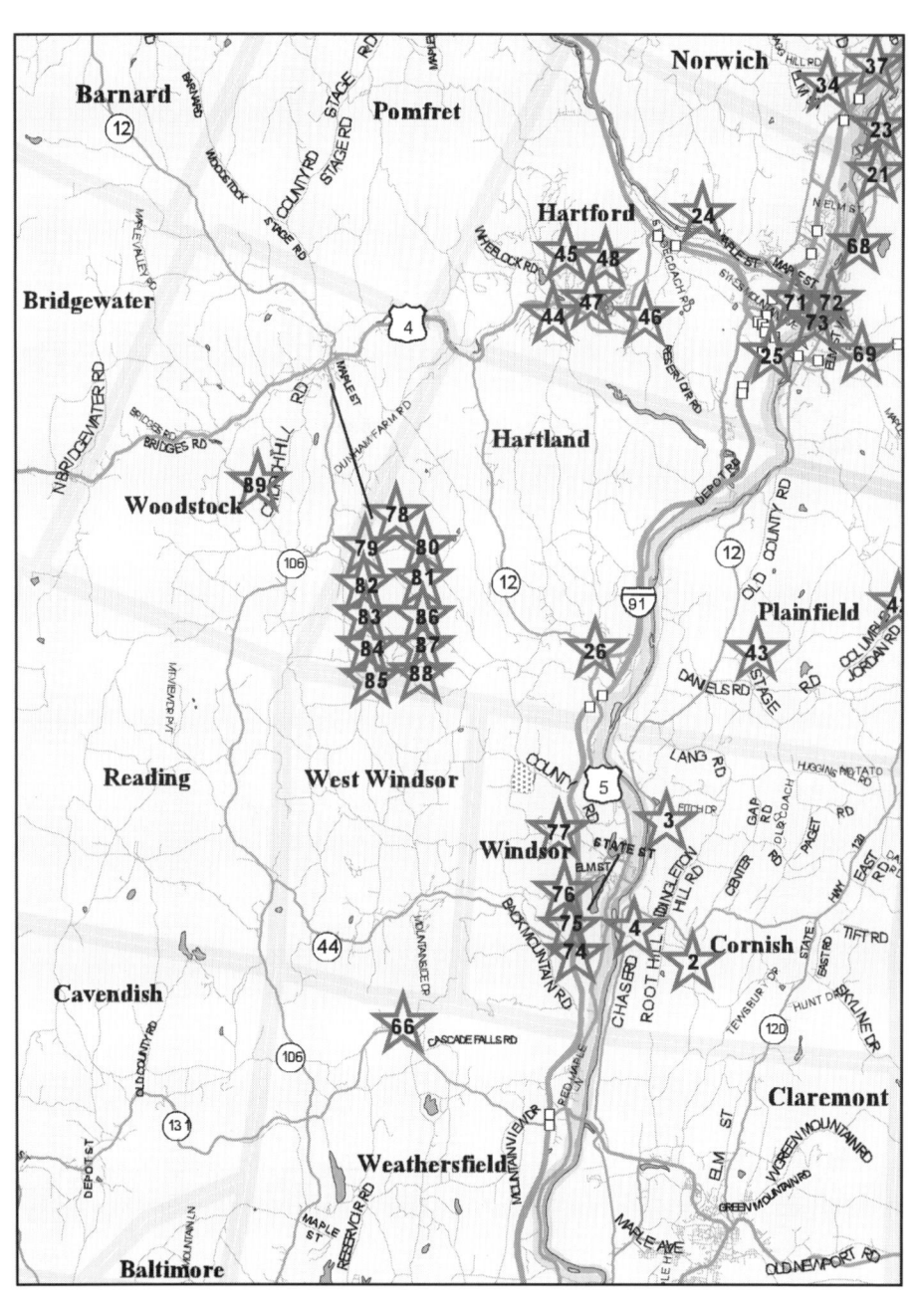

VERMONT CENTRAL REGION

NEW HAMPSHIRE CENTRAL REGION

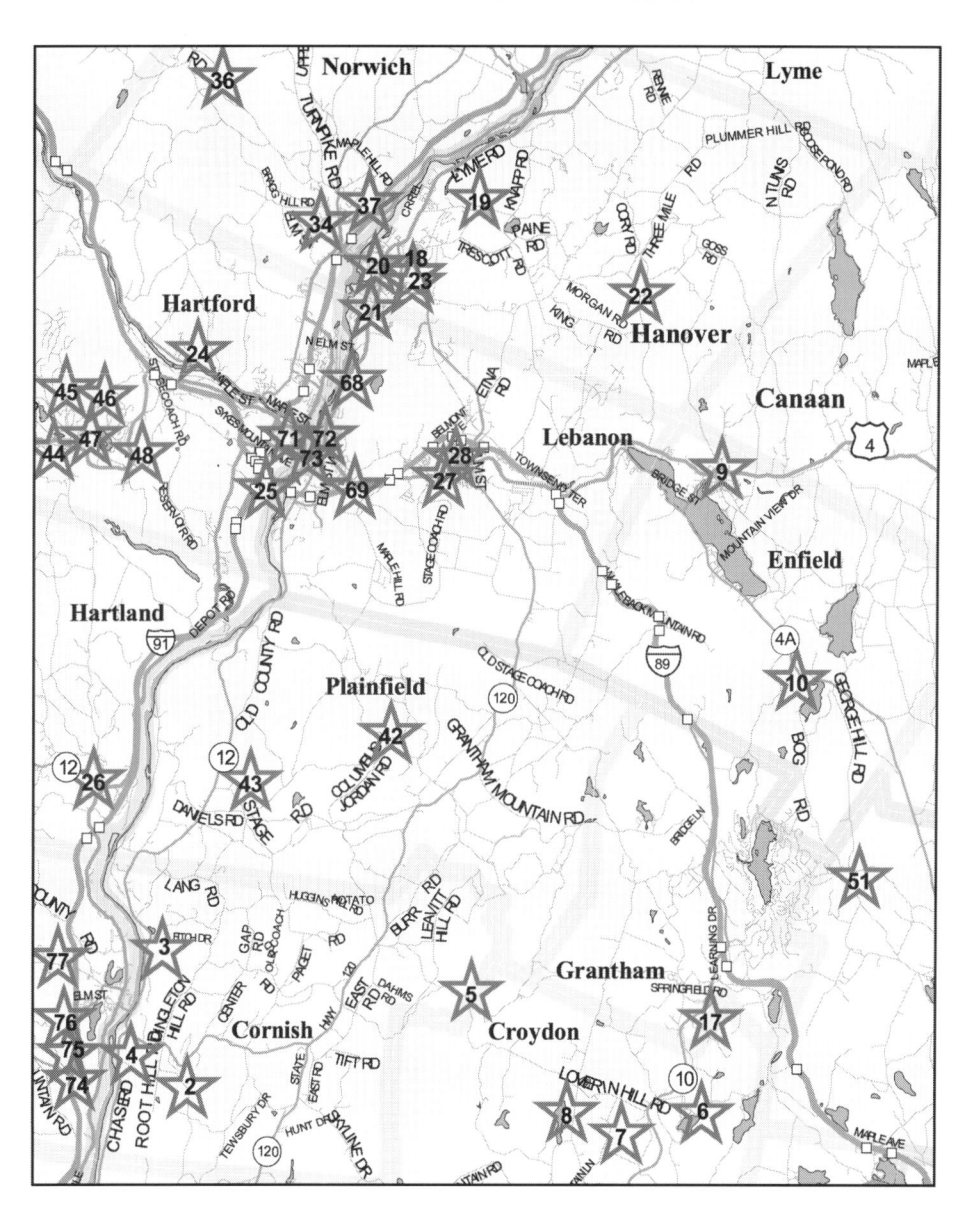

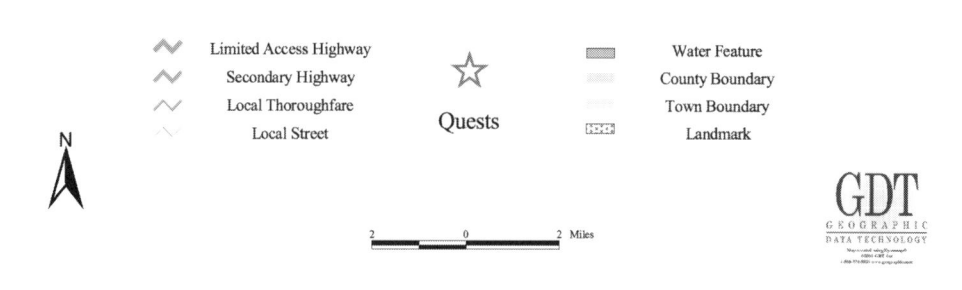

VERMONT SOUTHERN REGION

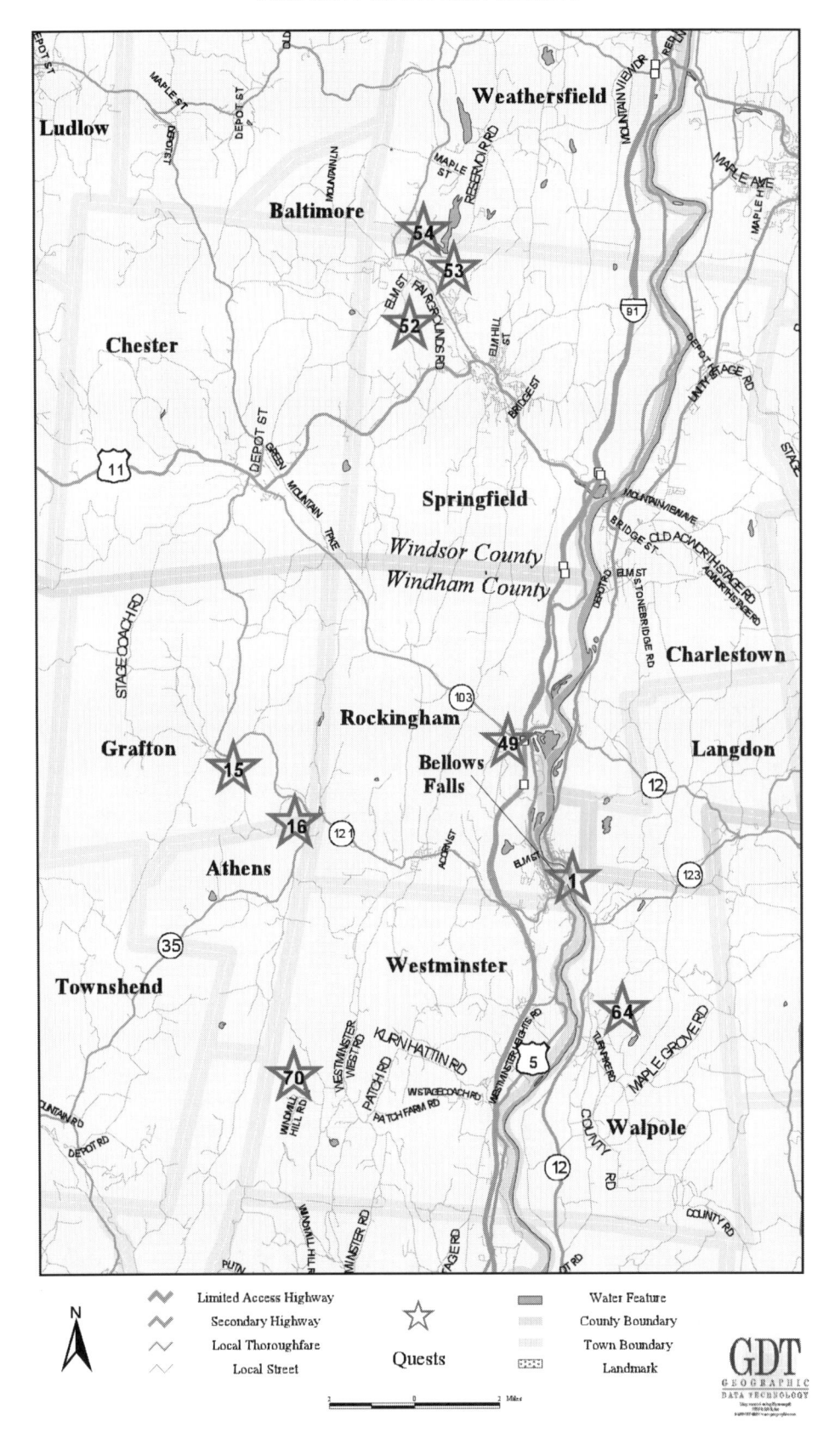

NEW HAMPSHIRE SOUTHERN REGION

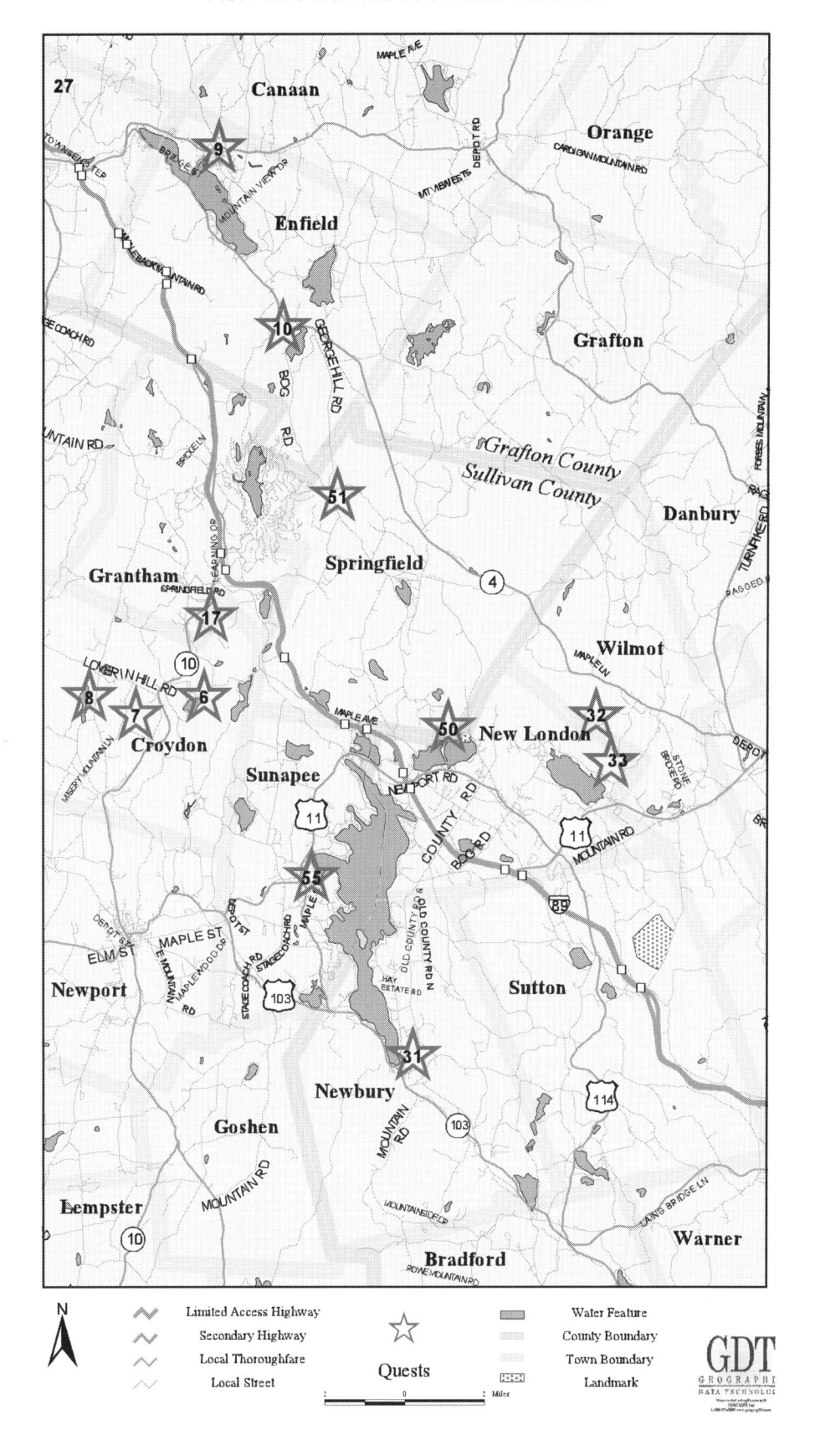

REGIONAL MAPS xxi

1
BELLOWS FALLS HISTORY QUEST

BELLOWS FALLS VT

To get there:
From the downtown square in Bellows Falls head south on Route 5 or Westminster Street, and park in the parking lot at the corner of Hapgood and Westminster.

Start at the Victorian house that is green, pink, and white.
   Built in 1892, the gargoyle on the roof is quite a sight,
   The house is on the corner of Hapgood and Westminster
   The gargoyle on top looks very sinister.
   Step back and look at the details from where you stand.
   A house with such style—isn't it grand?
   Look for the asymmetrical porch and steeply pitched roof.
   Find the delicate porch supports. Now, you're a real sleuth!

Walk north on Westminster Street,
   And at the fork bear right.
   Then, at the curve, right again.
   Soon the Bellows Falls Post Office will come into sight!
   The Post Office was built during the Great Depression
   In Spanish Colonial and Georgian Revival style.
   Look under the windows for a concrete tile.
   Record the number of letters in the architect's first name: ___

'... and this is where part of the movie the cider house rules was made.'

After the Post Office walk east to the fish ladder.
   As you cross over the first chartered canal in the U.S.,
   Imagine how the fish climbing up the river felt.
   Walk east for a while, until you pass the big yellow tanks.

Look over the south side of the second bridge where the balusters
      (supports) begin.
   You will see carvings marked by yellow paint on the right side
      of the rock.
   No one knows why they were made, who made them, or when.
   They may have been made by the Abenaki Indians.
   We know this spot was a place to fish and trade,

BELLOWS FALLS VT

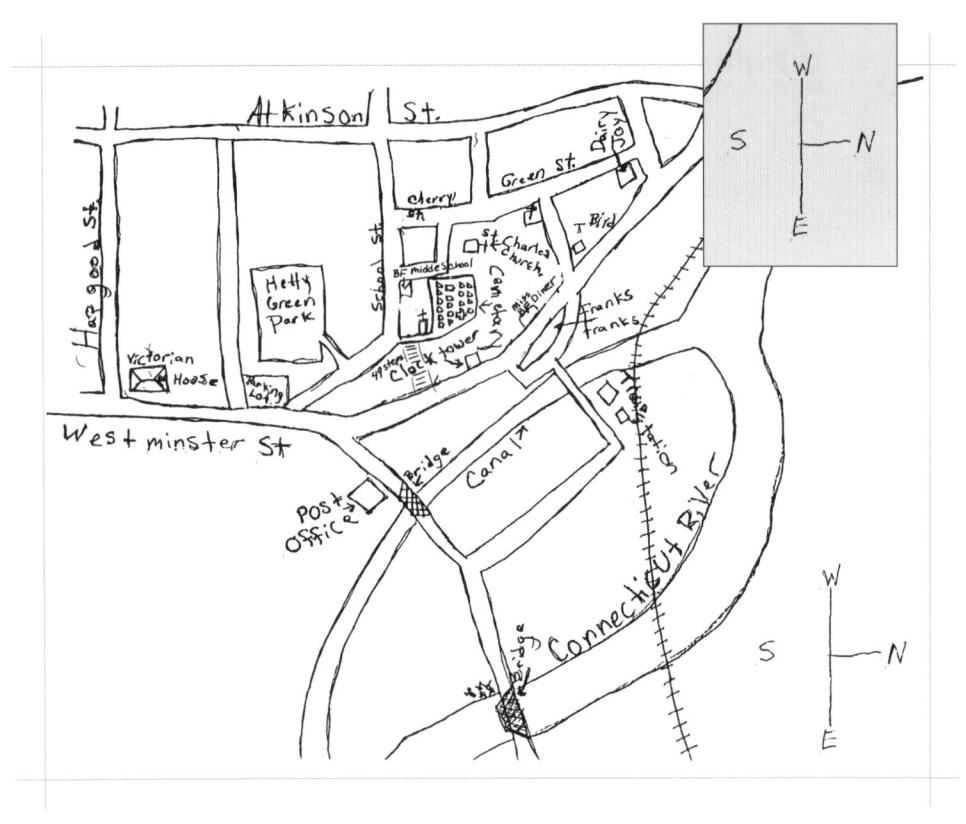

CONTINUED

It's amazing these markings did not fade.
Experts say they are three hundred to two thousand years old.
How imprecise we're told!

You might want to know on this bridge called Vilas,
    You stand in two states: New Hampshire and Vermont; pretty cool, huh?
    But be careful of the cars and trucks that drive too fast.

Turn around and walk west.
    Onto Island Street take the next right.
    Go past the old waxed-paper mill also built in 1892,
    Until a building named for the Green Mountains is in sight.
    A very important part of Bellows Falls history the railroad played
    And this is where part of the movie *The Cider House Rules* was made.

Next, go across the railroad tracks and past Island Park.
    Keep going over the bridge and turn left and then right at two arches.
    Cross the street into the tunnel and up the steps.
    Number of steps ___ - 4 ÷ 2 = ___
    You just passed through the Rockingham Canal House,
    Which was once a theater and hotel.

Now, cross the street and walk north past Miss Bellows Falls diner.
    This twenties-style restaurant with barrel roof has food that couldn't
        be finer.

Take the next left onto Williams Street, note and see
    On your left, a street named for Ms. Green's ex-husband's family

BELLOWS FALLS VT
CONTINUED

Who is Ms. Green? you may ask yourself now.
Continue the quest to learn more about Ms. Green
And see a beautiful place where people make their vows.
Go up the second flight of forty-eight steps.
Ahead of you is St. Charles Church.

In front of the Church, turn right onto the footpath not too far away.
Walk east up Cherry Street and turn right at the top of the hill.
Keep walking until you see the last gate into the graveyard.
Go thirty paces to the tall granite gravestone.
Remember! A pace is every other step.
Here lies Ms. Green who was once the richest woman in America.
She brought great wealth to Bellows Falls.
How many letters in Ms. Green's first name? ___ - 5 = ___

Continue through the graveyard and out the gate,
Turn south down the road and then go straight.
Ahead, you will see Ms. Green's Park.
Its granite statue is your next landmark.
In 1806, the house Ms. Green lived in was built
It was later torn down and is now a city park.

Turn north once more and find the forty-nine steps
That will take you down into town.
Now find your way back to the place
Where lots of letters can be found.
As you face the building
There are two sets of steps.
Look in the bushes for a box
To the right of the left.
Enter the three numbers you found: ___ ___ ___
If you got these numbers correct,
The lock on the letterbox should open, no sweat.

Now if you're feeling a bit thirsty or hungry
We know a fine place to plop yourself down
Walk north to the clock tower in the middle of town.
In 1753 it started its fate. It burned down in 1925
And then was rebuilt in colonial revival style.

Keep heading north to where the road divides.
Take the high road and take a look around.
This café's espresso is surely the best.
And this is the end of our glorious quest.
The sign on the side looks like a moon.
Go inside and buy coffee soon!

Ask there for a second quest box with more fun facts inside!

CORNISH NH

2 BLACKSMITH COVERED BRIDGE QUEST

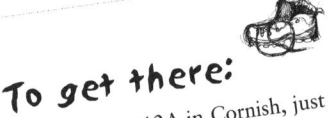

To get there:
From Route 12A in Cornish, just south of the Cornish-Windsor Covered Bridge, head east on Town House Road. In two miles the bridge will be on your right. On your way you will pass the Dingleton Covered Bridge, also built by James F. Tasker. You may wish to bring a compass for the last clue.

James Tasker lived on Parsonnage Road.
   He cut down trees by the cartload.
   Then brought them here to this Mill Brook,
   And built Blacksmith Bridge with posts and nooks.

Enter the portal, walk into this space;
   You will soon discover an exciting place.
   It is a very old bridge, 1881 to be sure
   Highly prized for its look, Tasker's legacy endures.

Look all around, past the King Truss beams
   Names you'll spy carved in wood above the stream.
   Look north near the hill—there is even a mill—
   With an undershot wheel that never stood still.

The bridge was built in 1881;
   One hundred years later it was redone.
   Milton Graton and his men labored long
   To make this bridge once again strong.
   Flooring and sheathing were replaced,
   And each side of the bridge was a little bit raised.

'**SLAB CITY** was once the name of this place . . .'

When you've crossed the bridge,
   Look to both sides,
   Past the guardrails, but not to your right:
   A trail leads down to the old mill site.

You'll be at the mill when you see some stones.
   There are good seats here, so find your own.
   Think of what it was like so long ago
   When the mill was running both fast and slow.
   "Slab City" was once the name of this place.
   The mill and the bridge kept an active pace.

If you walk back to and up the road (not down to the mill)
   You will spy some old walls on the edge of a hill.

CORNISH NH
CONTINUED

When you see walls ahead and the bridge and road behind,
    Look to your left—coppiced birches you will find.

Then on the left a boulder you will see . . .
    Now very carefully, listen to me.
    With your back to the boulder
    Facing 220 degrees SW
    Count and then take seventeen steps.

You'll be standing tall in the gap of the wall.
    Across from you—a wall in view;
    Along your left, another wall too!
    Where the two walls meet
    You'll find treasure at your feet.

BLACKSMITH COVERED BRIDGE QUEST

3 BLOW ME DOWN MILL QUEST

CORNISH NH

To get there:
Drive about 10 miles south of Lebanon on Route 12A and park at the pull-off on the east (left) side of the road at the Mill, approximately 1/4 mile north of St. Gaudens Road.

Walk to the green sign,
  as we say our rhyme.
  With the sign at your back,
  walk north 135 steps.

Look out at our pond
  of which we are fond.

   Cattails and lilies swing and sway.
   Blackbirds and fishies like to play.

Now walk south 180 steps to the blue railing.

You're at something blue,
  that doesn't stick like glue.
  So don't lean over the bar
  or you'll be too far
  Over the dam,
  on the rocks you will slam.

Walk 10 steps west, then 20 steps south.

Sit down on the wall.
  Make sure you don't fall.
  On this very sill,
  there used to be a mill.
  The water rushed on in.
  The mill wheel it did spin.

Now walk south to the end of the wall.
  Go down inside 25 steps to the door up high.
  Look up, look down, look all around
  to see and learn about what you have found.

Now back to the green sign.
  And then south along the railing—
  Keeping cars and traffic carefully in mind!

CORNISH NH
CONTINUED

Pass the mill, and the stone arch,
　And turn left when guardrail departs.

Follow the high wires to the brown walking square.
　And at the end of the curve of rocks—look under there.

BLOW ME DOWN MILL QUEST

CORNISH NH

TRINITY CHURCH QUEST 4

To get there:
From the New Hampshire side of the Cornish-Windsor Covered Bridge, travel south on 12A past Town House Road. Stay south on 12A. The church is on the left as you climb up the hill, approximately 1/4 mile south of the bridge.

Park your car
   Don't go far.
   Head for the stones,
   Look out!
There are some bones
Below you.
Trinity Cemetery is where you'll be.
An obelisk stone is what you'll see.
It is real tall,
Old Israel Hall.
Count five rows back and please don't slack.

Look to your right,
   A flat stone's in sight.
   A big eye can be found
   Just above ground.
   You should be in the place
   Where Jonathan Chase
   lies underground
   Six feet down.
   A key, a cross
   of skull and bones
   These are the things
   That Jonathan now owns.

Go back to the Church
   Toward Mount Ascutney
   Red, white, and blue is what you'll see,
   And a stump of a tree near Church Trinity.

Shining lights, big green door,
   Three tall windows, shutters galore.
   Walk through the door,
   And then one more—
   To where ministers stand, pray with their hands.

CORNISH NH
CONTINUED

Turn around and walk west,
   Head for the chest.
    It's on the right—
    Treasure's almost in sight!
   Open a drawer,
   And there's your reward!

TRINITY CHURCH QUEST

CORNISH NH

5 JONATHAN WYMAN SAWMILL QUEST

To get there:
Travel on Route 120 to Cornish Flat. Find the corner of Upper East Road and School Street, at the east side of the triangular common area, across from the Cornish General Store. Proceed up School Street to the G. H. Stowell Free Library, a large, red brick building on your right. After .2 miles, bear left onto Leavitt Hill Road. Continue up the road, bearing right, for another .4 mile until you come to a fork and see the sign for West Pass Road on your right. Take West Pass Road .6 mile, until you come to the stone bridge with a waterfall on your left. Park in the small parking area on your right, just before the bridge. Your Quest begins there. Please note that the waterfall is privately owned and not part of this Quest. *Please bring a compass.*

After you park, take a quick look
   Where a fall of water becomes a brook.
   It's privately owned, so to do what's best
   Just eyes should admire this part of the Quest.

Walk down the bank, right near your car,
   Look to your left, but not too far.
   A sight to behold, with moss like mold.
   There is a bridge, the oldest of stone,
   In these here parts of our Cornish home.

Back up to the path where brambles grow,
   Ancestor of brambles that long ago
   Knew men who worked, come rain or snow,
   Making these woods what we now know.

Walk past logs, long been felled
   Their neighbors know the secrets held.
   Head down the hill to the mill,
   All that is left, stones standing still.

Around to the right, footbridge in sight,
   A slippery flat rock, a sign that says "Bach."
   You're on your way for a day of play.
   But before you rest there is more to this Quest.

Cross the bridge, and walk on 'til you come to a fork.
   The path divides, choose the right and head down by the brook.
   Ninety steps more to the base of a hill
   A stump and a stone downstream from the mill.

Take a compass bearing 153 degrees south.
   (Turn 180 degrees, if compass you doubt)
   Look through the trees, past the thick forest floor.
   A semicircle of stones awaits by the shore.

CORNISH NH
CONTINUED

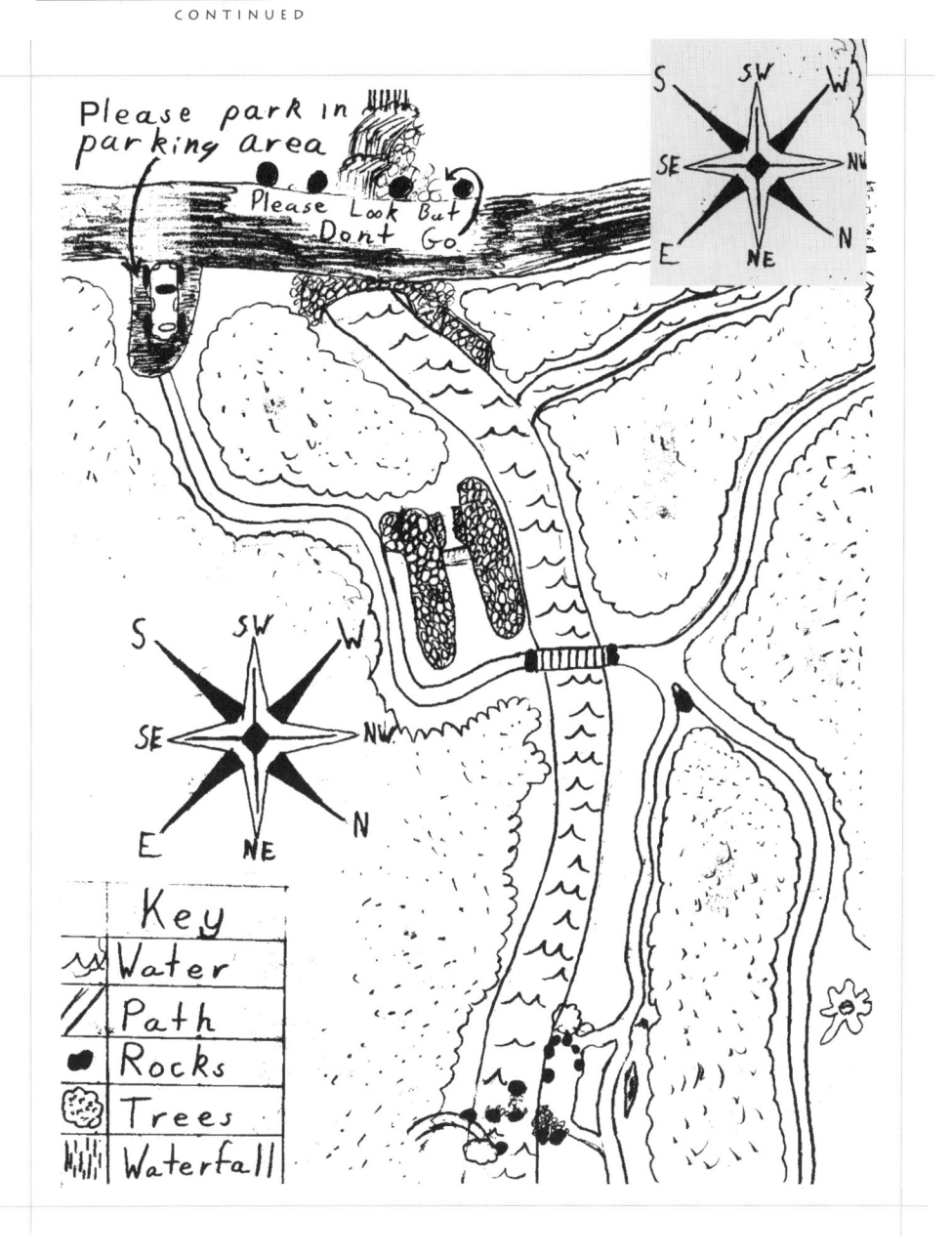

Feel peace surround you as you walk in,
    For you are someplace you have never been.
    A brook and a waterfall are things you will hear,
    A birdsong, leaves crackle, a glimpse of a deer.
    A nice place to picnic would be right here.

Retrace your steps back to the stream.
    Recross the bridge as if in a dream.
    Heading south, the mill wall will be on your left.
    Its tower still stands, looking bereft.

Climb up the step in the mill; from there, five steps more.
    Watch out! Don't fall! Find the hole in the wall.
    Your eyes looking left, about five feet tall—
    The box will be there, the treasure and all!

JONATHAN WYMAN SAWMILL QUEST

6
CROYDON SCHOOLHOUSE QUEST

CROYDON NH

To get there:

Take Exit 13 off I-89 and follow Route 10 south through Grantham until you reach Croydon village. The schoolhouse is surrounded by a white picket fence, on your right.

Built in 1790,
    Our school is very old.
    You can tell by the bricks,
    We're sure you've been told.

Park by the green dumpster,
    And walk 15 paces.
    Now turn to the right,
    Our playground your body faces.

On your way to the building's end
    A chimney you will see.
    A woodstove they used,
    That is where it would be.

When you've reached the corner,
    Left is how you should face.
    Do you see the picnic table?
    Go to that place.

Now go past the big tire
    To the left of the path.
    Count up 35 paces,
    Count as if you're in math.

CROYDON NH
CONTINUED

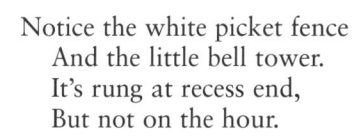

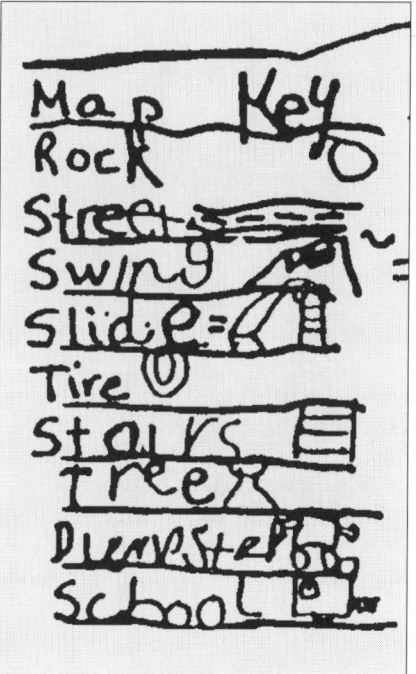

Notice the white picket fence
   And the little bell tower.
   It's rung at recess end,
   But not on the hour.

You've walked the size of our school,
   Now face the red door.
   The Valley Quest treasure you seek
   Is under the porch floor!

CROYDON SCHOOLHOUSE QUEST

CROYDON
NH

7
CROYDON'S PAST QUEST

To get there:
Take Exit 13 off I-89 and follow Route 10 south through Grantham until you reach Croydon village. The Quest begins at the schoolhouse, on your right, surrounded by a white picket fence.

All of our Quests deal with
    Croydon's past
    In a century where things
    happened so fast.

This quest, you'll see,
begins at school,
Where we have learned
the golden rule.

To the right of the dumpster
you'll find Forehand Road,
made of mostly dirt and
maybe a toad.

The hike is beautiful
with flowers from the wild.
They blossom and bloom
when the weather is mild.

You'll hike by four turnoffs
that are on your right.
Don't get too lost;
there's a possibility you might.

Go past a left with a sign:
    Patriot's Drive.
    Some summer people live there.
    They are still alive!

The first graders dig
    is at the fifth intersection.
    Look, once you find it
    you'll be bit by the infection.

CROYDON NH
CONTINUED

The next dig is where you'll find the treasure
   From this one you'll get a lot of pleasure!
   Just a little bit further past a trailer up the road.
   The treasure dig's up there where the grass is not mowed.

It's on the left side, so keep your eyes open.
   No time to be discouraged; and no time for moping.
   Look for two big trees. Across the road is a stone wall.
   Moving those big stones was not a ball!

This is the best foundation; it's in good condition.
   Looking for our treasure is an easy mission.
   Look on your map, you'll see s, h, and k.
   There's our treasure—the rest we took away!

CROYDON'S PAST QUEST 15

CROYDON NH

8 FOUR CORNERS CEMETERY QUEST

To get there:
Take Exit 13 off I-89 and follow Route 10 south through Grantham until you reach Croydon village. Continue south on 10 to the fire station. Turn right onto Loverin Hill Road. Go to the end of Loverin Hill Road. The cemetery is past the pond on the right.

Cemeteries are spooky,
   filled with the dead.
   But believe it or not—
   it's history fills our head.

A lot of our streets
   were named after the people.
   Nearby was a church
   built with a white steeple.

The church is now gone
   but the cemetery remains.
   There are quite a few families
   with unusual first and last names.

Pass the first two rows
   and then take a right.
   Continue down to the end,
   a rock with "Fogg" will come into sight.

The Fogg family's buried there.
   It's the only rock of its kind.
   No other rock like this
   in the cemetery you'll find!

Look on the other side
   and over the wall.
   Your treasure is there.
   Stamp your passbook, don't stall!

Take time to read the stones.
   The earliest person born in 1813.
   The youngest child died
   age three weeks; too young it seems.

'Stamp your passbook, don't stall!'

16   VALLEY QUEST · 2001

CROYDON NH
CONTINUED

Four Corners Cemetery

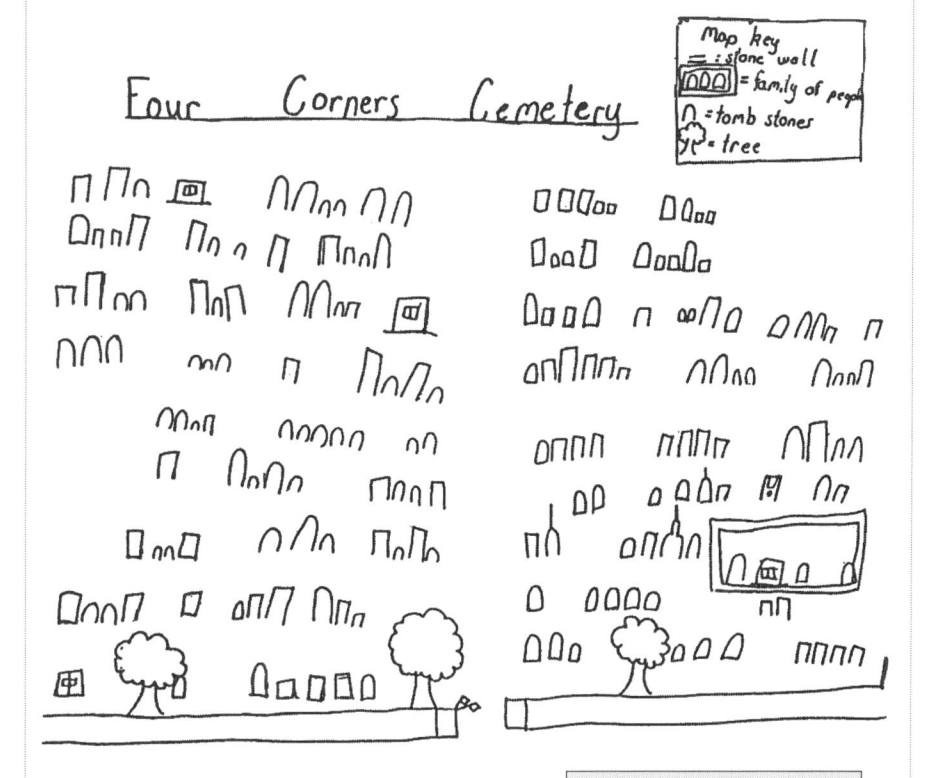

[hand-drawn map of the cemetery with tombstones, trees, stone walls, and family plots, with a map key indicating: stone wall, family of people, tomb stones, tree]

There were families with many kids.
  Husbands had lots of wives.
  They died very early.
  They lived quite short lives.

Enter the cemetery
  from the front gate.
  Go straight down the path.
  Check each stone and each date.

FOUR CORNERS CEMETERY QUEST

ENFIELD RAIL TRAIL QUEST

ENFIELD NH

To get there:

Take I-89 to Exit 17. Take Route 4 east 4 miles to Enfield. Take the second right past the Enfield Garage (High Street) just as Route 4 makes a sharp left into town. At the first stop sign, go straight through the intersection. Take the first left onto Depot Street. Park at the end of Depot Street in the parking lot to the left of the red building. This building is the old Enfield railroad depot, but now houses the town ambulances. Please make sure not to block the emergency vehicles in any way.

1. In eighteen hundred and forty seven,
    Enfield folk thought they'd gone to heaven.
    To this depot they and their cargo could now roll
    To ride the brand-new Northern Railroad.

2. Whistle stops and train rides are long gone,
    Victims of highways and air travel throngs.
    Out of sight are rotting ties and rusty rails,
    Now there is gravel and the Northern Rail Trail.

3. Enfield village is your first destination,
    Hiking or biking, get on with exploration!
    Head to the right or, with a compass, go west!
    All aboard this historical Rail Trail Quest!

    Before the railroad came, this area, it is said,
    Was mostly farms and a few homesteads.
    The train was a magnet for prosperity,
    Thus the shops, mills, and village that you see.

4. Next stop is the bridge over Mascoma River,
    The bridge or the rapids might make you quiver.
    Instead think back to how water helped fill a hole
    Left behind by a glacier, before humans strolled.

5. On the left is Mascoma Lake, long and deep,
    Named after an ancient Squakheag Indian Chief.
    His village was in Mass., far away in those days,
    But his tribe hunted this far north, anyway.

6. The trail up ahead appears flat and straight,
    But look to the sides, you are gaining height.
    You're on top of what's called an embankment
    Built for the railroad's advancement.

ENFIELD NH
CONTINUED

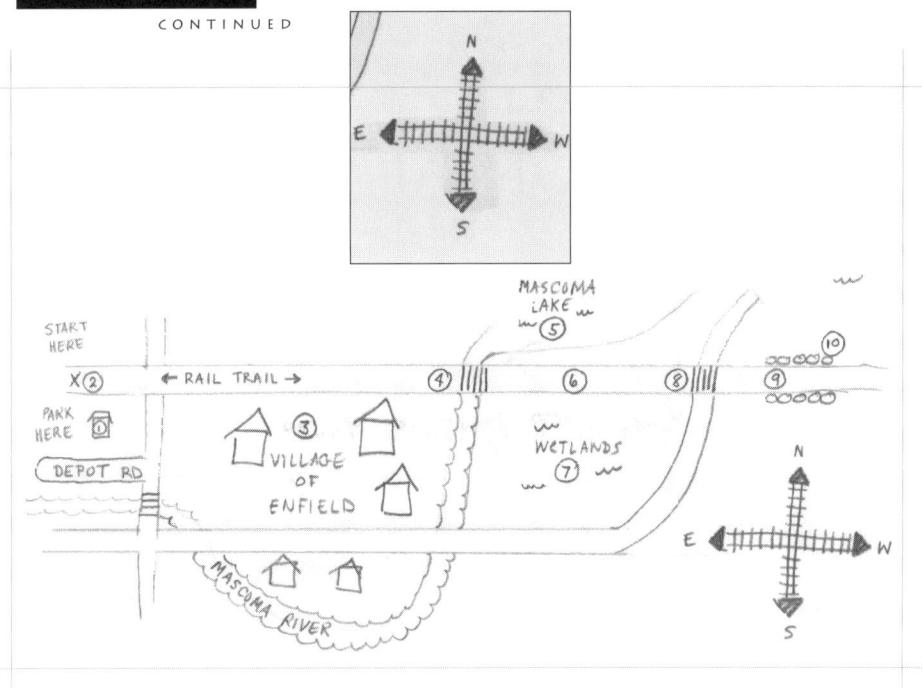

This area was once marsh, soggy and wet,
With no place to run a train through . . . yet.
Rail workers piled dirt high across this wet spot,
Until it was set and their backs were in knots.

7   To the right of this bank is a rich habitat,
    A wetland home for many a duck, in fact.
    Explore a little and you may see
    A frog, a turtle, a heron . . . lucky thee!

8   The next bridge makes us stop and wonder:
    Who built this so cars take turns going under?
    The Shakers built the big bridge across the lake
    To get to the rail depot without effort great.
    Did they tunnel under here and thus this bridge?
    Give a friendly wave to those who way give.

9   The Quest is over, when rock walls appear.
    "Ledges Pass" they are called; the end is near.
    Two gangs of workers, forty men, they say,
    Took a year to carve this cut, with nary a stay.
    Gas or steam engines were not yet the rule,
    Hand drills and explosives their only tools.

10 Upon these walls are etched names and dates,
    By workers whose sweat this passage did make.
    At the end of the pass on the left is a rock,
    Behind "1893" you will find the Quest box!

> **QUESTER PLEASE NOTE:** *At the far end of the pass, a trail leads to the shore of the lake. Once you are on the trail, you are on the private property of Mr. Earl Farnham. Please respect his beautiful property, and be aware that you are passing at your own risk.*

ENFIELD RAIL TRAIL QUEST

ENFIELD NH

SHAKER VILLAGE CEREMONIAL SITE QUEST 10

To get there:
Take I-89 south of Lebanon to Exit 17. Take Route 4 east to Route 4A. Make a right onto Route 4A and drive south 3.3 miles. Park in the driveway with a sign for Stone Mill on the right (west) after passing the Shaker Museum.

1. Look west toward the hill and you'll see a sign
    that shows Enfield's Conservation line.
2. Follow the well-beaten path up the hill.
3. Right at the fork to stay on it still.
4. Where the trail turns left, ruins of a bridge you'll see
    to a field where merino sheep used to be.
    (Pass the bridge, staying on the trail).
5. The trail turns northwest, as up you go,
    with a beautiful view of the lake below.
    (Observe bluebird houses).
6. Across the top of the hill and then you'll see
    an old granite post and a big locust tree.
7. Walking on, look down.
    Below was once found
    the end of a run
    where skiing was done.
8. At the little white post, take a short break
    for a compass reading you may take.
    Head west at the bearing of 268
    (Hint: due west is 270 degrees).
9. Go a hundred yards heading west.
    You're almost there—the end of your Quest.
10. March up the hill like a Shaker would
    and come to a grove set back in the woods.
    You'll see a gate and a sign.
    Here is a place of quiet and prayer
    Take some time of reflection whilst there.
11. At the southeast corner of this spiritual place
    you'll find our box's special space.

ENFIELD NH
CONTINUED

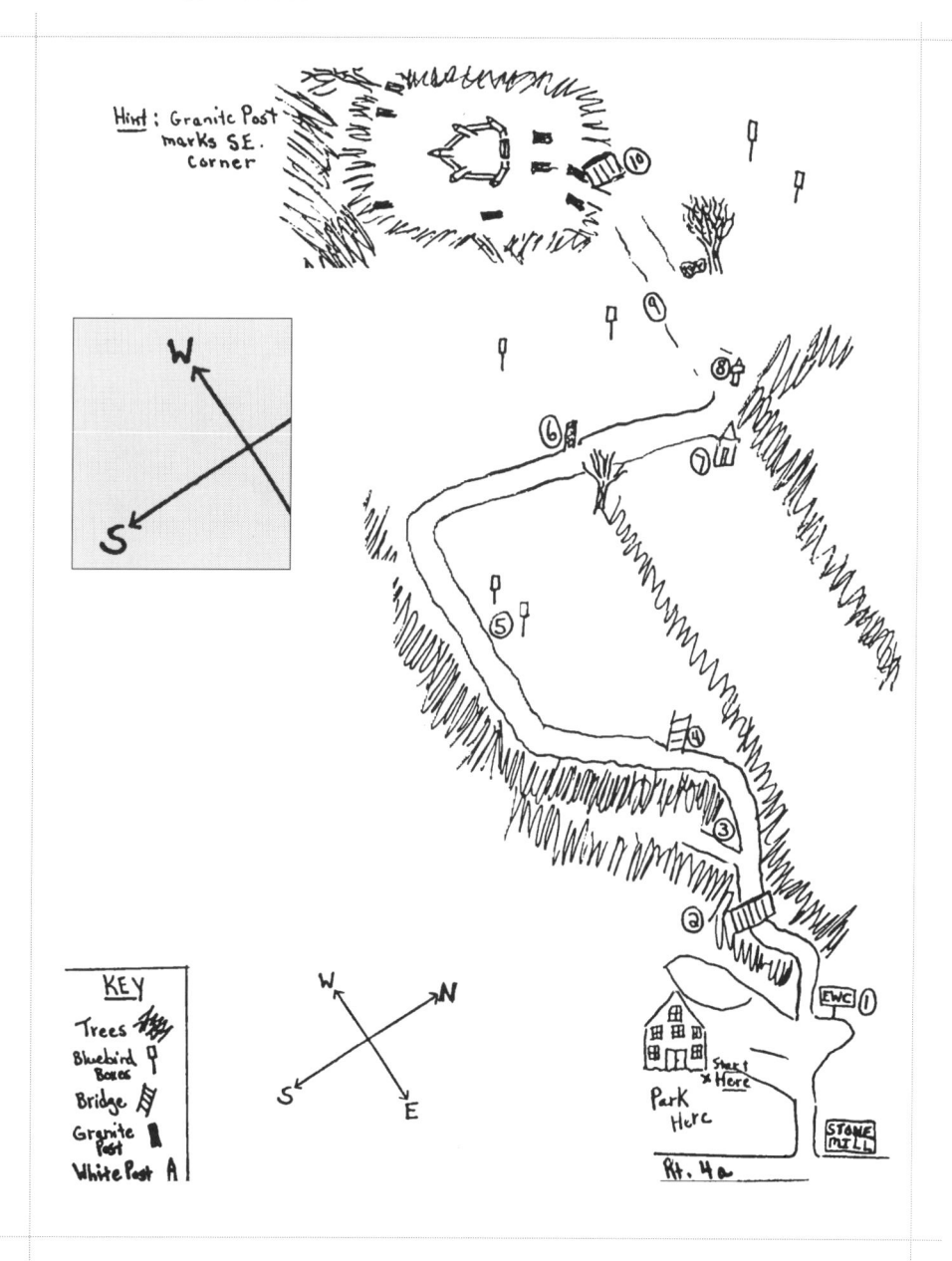

Hint: Granite Post marks S.E. corner

KEY
- Trees
- Bluebird Boxes
- Bridge
- Granite Post
- White Post

SHAKER VILLAGE CEREMONIAL SITE QUEST

FAIRLEE DEPOT QUEST

11

FAIRLEE VT

To get there:
Take I-91 to the Fairlee exit (Exit 15). At the bottom of the off-ramp, turn east, and then turn left at the T onto Route 5 north. The Quest begins at Fairlee Feed Store, just south of the Depot in the heart of Fairlee.

Welcome to the Fairlee Depot Quest!
   We'll send you north, east, and west.
   You'll learn about railroad history
   While you seek our treasure-box mystery!
   Before the railroad came to Fairlee,
   People didn't travel merrily:
   They had to go by river raft
   Or stagecoach on a bumpy path.
   The Green Mountain Boy in 1848
   Was the very first train. It sure was great!
   Connecticut & Passumpsic the company's name,
   Moving freight and passengers was its game.

Now put your left side to Route 5
   And walk 'til you reach a gravel drive.
   You'll see a row of trees.
   Go to the fifth one, if you please.
   Joseph Alger kept the trees trim,
   We have learned a lot about him.
   He was the master of this station
   And made it a wonderful destination.
   He planted flowers and vegetables, too,
   Displayed fool's gold and mica for travelers through.

> 'This is the floor the old creamery had back when dairying in Vermont was really rad!'

Now walk to the tracks keeping the depot on your right
   And we'll point out a special site.
   Stop at the corner and look to the east
   And you'll see where hobos could get a feast.
   It was the time of the Great Depression,
   Which taught our country a great big lesson.
   Hobos rode the train from around the U.S.
   Joseph gave them food and a place to rest.
   They'd go to the river following a path
   To shanties that kept out the weather's wrath.

Now follow the tracks to Bradford (north)
   On this Quest by the third and fourth.
   After seventy-three ties, turn west and stay loose
   Then walk 'til you reach a line of spruce.
   Follow the trees along toward the steeple
   At the seventh tree, look west, please, people!
   Our stationmaster's house was number 1910.
   The Depot was Fairlee's town center then.

Now retrace your steps to the Depot's front door.
   Go to its south wall—we'll show you some more.

FAIRLEE VT
CONTINUED

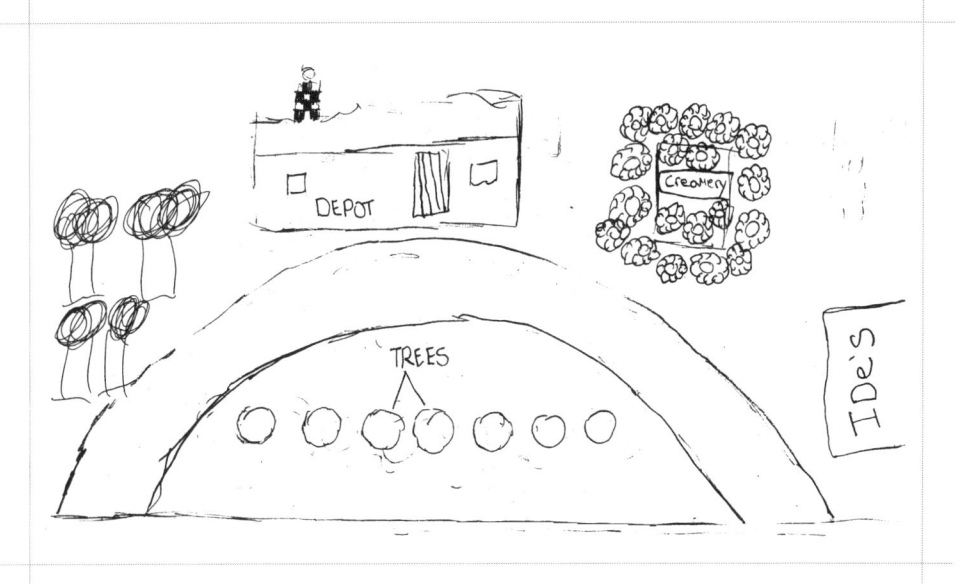

Go to the tracks and walk south twenty-eight ties
   There you will find an archeological surprise.
   Go a few yards west and dig lightly with your feet
   And beneath you will find a slab of concrete.
   This is the floor the old creamery had
   Back when dairying in Vermont was really rad!
   The creamery sent milk to other places—
   To put white moustaches on people's faces!

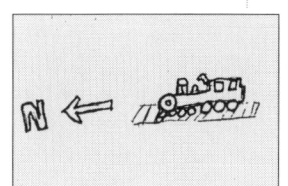

Go to the tracks and walk forty-six ties back
   To a wide wooden door beside the track.
   Luggage was loaded through that rolling door
   And steamer trunks piled up, ceiling to floor.
   When campers arrived for Lakes Morey and Fairlee
   The trunks all arrived about ten days early.
   Camps' horses came, too, and went wild when they arrived
   And would tear down Main Street from the Depot's drive.

Now look for a pole that is tall, wooden, and long.
   It helped keep things from going wrong.
   It used to be a semaphore,
   Whose signals prevented a lot of gore.
   It told the trains to go or stop
   With red and green lights mounted near to its top.
   The station master got telegraph signals that said
   When a train would be straight ahead.

From the semaphore, go north fifty-six ties,
   That's where what's known as the sidetrack lies.
   When two trains were coming, one would make the decision
   To pull onto the sidetrack—and avoid a collision.

Now that we've given you facts and pleasure,
   We will lead you to our Valley Quest treasure.
   Go north up the tracks looking to your left side
   In a wall made of wood the treasure box will hide!

FAIRLEE DEPOT QUEST

FAIRLEE GLEN FALLS 12

Park at the boat launch,
   Be sure you're all set,
   Step o'er the "road-fence"
   And turn to the left.

Walk about seventy steps
   (From the sign)
   And cross the street.
   The woodland opening
   Should be right at your feet.

You'll see a white rock,
   But please do not stop.
   If you keep on the trail,
   We're sure you'll not fail.

A tree broken in half
   Crosses the path.
   Here comes some water,
   But don't stop for a bath.

Keep on the path . . .
   You'll see a waterfall.
   But it's just the lower one
   And not tall at all.

Pass the orange marker, then pass the gall.
   It looks like a beach ball!

When you find the second orange marker
   Along your way
   "Turn right and thirty steps,"
   that's what we say.

Now find an upturned root,
   Such a beautiful sight
   (Like a giant's hand,
   But please don't feel fright).

Facing toward the Upper Falls,
   A slanted stump will appear on your right.
   Walk twenty-two steps there and look down
   for that is where our treasure is found.

Visitors have enjoyed
   Fairlee Glen Falls
   For more than one hundred years.

To get there:

Take I-91 to the Fairlee exit (Exit 15), turn west, and take Lake Morey West Drive 1.4 miles (around Lake Morey) to the Boat Launch. The Quest begins there. Please do not park in the driveway across from the trailhead—this is private property.

FAIRLEE VT
CONTINUED

Lake Morey Summer Resort...

1896

Glen Falls House, Lake Morey.

After signing our
guest book,
Go close, take a
look for yourself,
And give it three
cheers!

FAIRLEE GLEN FALLS QUEST 25

13 MIRACULOUS TREE QUEST

FAIRLEE VT

(IN THE VILLAGE OF ELY)

To get there:
Take Route 5 either south from Fairlee or north from East Thetford to the village of Ely. From Ely, take Route 244 west underneath I-91 to Bragg Hill Road. Turn right on Bragg Hill Road and follow it to the end. Park at the cemetery—your Quest begins there. *Remember to bring a measuring tape.*

I stand in back with wide, stretching arms,
   Protecting all here from harm.
   My family is oak, my color white—
   A compatriot stands next to me on the right.
   Rounded, lobed leaves can be found
   Either upon me—or upon the ground.
   Please measure my waist, up four feet,
   In order to calculate the DBH[1]—hey that's neat!
   Record the white oak's DBH here: _____

Leaving the highway noise behind,
   Seven feet up on Allbee a finger pointing up find.
   Then a baseball diamond sitting on home
   Slink under the line, and left up the road roam!
   We're now in a mast-producing zone—
   A fancy way of saying nuts call this place home.

Curving to the right,
   Look through beech on your left.
   A road meanders lower, tracing the ravine
   Where during the Pleistocene[2]
   The Ely River could be seen.[3]

The road curves right past a pole
   And the tall, twin hemlocks.
   Hemlocks are one of the four
   Dominant northern forest trees
   Growing up here among the rocks.
   Measure the first hemlock's DBH: _____

Onward! Sugar maple, beech,
   And yellow birch are the other three—
   Oh say how many can you see?
   Curve left. Threadbare from the years,
   An old yellow birch stands right near 675
   Looking ragged—yet it is still alive.
   Calculate its DBH: _____

---

1. Foresters use a standard measurement for the girth of trees, known as diameter at breast height or DBH. To calculate DBH, measure the diameter approximately four feet above the ground.
2. Better known as the "Ice Age."
3. The Ompompanoosuc is a descendent of the Ely River that used to drain out through this valley, approximately tracing the path of Route 244.

FAIRLEE VT
CONTINUED

DIAMETER

Our fork holds two poles in its crest—
    Veering left I think is the best.
    The next big tree on the right is a white ash.
    How do we know?
    Like muskmelon its bark does grow!
    What do folks do with a tree like that?
    Make hockey sticks or a baseball bat.
    The ash's DBH: _____
    You'll pass a sugar shack on the left,
    And a front-yard spruce on the right.
    But stay straight ahead
    With your goal still out of sight.

An apple tree looms left flanking the road.
    In fall it will bear a tasty load.
    If soon you pass the numbers 369
    I can tell that you are doing fine.

Then, uphill on the right
    Three white birch sit tight.
    Just past them is a driveway
    Which we will turn up today.

Beyond the birch is a majestic tree.
    Oh tell me what you think it might be?
    Despite a very terrible blight,
    This century old _____
    Still stands living in our sight!
    A miraculous tree!
    A sight rare to see!
    Record the miraculous tree's DBH, please: _____

Now examine the nuts, the bark, buds, and leaves—
    For then you will see how to *see* this rare tree!
    To find out the name of the tree you have found,
    Add up the DBHs and then measure the ground.
    Taking that distance, look 'round for a hole
    Where you'll find your answer—but don't tell a soul!

MIRACULOUS TREES QUEST

FAIRLEE VT

PALISADES QUEST

QUESTER PLEASE NOTE:
This Quest is near a falcon's nesting site. Peregrine falcons are an endangered species and this is a protected area during the nesting season. Don't go beyond the Quest box.

14

To get there:
Take I-91 to Exit 15. Go west off the exit ramp, and take a right onto Lake Morey Road East. Park in the parking lot of the fire station on the corner on your right.

1. Park the car in the lot. Don't stop to rest.
   Follow the fence, there is no bench.
   Walks towards the highway,
   U-turn, and look ahead for the pathway.

2. Along the off-ramp, look on a tree,
   A Lake Morey marker is what you will see.

3. Look up high, there's a long-needled pine branch.
   Take a turn to the left, while you do a dance.
   This is the path to follow to find the treasure.

4. Caution, when you climb this mountain.
   Be careful you do not disturb the falcons here.
   They are a protected species and are nesting near.

5. Follow the fence; it's on your left.
   The path is steep, so do not weep.
   Through the break, don't let the barbed wire bite.
   Now look, it's on your right.

6. Take a break, to see our lake. It's on your left.
   After a few steps, stop! We don't want you to drop.

7. Horray, horray, you're on your way!
   Zig, zag, zig, zag for this part of the day.

8. At this egg, we named her Meg.
   No need to whine, it's time to dine.
   Sorry no diner, this place is finer.

9. On your feet, slow and sweet.
   Walk across the bridge you meet.

10. Out of the woods to a clearing,
    Don't touch too high, or you'll fry.
    Stand under the wire. Go to front support cable.
    Turn to left and walk four steps.
    Turn to view, walk twelve steps to the rock pile.
    Dig around and you will come upon our treasure box.
    Look inside; it's stamping time.

FAIRLEE VT
CONTINUED

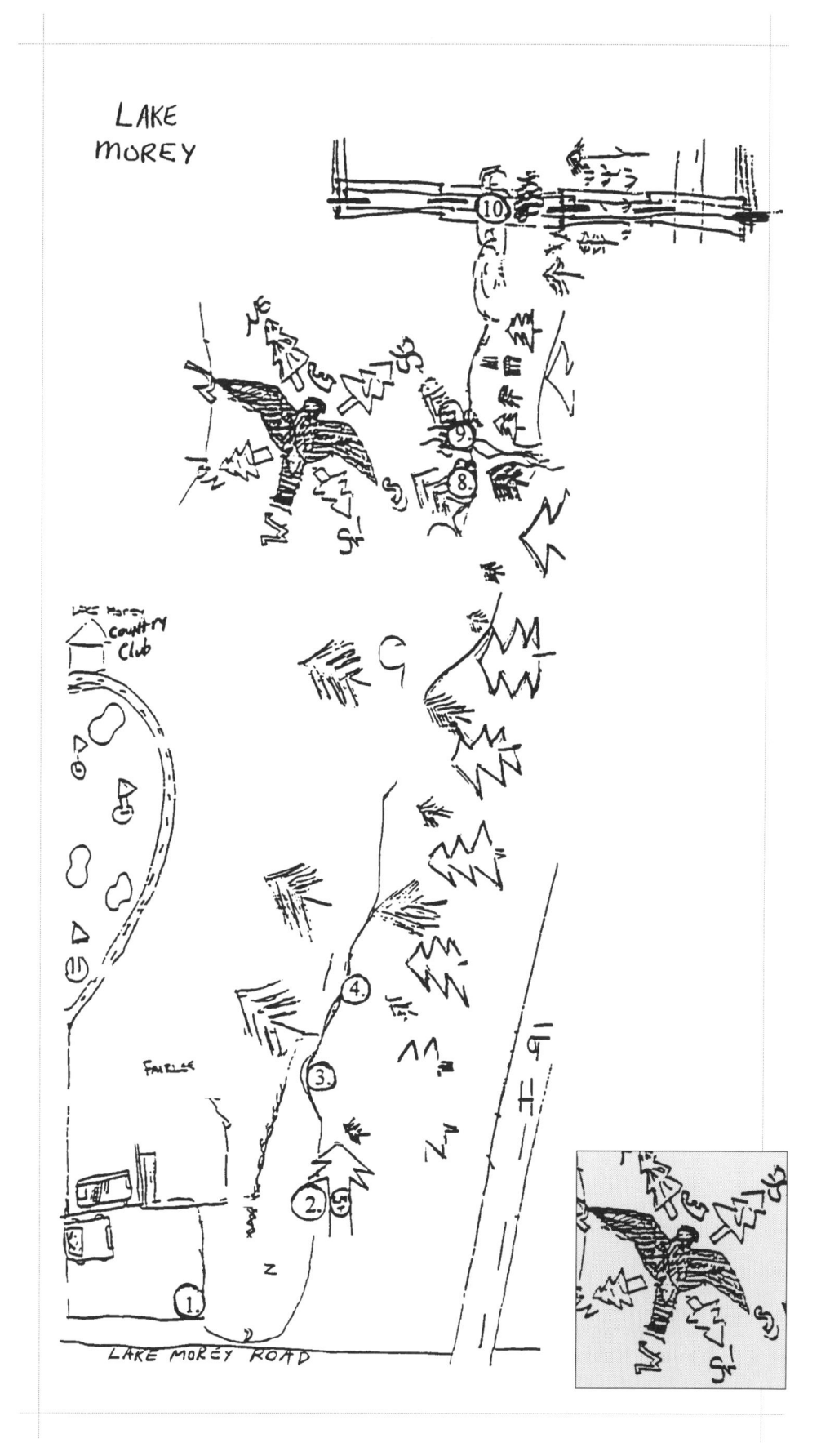

LAKE MOREY

PALISADES QUEST

15 GRAFTON PONDS QUEST

GRAFTON VT

To get there:
Take Route 121 west to Saxtons River. Past the post office there will be a fork in the road. Take a left and keep on going until you get to a little town with a general store. Cross the bridge, turn right after the bridge, and follow the signs to Grafton. In the heart of Grafton, turn left just before the Tavern, and proceed until you see a sign that says Grafton Ponds. This Quest can be walked, biked—or ski it in the winter!

Welcome to Grafton Ponds!
   This area was created around fifteen years ago
   Because the Old Tavern at Grafton wanted their guests
   To have something recreational to do.

Start in the parking lot. Go up the steep slope,
   This trail was a logging road a long time ago.
   Around 1860, Grafton had three lumber mills
   So lots of timber was cut down from these hills.

At the top of the little hill, take a right
   And go until the tubing hill is in sight.
   The pond below was made by men not long ago
   It is used for wildlife, skating, and making snow.

Look for the small building down by the pond.
   It was originally designed
   As a warming hut and picnic place.
   Now it is also used to sell food and rent skis.
   What type of building is this?
   It is a __ __ __ __ __ __
   Hint: This type of building ends with an "N,"
   but you need to remember the letter with which it begins!

When you're done at the first stop,
   Turn around and go straight up the hill.
   No humans have lived here and this we know
   Because there is no evidence of old cellar holes.

A lot of animals live in these woods,
   There are woodchuck, deer, bear, and raccoons.
   As you move down the trail, look for a trail sign.
   The sign will be on your right.

Don't go down that trail, but read the sign for your next clue.
   The sign says that this trail is used for something specific to do.
   It is a __ __ __ __ __ __ __ __ __ trail.
   The third and seventh letters are the same; remember this letter!

GRAFTON VT
CONTINUED

Continue past the leaning tree
    Whose two trunks come together in the shape of a V.
    Keep moving north.
    You will see two trees in the middle of a three-pointed fork.

As you move down the trail
    Note the blackberry bushes everywhere.
    They are a sign that this place was cleared
    For sheep farming in long-ago years.
    Some of the trees that you see
    Are used to make a famous Vermont product.
    Remember the first letter of this sweet treat:
    __ __ __ __ __ __ __ __ __ __!

Keep moving north.
    Trails branch out leading east and west.
    Don't take them, though;
    North is best.
    Notice that the trail is wider then it used to be.
    This is because of the invention of a new style of ski.
    You'll know you are on the right trail if on your right you see
    The deep-ridged bark of an uprooted oak tree.

Take the NEXT left and move toward the village overlook.
    This property used to be owned by a man named Ed McWilliams.
    This spot may be
    Where he used to see his sheep grazing peacefully.

GRAFTON PONDS QUEST

GRAFTON VT
CONTINUED

Look in the distance for the two pointy towers.
   The official name of these architectural features is:

   _ _ _ _ _ _ _

   HINT: The word begins with an "S," but it is the fifth letter
   You need to remember!
   The name of the town that you see is important too.
   Use the third letter
   in the name of the town:

   _ _ _ _ _ _ _

Off to the field and look for a few birdhouses as you go.
   To get to the field, go down the trail and take a right.
   Stonewalls surround this field.
   The stones are big and that's how we know

The field was used for grazing animals, instead of to grow
   Vegetables. If the stones were small then we would have found
   That they were probably dug out of the ground.
   Use the first letter of the animal that used to be raised here:

   _ _ _ _ _

Look at the beautiful field and take a rest
   Head down the hill, there is not much left.
   Follow the river to the covered bridge.
   The first letter of the name of the river below
   Is the last clue that you need!
         _ _ _ _ _ _ River

In 1892, the building in front of you was termed
   the Grafton Cooperative Cheese Factory.
   Dairy farmers brought their milk here and got cheese in return.
   In 1912, the Cooperative burned down.
   And for a while there was no cheese in this town.

In 1967, this place was rebuilt
   With the friendly help of Ed McWilliams.
   Now, this world-renowned factory of cheese
   Holds your treasure, so go in and buy yourself a Gold treat!

Congratulations! You've finished our quest!
   Write all of the letters below in the order that you found them.

   _ _ _ _ _ _ _

If you go into the cheese factory and ask for your treasure box,
   They will ask you for a password.
   The letters that you have written above
   Will spell your password.

VALLEY QUEST · 2001

GRAFTON TOWN — THE CAVE QUEST

GRAFTON VT

16

To get there:
Follow Route 121 to Grafton. The Quest begins near the "Old Fire Barn," just west of the bridge and near the intersection of Main Street (121) with Townsend Road (35).

Start your quest on Main Street.
　It starts two houses west of the bridge
　Go to the building where people go to buy houses.
　Built in 1855, it was originally used for the town's post office.
　Write down the first letter on the small rectangular sign
　With phone numbers on it.
　Write the letter here: ___

Face this building, turn left, and continue up Main Street.
　On your left will be the biggest building in town.
　This is the Old Tavern. It was built in 1801
　and then doubled in size in 1820!
　It used to be called the Phelps Hotel.
　The Phelps brothers bought it in 1865.
　They fixed it up with $4,500 worth of California gold.

Go inside to the desk and look up on the wall
　for a famous Civil War general's name.
　Now write the fourth letter of his last name here: ___

The next stop on your quest is The Brick Church.
　Take Townsend Road, which is off Main Street, on the left.
　When you get to the Daniels House, go right.
　Go through the ball field and past the bleachers and scoreboard.
　When you get to the split-rail fence on your right,
　Take a right onto the path.
　(Make sure you follow the rail fence near the rock wall.)

Soon you will see a place of prayer.
　This brick church was built in 1833.
　It used to have sheds behind it
　for church goers to park their horses.
　People bought the stalls behind the church,
　just like they used to buy the pews inside it.

There are only two church buildings in town.
　Both churches united in 1920 and
　became the Church of Grafton.

'Here our oldest firepit rocks are surrounded by beautiful hemlocks.'

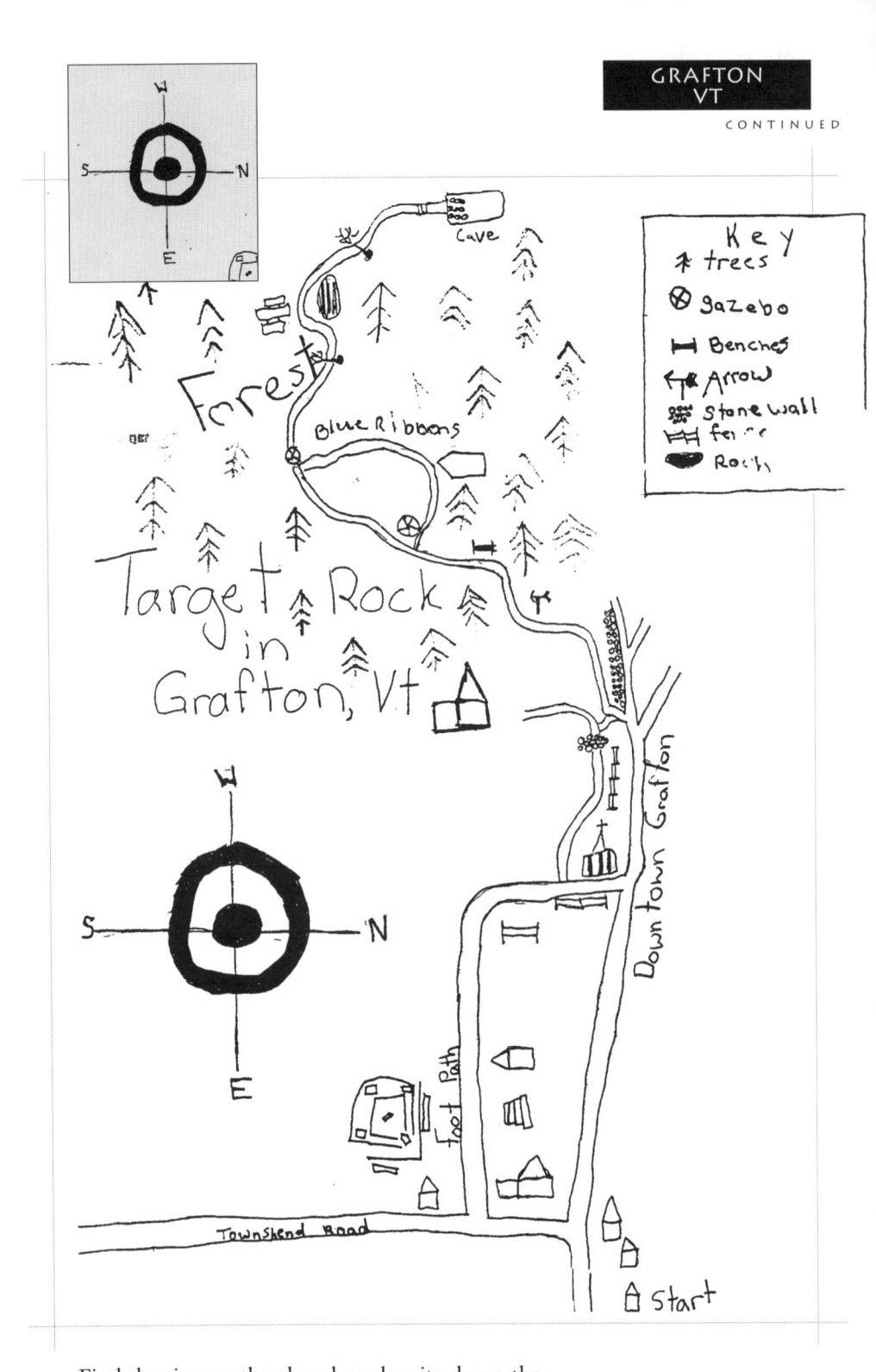

Find the sign on the church and write down the
   Fifth letter of the fourth word.
   Also, write down the fifth letter of the first word.

___ ___

Now, to find your next clue,
   You need to get to the main entrance of the village park.
   How you do that is up to you, but
   We suggest that you find a friendly
   Native and ask for directions.

GRAFTON VT
CONTINUED

But if you are feeling shy
    Circle round the building counterclockwise.
    Where bricks end and wood begins
    Look for two brick chimneys.
    Proceed that-a-way and find the village park.

Once you're at the main entrance,
    Walk about six steps and look out ahead
    And slightly to your right.
    You should see a path.
    Take the path for a while
    (This path could be covered with snow in winter)
    You will see red markers soon.

Passing by 1999, go to the place where you can read.
    Have a seat and try to succeed
    Find the second letter of the first word
    Write it here: ___ (built in 1925)
    Then on and not up to another room.

Take another rest and think of
    Success. Look for the sign that has a tree name in it.
    Write down the fourth letter of the second name: ___
    Surrounded by maples and birches,
    Follow the path to where you can eat.
    (Gazebo built in 1926).

You can sit at the table and cook up a meal.
    For now for our town you will have a feel.
    Here our oldest firepit rocks
    Are surrounded by beautiful hemlocks.
    Now write the third letter of the name of this town: ___

Go around the huge rock. Look for the blue
    Ribbon on a tree. Then get back on the trail.
    Follow the red blazes until you get to the steps.

At last you have made it to the end
    Of the quest. Hope you had fun and
    Reaped a lot of good.
    Check out the entrance to this natural shelter in front of you.
    What shape and letter do you see? Write that down, followed
    By the letter "e." Surrounded by huge ledges.
    Put all the letters together and see what it spells.
    Write the letters here: ___ ___ ___ ___ ___ ___ ___ E
    Now can you find the Quest box?

GRANTHAM
NH

DUNBAR HILL CEMETERY QUEST
17

To get there:
Take Exit 13 off Route 89 and travel south on Route 10 toward the center of Grantham. From the center of town, look for a sign for Grantham Village School and turn left onto Springfield Road/Route 114. Continue until a sharp bend in the road and another sign for the school. Continue on Learning Drive into the school's parking lot.

Our school used to be only four rooms—
   1983 was that year—
   Until the addition came along
   Creating the school you see here.

On top of a boulder, near the cemetery,
   There is a plaque filled with history.
   It's hunter green with white letters
   Declaring us to be free.

Over the flowing Sugar River,
   Cross the bridge of steel,
   It winds its way north and south,
   A trout haven to conceal.

Find the house with the number 52,
   A very old house it is.
   Mr. Walker's parents lived there long ago,
   This house now is his.

Our town has been standing over 200 years,
   It certainly has been a long time,
   We settled here the 8th of June,
   When wages were close to a dime.

Cross Route 10 over to Dunbar Hill,
   There you will find many signs.
   Walk up along the paved road,
   You'll find words and letters of all kinds.

This structure was built during the Civil War.
   It once was a two-room school.
   The building now houses the town offices,
   And the police that enforce the Grantham rules.

GRANTHAM NH
CONTINUED

Climb a quarter of the way up the
    Enormous hill, you'll find two rocks to rest.
    In case you are tired, you'll want to know,
    You are halfway through our Quest.

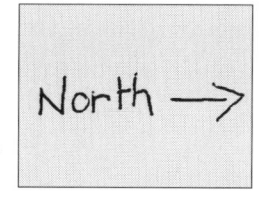

You'll see a house of gold
    Going halfway up the hill.
    A windmill spinning round and round,
    And ornaments the lawn do fill.

Look for the Field and Sons' trucks,
    Over on the right.
    Follow the road that bends 90 degrees,
    Your Quest is almost in sight.

Twisting and turning,
    A driveway like an "S"—
    The person who lives here,
    Helped developed the Quest.

Two brown houses up a long driveway,
    Lined with many trees,
    Upon a steep and hilly lawn,
    A stone wall surrounds these properties.

Dunbar Hill Road becomes
    Cote Road, joining together to become one.
    If you find the Sugar Springs Farm sign,
    Your Quest is almost done.

You'll see a stone wall across the way,
    Go through the lower gate.
    The graveyard here is very old,
    It is filled with stones of slate.

Go to the slate grave with two rusty bars,
    Treat this site with respect and care.
    The stone bears the year 1866.
    Hannah is buried there.

Their monument is made from granite,
    It is the tallest in the yard.
    Upon the top is an urn
      and shroud,
    A Smith family memorial
    Standing guard.

Carved in smooth stone,
    French was their last name.
    Look behind the big maple tree,
    You'll find the Quest Box to claim.

DUNBAR HILL CEMETERY QUEST

HANOVER NH

AMPITHEATER QUEST 18

To get there:
This Quest starts in the middle of the Dartmouth College green. Take I-91 to Exit 13, travel east across the Connecticut River, and up the hill on West Wheelock. The green is at the top of the hill on your left.

Start in the middle of the green
    Where a lot of students can be seen.

Now find the building with a pine tree on top
    Then look below to find a clock.

If the hour hand is facing III
    You'll be heading in the direction of the place with a "B."

To get there pass the columns four
    And you'll find yourself at the chapel next door.

Bells and arcs and faces hidden behind colored glass
    Will look at you as you casually stroll past.

The stone walk you're on will lead you right by
    Four tall white houses sitting on your right side.

Straight ahead a dirt path doth lie
    With tall white pines over to one side.

Foot travelers know they are headed the right way
    As they pass a crooked "arm" reaching up and away.

Enter a clearing and lying straight ahead
    Two trees: one a memory, and one tall and not dead.

Walk straight through the amphitheater to the other side
    Through a rectangular opening where the treasure hides.

Near the wall without graffiti there is a pipe on the ground.
    From there, turn around.
    Within the deep darkness, under stairs, your treasure can be found.

HANOVER NH
CONTINUED

'Bells and arcs and faces hidden behind colored glass'

AMPITHEATER QUEST

19 BALCH HILL QUEST

HANOVER NH

'look at the great grandfather trees'

To get there:
From Hanover, take Route 10 north. Turn right on Reservoir Road. Go about 1/2 mile and park in the parking lot for the Ray School on the left.

Along Reservoir Road, east you will go
   To a bike path that doesn't quite show
   Unless you look for mailbox #29
   Then to the left of the driveway, the path you will find.

Follow this path to the trail on the right.
   Just be careful, and please don't fight.
   Up the hill, follow blazes of white and blue
   But be sure not to miss the arrows too.

Continue on to almost the top,
   For it is there that you will need to stop.
   So pause and look at the great grandfather trees
   because your treasure is hidden in one of these.

After finding the treasure, continue on to the top.
   There's a beautiful view that will cause you to stop.
   Nearby, too, is an amazing oak,
   Seventeen feet around—this isn't a joke.
   See Mt. Ascutney from the top, Baker Tower too.
   And on your way down follow blazes of blue.

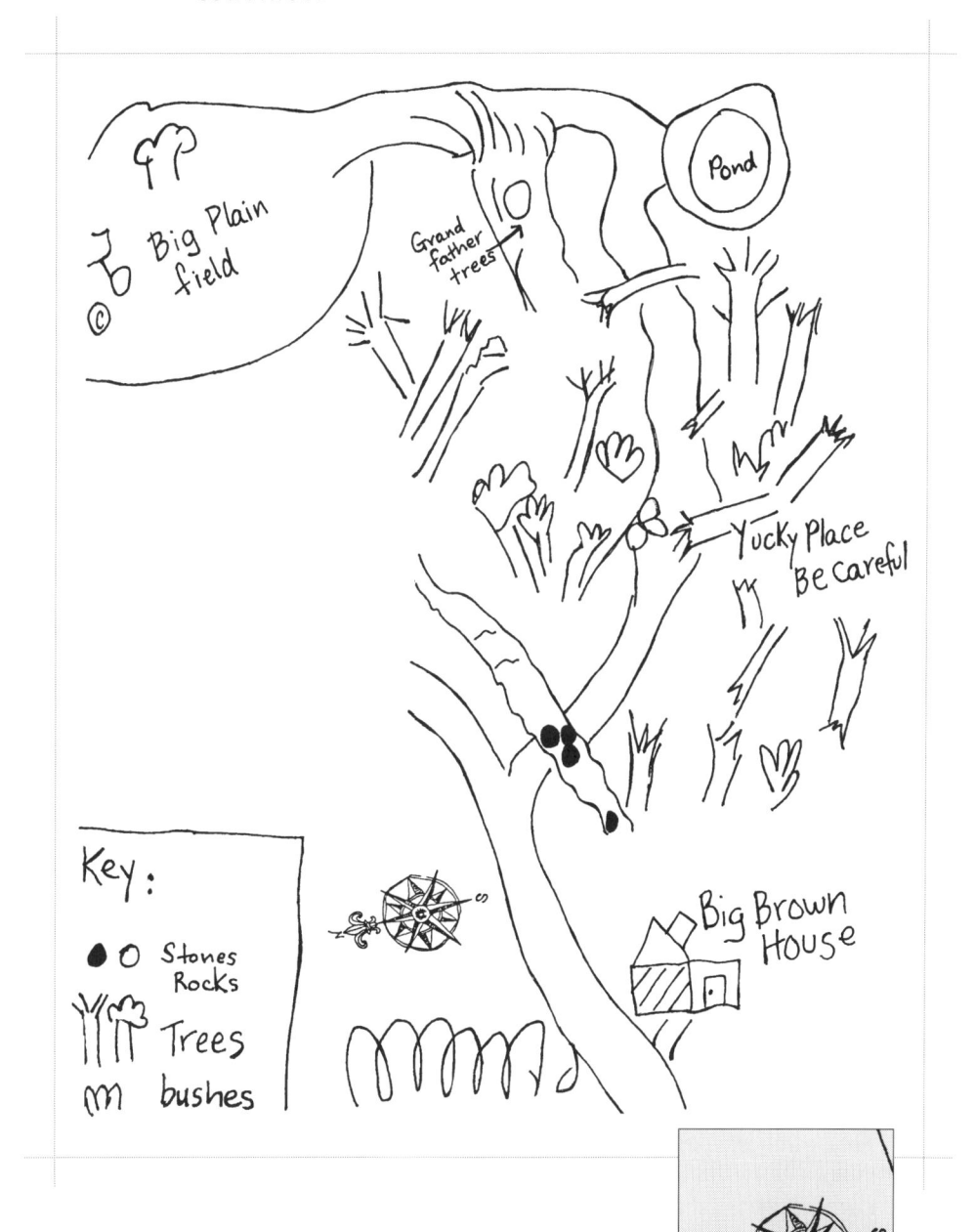

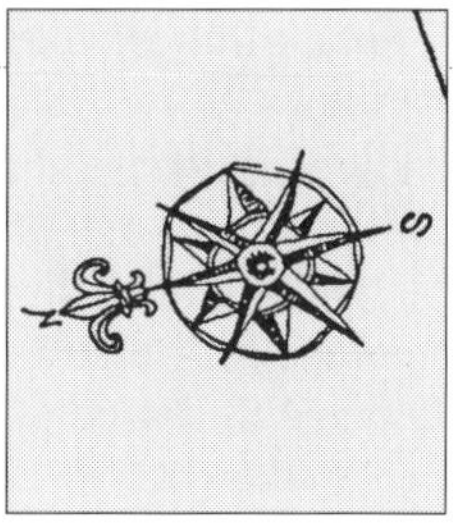

HANOVER NH
CONTINUED

'follow blazes of blue.'

BALCH HILL QUEST 41

LIBRARIES OF HANOVER QUEST 20

HANOVER NH

To get there:
This Quest starts in the middle of the Dartmouth College green. Take I-91 to Exit 13, travel east across the Connecticut River, and up the hill on West Wheelock. The green is at the top of the hill on your left.

From where you park go to the green.
   Meet in the middle where a clock is seen.
   Then turn to the east. Walk to a building tall
   It is on a corner and its name is Reed Hall.
Before Reed Hall was built
Eleazar Wheelock was the one
Who had the first library—
In his home it was run.
A mystery in 1838! This very same home
disappeared! Oh WHERE did it roam?
Our mystery will be solved later in the day,
But first we go off in another way.
Walk north to an architectural treasure
Whose stones are too huge to measure.
Be sure to count the arches all
Before you turn to the four-columned hall.
Two Dartmouth libraries side by side.
One of columns to view with pride
The other one with a weather-vane tower
That chimes for you at every hour.
Proceed west. Four brick buildings you will see.
Then walk south: at the corner an eatery.
Cross West Wheelock. Go right—We're almost there
And the mystery solved about the house that went WHERE?
Keep going, keep looking, and follow your noses.
Open your eyes wide—can you smell the roses?
Go in (if it is open) four columns you've seen before
Two located on either side of the door.
The inside wall has a plaque, giving some insight you might lack.
While a flower shop now, it used to be a library . . . HOWE!
Now back to the corner, and stroll south to where awnings abound
Dartmouth, Ledyard, Wheelock are names to be found.
Stop at the ivy-covered building in the middle
Then go to the second light to soon solve this riddle.
Turn left and go east straight on your way
Past a new place to park—don't be tempted to stay!
Crossing beyond to Maloney's right there

HANOVER NH
CONTINUED

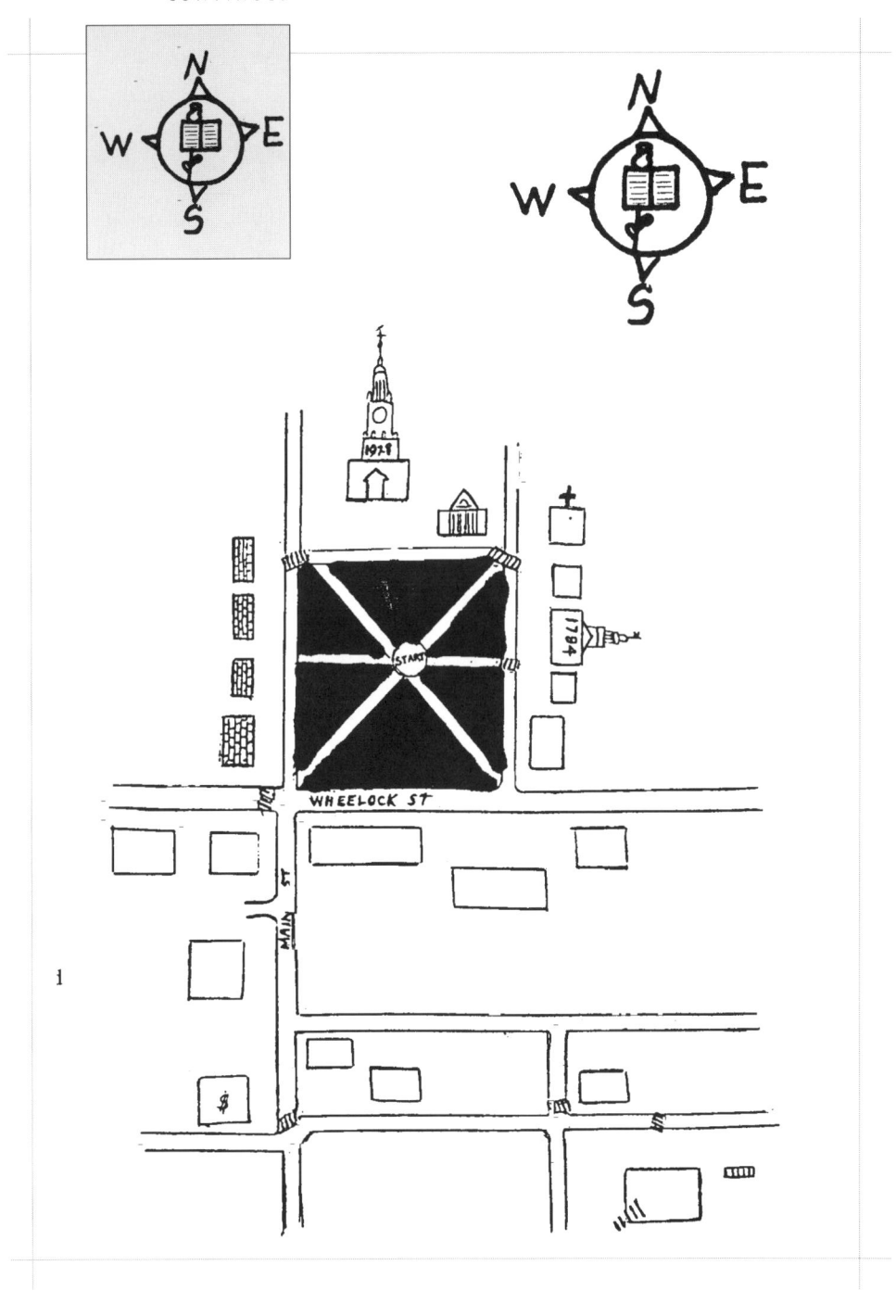

Then cross once again and stop! We are WHERE?
Yes, in 1975 it happened once again
—all of those books were moved to a different spot!
To this place, the Howe Library,
that we enjoy a whole lot!
Go down the stairs and 'round the back,
looking for the bicycle rack.
Then find the back door. A large push button you'll see.
Behind it, open the hinge and you will squeal with glee!

LIBRARIES OF HANOVER QUEST

21
MINK BROOK QUEST

HANOVER NH

To get there:

Get off at Exit 13 on I-91. This is the Hanover, New Hampshire/Norwich, Vermont exit. Go toward Hanover, crossing the Connecticut River. At the top of the hill, turn right at the light onto Main Street. In .6 miles, turn left onto Brook Road. Continue on Brook Road for .2 miles. Parking will be on your right.

Leave the parking lot and please come learn
　About mink, suckers, grape, and fern.
　Soon there will be a small trail on the right
　Go see the view of Mink Brook—it's a sight.
　Wonderful at rodent control, mink can kill and store prey.
　You may see mink hunting this shore one day!

An alder tree will be on your left as you look at the view.
　On the right are tall willow trees, of which there are two.
　Both of these tree species can be found by brooks.
　They need soil this moist, to help their good looks.

Each alder tree leaf scar has a round face with eyes
　And a tiny nose looks at you with surprise.
　Alder trees anchor stream banks, containing the motion.
　Their roots are essential to preventing soil erosion.

Willow　*Alder*

Return back to the main trail and continue 'til a house.
　Listen to the sound of the water. Be as quiet as a mouse.
　This sound is made by bubbles breaking.
　Under the rocks, animal homes in the making.

Little face

Mayfly　*Live in Ripples*　*Water Penny*　*Stonefly*

Riverside Grape — dark blue berries

Continue on the main trail, not two trails right.
　Bend to the left where the crabapple tree is in sight.
　Look on both sides for the riverbank grape, a vine with tendrils to climb.
　Grouse, fox, turkey, and other wildlife upon its fruit dine.

The trail continues to a small meadow where ripples abound,
　A place where animal tracks can be found,
　On the sandbar, raccoons, foxes, mink . . . even bear,
　Have left footprints when drinking and hunting with care.

44　VALLEY QUEST · 2001

HANOVER NH
CONTINUED

As you go on, European buckthorn is on the right,
   When it's thick it out-competes native plants for sunlight.
   It also is a glutton for nutrients and space,
   So wildlife loses native food at a far too rapid pace.
   To help with the problem, use native or non-invasive plants at home.
   Never release aquarium plants into streams, for the plants might roam.
   Be careful to remove all plant material from boats as well.
   This keeps water milfoil, water chestnut, and zebra mussels from spreading, I tell.

On the trail a little further, pine and hemlock abound.
   Continue up the rise past a stone wall that follows the ground.
   Take a right onto the Brook Loop and enjoy the water again.
   In early spring you'll find a lot of suckers here and their kin.
   In the last week of April and first week of May,
   Suckers move up the brook, jumping up waterfalls so gay.
   Continue on this trail—following the blue arrow.
   It's the main trail you want, not the one that is narrow.

One of this region's natural wonders is the sucker migration.

Now at the intersection, the Quest you will not fail.
   You must continue straight and take the Forest Trail.

Animals move through here to the brook where they drink,
   To their lives this habitat is a key link.

Walk until you find some giant pines, then cross a buried log bridge and find equisetum there.
   Horsetails is another name for this plant that is not rare.
   It is useful for anchoring the soil. Look at it close.
   See its jointed stems. It can poison livestock if they get too high a dose!

As you make the bend the land slopes up quite a bit.
   In the springtime the wildflowers will be quite colorful, so sit!

a. maidenhair fern
b. red trillium
c. blue cohosh

Cross another soggy bridge and notice moss-covered logs, some old and some new.
   Find the oldest you can and the youngest one too.

Now soon you are at an intersection again. Walk back eight paces.
   In the stone wall is a hole, where the Quest box now faces.

(To return to the parking lot, take a right.
   A "Mink Brook Nature Preserve" sign is in your sight.)

MINK BROOK QUEST

MOOSE MOUNTAIN QUEST 22

HANOVER NH

To get there:
From Hanover, take East Wheelock Street over the hill and down to Etna, about 4 1/2 miles. Where the road ends, turn left, onto Etna Road. Continue 1/2 mile, past the Etna General Store, to Ruddsboro Road, and turn right. After 1 1/2 miles, turn left onto Three Mile Road. Continue about 1 mile, until you see a small parking area on your left, where the Appalachian Trail crosses the road. Park here. The trail is on your right.

'... Commit time and effort and desire to DO'

Cross the road and look for the sign.
    There are the colored blazes you must find.
    Start here for adventure and soon you will see
    A great, big, old "W" tree.

Continue along, and you will have found
    That when you climb up THIS mountain
    First you go DOWN!

Across a creek, then you must creep
    But be careful—don't wake the moose
    From his sleep!

Walk half a mile, past Harris Trail
    Then follow white blazes—you will not fail
    To pass a swamp and begin your climb.
    Now it becomes a strenuous time!

Nearing the top are hemlock trees.
    At the summit turn south and you will see
    A most marvelous view: mountains, rivers, and ponds
    A view created, it seems, as if by a magician's wand.

Now look for a large, southerly pine.
    Under some rocks our box you will find.

You have succeeded in your Valley Quest hike
    Armed with willpower, strength, and the like.
    Success is gratifying to all of us who
    Commit time and effort and desire to DO!

HANOVER NH
CONTINUED

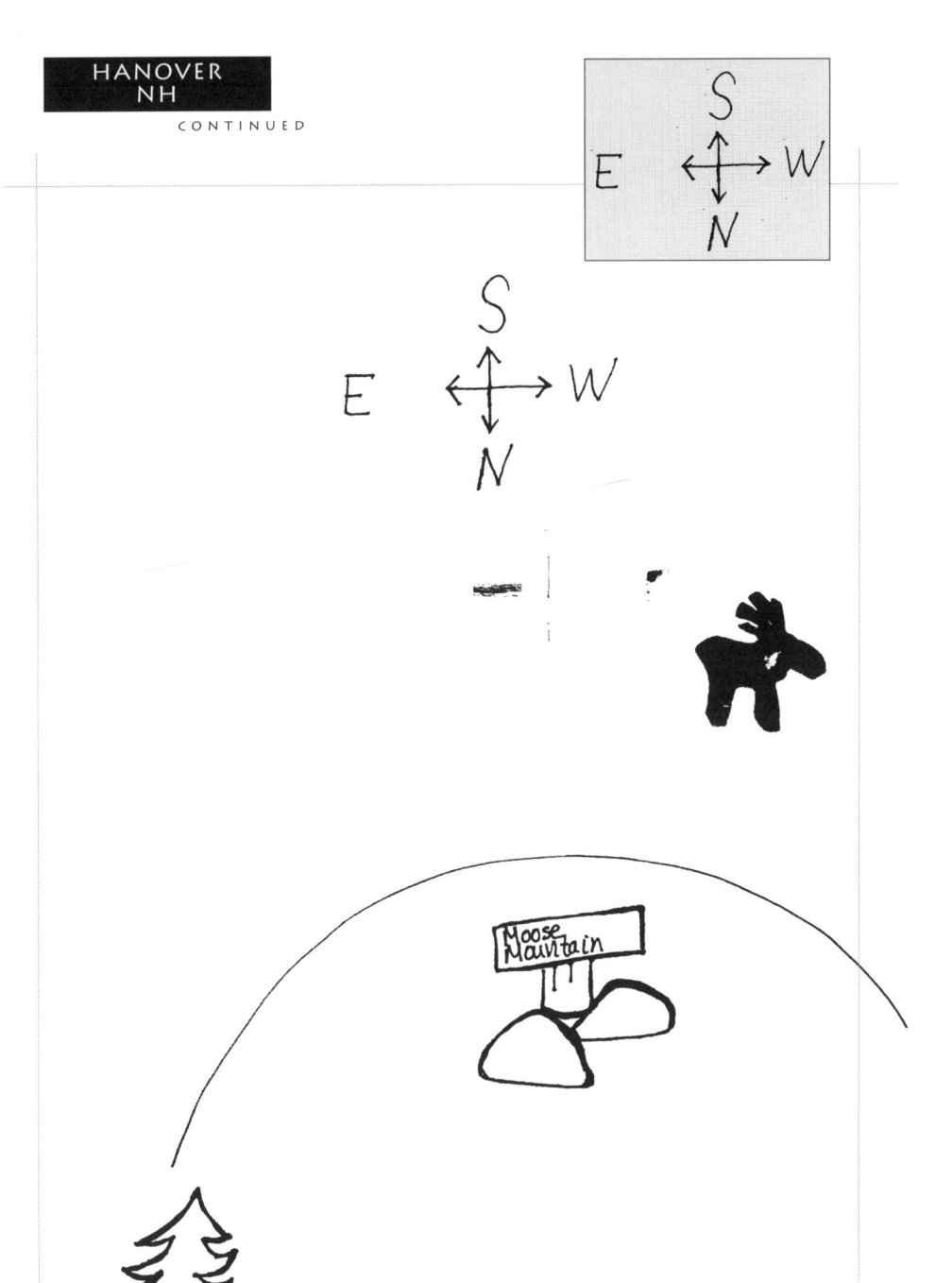

MOOSE MOUNTAIN QUEST 47

VELVET ROCKS QUEST 23

HANOVER NH

To get there:

From Exit 13 off I-91, travel east across the Connecticut River into Hanover. Continue straight through the traffic lights to the second set of lights. Turn right onto South Park Street/Route 120 and continue to the first major intersection. At the intersection, turn left into the parking lot for the Co-op Service Center.

As you are driving on Lebanon Street,
   A five-way stoplight soon you'll greet,
     To the east, a grocery store, gas station, and field
   Beyond, a forested hill will our treasure yield.

Behind the gas station, you may park.
   Head east by foot, and look for the mark.
   On the far side of the field, look to the right.
   Where the forest starts are blazes of white.

For maybe a mile follow white blazes
   Over rocks and roots.
   You might be glad if you're in hiking boots.
   When it seems like you've reached a high ridge top,
   Keep looking for a blue blaze where you should stop.
   Follow these spaced-out blue blazes
   To another hill top and see
   A hole in the middle of a very old tree.

If you look to the middle of this welcoming space,
   A campfire site, you will also face.
   A wood shelter for hikers will be there, too.
   And, a rock outcrop boasts a beautiful view.

From here, all of Hanover used to be seen,
   Now it is blocked by the trees so beautifully green,
   But, the sky so blue, you will also see.
   Among the rocks here, your treasure will be.

After a short rest, to the right you may wish to go,
   A few hundred paces to a place you should know.
   Now, here on the right, the trees open for you—
   A view of Etna, with mountains green and sky so blue.

HANOVER NH
CONTINUED

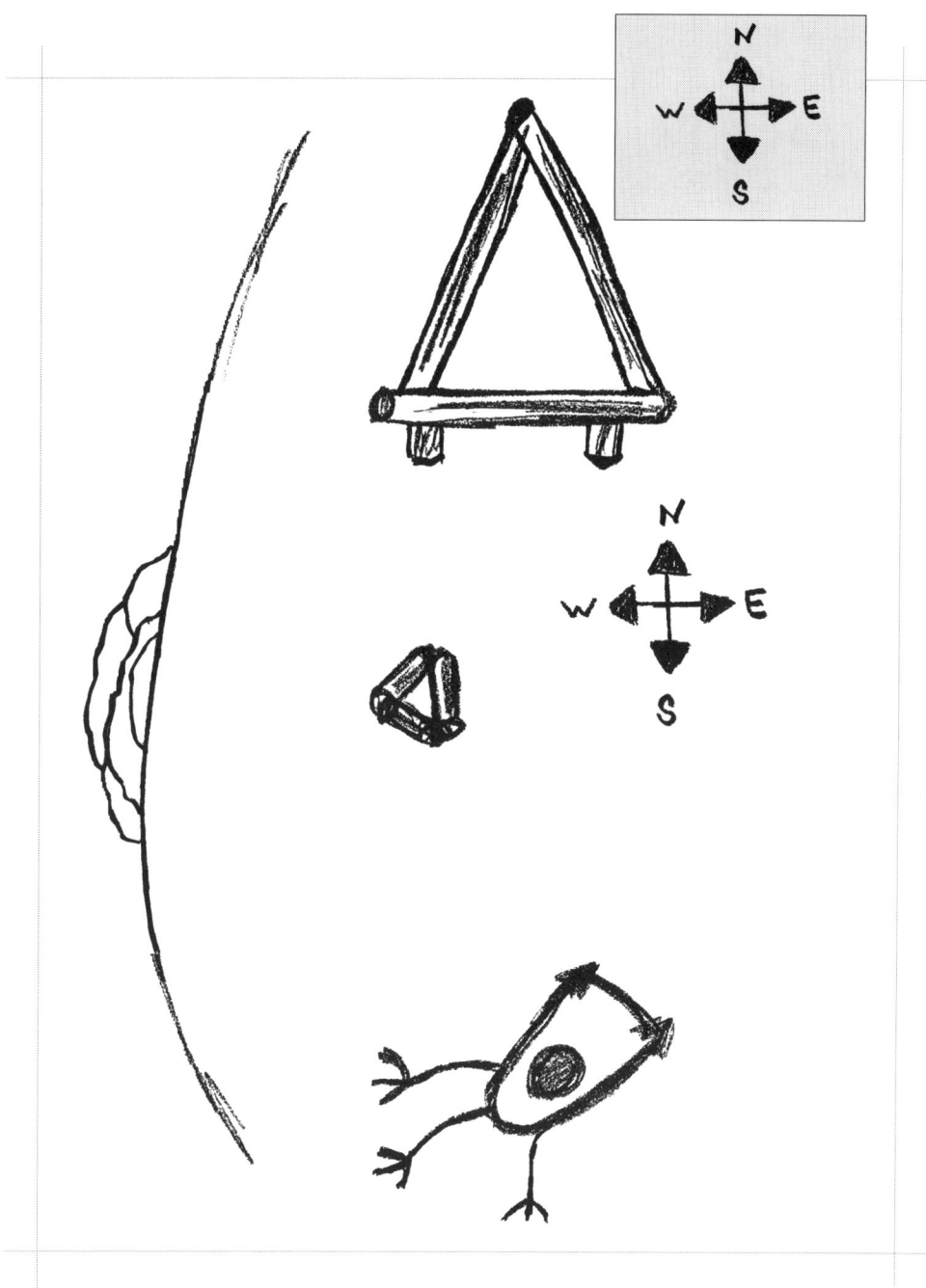

From here, the blue blazes go vertically down.
   Go right at the AT sign you've found.
   Follow these blazes onto the right.
   When you pick up the old trail—what a welcoming sight!

You will once again pass the velvety rock,
   Pass the forest, the field, to a parking lot.
   We hope you hike this on a beautiful day:
   And, that you find peace and rest—
   And a chance to play!

VELVET ROCKS QUEST

24 HARTFORD HISTORICAL MUSEUM QUEST

HARTFORD VT

To get there:

Take Exit 11 off I-91 and travel south on Route 5 to Route 14 in White River Junction. Travel west on Route 14 for approximately 1 mile to Hartford Village. Park across from, or behind, the Historical Society building (1461 Maple Street), which is on the right across from the left turn to the Hartford Bridge. Please note that this Quest can only be completed when the historical society is open, the first Tuesday of every month, 6 to 8 pm, and the first Sunday 1:30 to 4 pm.

Welcome to our home and collections.
We hope you enjoy your explorations.
Built between a century's beginning
And the "war to end all wars" ending,
This house was given to us to preserve
Our historic treasures for all
    to observe.

(The oldest artifacts date from before the town's charter in 1761)

Count the entrances to this interesting hall
    But please don't look at any of the stains!
    Names of many businesses are on the wall
    Find the sketch of the Quechee bridge for trains.
    (All the wallpaper in the house is over 50 years old!)

WRITE the first letter of the second word
    under the sketch: ___

Eating was the intended activity here
    Not the use of instruments percussion.
    A site of laughter and good cheer
    Find the dish with a two-way discussion.
    (Some of the dishes date from the 1830s.
    Now look around the room.)

WRITE the second letter on the
    old street sign: ___

Go now to a case with metals to please.
    Look for some small wooden pieces all in a bunch.
    Children are told not to play with these.
    You'll have to break one off before starting lunch!
    (Look nearby at the items from
    early businesses in Hartford.)

HARTFORD VT
CONTINUED

WRITE the last letter of the word found after
"EATAGOOD PEANUT": ___

The room with a fireplace
   Has a picture of a real nice face.
   Back in silent movie days (I'm told, at least)
   She starred in a movie called *Way Down East*.
   (Some of this movie was filmed in Quechee,
   Hartford, and Wilder.)

WRITE the second letter of her name: ___

'the railroad "made" White River Junction and was important for over 100 years'

In the case with sides of many crooks
   Are many items used to promote good looks.
   One is a "bird" designed for sewing
   It is blue and white and not crowing.
   (Why do you think it was called a "bird"?)

WRITE the first of the three letters
   spelling something that would be
   stuck into part of it: ___

Now we move on just a few more paces
   To find something that once would send us many places.
   Today a computer might fill this function
   Of getting us a ticket out of White River Junction.
   (The railroad "made" White river Junction
    and was important for over 100 years.)

HARTFORD HISTORICAL MUSEUM QUEST 51

HARTFORD
VT
CONTINUED

WRITE the second letter of the name
   of the town we're in: ___

Up the stairs there's a small room on the right.
   Is it dark? Then please turn on the light!
   Here worked a man who many came to see
   Even though he might hit them in the knee!
   (Take time to look around Dr. Garipay's office.)

WRITE the first letter of the word "yell": ___

Return down the stairs
   (did you turn off the lights?)
   Are you sure you have seen all our sights?
   WRITE all your letters down in a row
   now you've spelled out the name of our home
   Find the most modern thing in the house
   Look for the TREASURE BOX
   but watch out for the mouse!
   (You'll have to open something to find it.
   It will be labeled with the name
   you have spelled.)   ___ ___ ___ ___ ___ ___ ___

HARTFORD VT

HARTFORD RECYCLING QUEST 25

To get there:

Take I-91 to Exit 11 in White River Junction. Go south on Route 5 for about 2 miles. When you pass the Maple Leaf Motel on your left, watch for the Hartford Community Center for Recycling and Waste Management just ahead on the left (east) side of Route 5. This Quest can be done 8 to 4 Monday through Saturday.

Your Quest starts at the parking lot,
   Walk to the display where many things rot.
   Full of rotting leaves, apple cores, and weeds,
   Compost provides what a garden needs.
   Don't throw your food scraps in the trash!
   Compost is like gold—as good as cash.

Facing the bins, turn to the left,
   Enter a room and follow your Quest.
   Look at the walls of this entryway—
   It was children who made this display.
   What did they use to make the forest creatures?
   The eyes, the noses—and the other features?

Open a door to see a dragon with wings:
   She's made of plastic jugs and other things.
   Get on the bike and pedal 'til you're sore.
   Which takes more energy? Recycling or mining ore?
   There're lots to do and learn in this room,
   Have fun now—for your next stop is a tomb!

Follow the porch and cross the drive here—
   But look both ways to make sure that it's clear.
   Look at the land going up a slope,
   There's a stone here that's kind of a joke.
   It is a tombstone for a mountain of trash,
   A huge, mummified garbage stash.

Now turn around and read the signs.
   We collect hazardous wastes here—all kinds.
   Bleach, batteries, chemicals to kill aphids and ticks—
   Don't throw 'em in the trash! They'll poison the groundwater, make us sick.
   Now stop, close your eyes, and please think . . .
   What hazardous waste is under your sink?

HARTFORD VT
CONTINUED

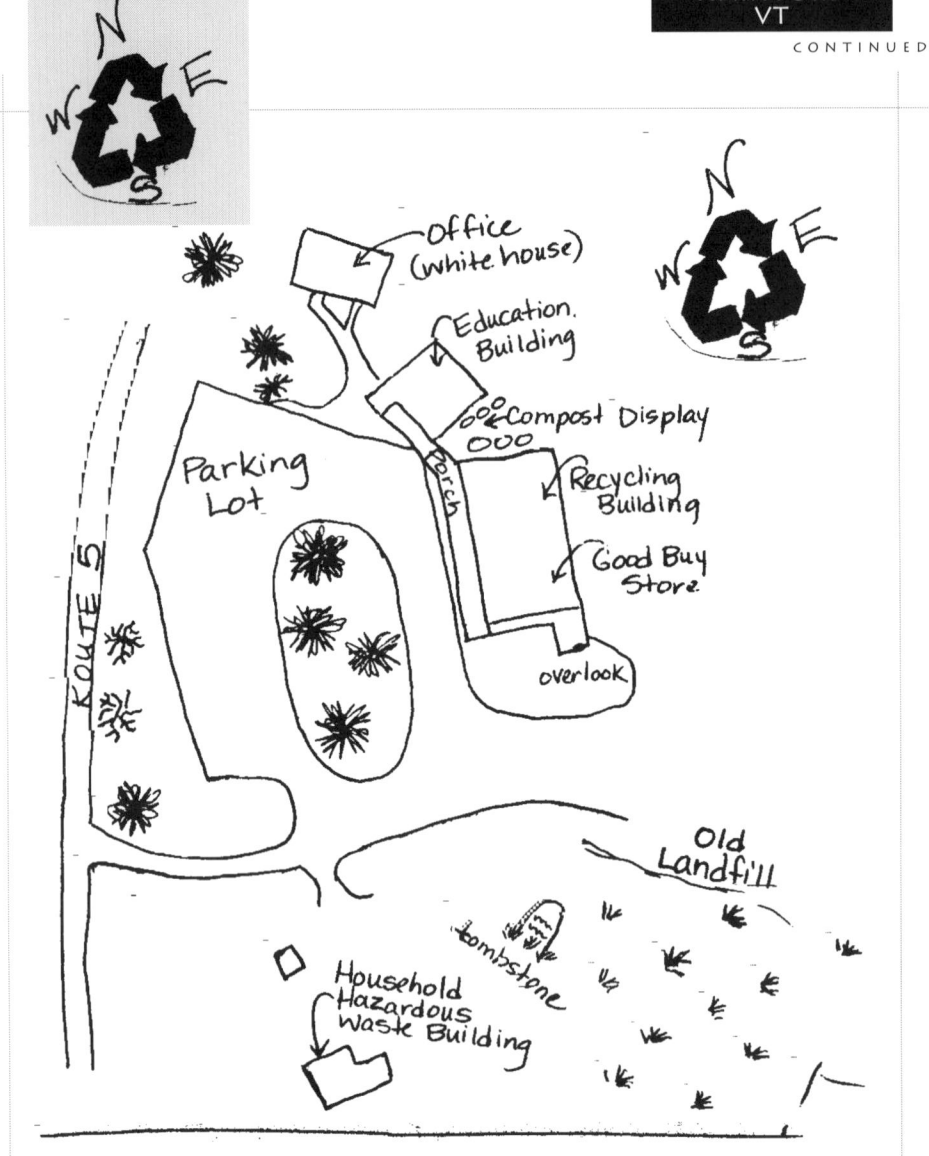

'... a tombstone for a mountain of trash, a huge, mummified, garbage stash!"

HARTFORD VT
CONTINUED

Turn back and carefully cross the drive again.
    Follow any people you see carrying bins
    To a room where we take used cans, bottles, and paper.
    It's all sent away to factories where they remanufacture—
    New cans, glass, and paper for all to use.
    Recycling saves resources and reduces refuse.

Want to see the cans and bottles fall down?
    You're near the treasure so don't clown around.
    Enter the far door to the "Good Buy Store."
    Here are used clothes and trinkets galore!
    Look for the "observation balcony" sign,
    Enter, and look around for what you can find.

The treasure box is very near.
    It is in the corner—so your Quest ends here.
    Hope that this Valley Quest was a blast
    And you learned to choose disposal last.
    It was a pleasure to have you here as a guest.
    Remember: "Reduce, Reuse, and Recycle" are the best!

We lost our way but found our way again. Sin

26
HARTLAND THREE CORNERS QUEST

HARTLAND VT

To get there:
From Exit 9 off I-91 go north on Route 5 to Hartland Village. Turn left onto Route 12 west and immediately turn right onto Quechee Road. Park in front of Damon Hall, the brick building on the corner of Route 12 and Quechee Road.

Start here at me
   Built in 1930
   Made out of stone
   not of bone
   I fought for my country in 1861
   I honor those who fought through 1941

Slowly look around
   To where a hotel was once found
   Deeded in 1774
   Who knew then what it would be for?
   The Pavilion Hotel is what it once was
   Rebuilt by Sir Damon
   (His name lives on)
   Right next to a tree.
   Dedicated in 1915
   Now is a place
   For a town meeting

Facing Damon Hall, make a right
   Up Quechee Road with your
   Next turn out of sight.
   Look for a road with
   The double ff's . . .
   That's the next task
   On this Valley Quest.

Take a left onto this road (ff's) for here you will learn
   Of a free standing staircase in a house near a turn.
   Down over the hill at the end of Bischoff's Lane
   High on the right, out of site, and not quite plain
   Is the grand house, once filled with fancy ladies and gents,
   Surrounded by a simple wooden picket fence.

Take a left on Route 12
   Near sign-maker and elve.
   And can you search
   For what once was a church?

HARTLAND VT
CONTINUED

Go to the East for 2/10th of a mile
    Looking for a house which caused quite a trial.
    Here lived a Doctor who shot at his friend.
    They divided the house and that was the end.
    This house you can find in plain black and white
    A house that is halved, almost, but not quite.

Next on this Quest is a Memorial Hall
    That once held books, but alas no more.
    This place of learning and books (did I say?)
    It now is a place of History, literally.
    Make sure you check out six over six
    When you look at this building that is built out of bricks.

Now it gets tricky so pass Damon Hall
    Carefully crossing to the old General Store.
    Now bypass Sumner
    And look for a sacred place up yonder.
    I know you are eager to find the end of the trail
    So follow "Station" looking for a white rail.
    Follow the fence around to a large tree that is fenced
    From the Ghosts, I hope this makes sense.
    In the fork of this tree that is close to the Church
    You will find that this box has a most perfect perch.

HARTLAND THREE CORNERS QUEST

27
COLBURN PARK QUEST

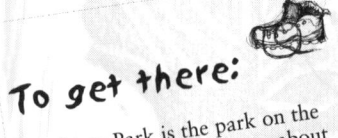

LEBANON NH

To get there:
Colburn Park is the park on the downtown Lebanon green about 5 miles south of Hanover on Route 120. Please note that this Quest box is only accessible weekdays from 9 am to 4 pm.

Welcome to our Valley Quest.
Please walk our map to our treasure chest.

1. Our map takes you places around our town green.
    Enjoy the stops that are part of our Lebanon scene.

2. Look across the road and look for a clock big and tall.
    Go to it; you'll feel very small.

3. Make a left past the gas station and down the road a bit to the brick building.
    That's for recreation with steps where you can sit.

4. Go back to the corner. Take a left. Go up to the big yellow building.
    There you'll see a gallery where some people get their salary.

5. Go back up to the corner. Take a left. Go up to that first building.
    You can go here to get a book or take a look.

6. Go across the street to the middle of the park and face Sweet Tomatoes.
    Go to the place Sweet Tomatoes is in. (Hint: Go northwest. This place rhymes with ball.)

7. Pass Village Pizza, then cross the road. Heading north is where you should go.
    But take a look before you start and see the place with the big heart.

8. Go past the Listen Center to the next street. Cross the road and there you'll meet the end of our Quest.
    Go inside to the front desk and ask for the treasure chest.

LEBANON NH
CONTINUED

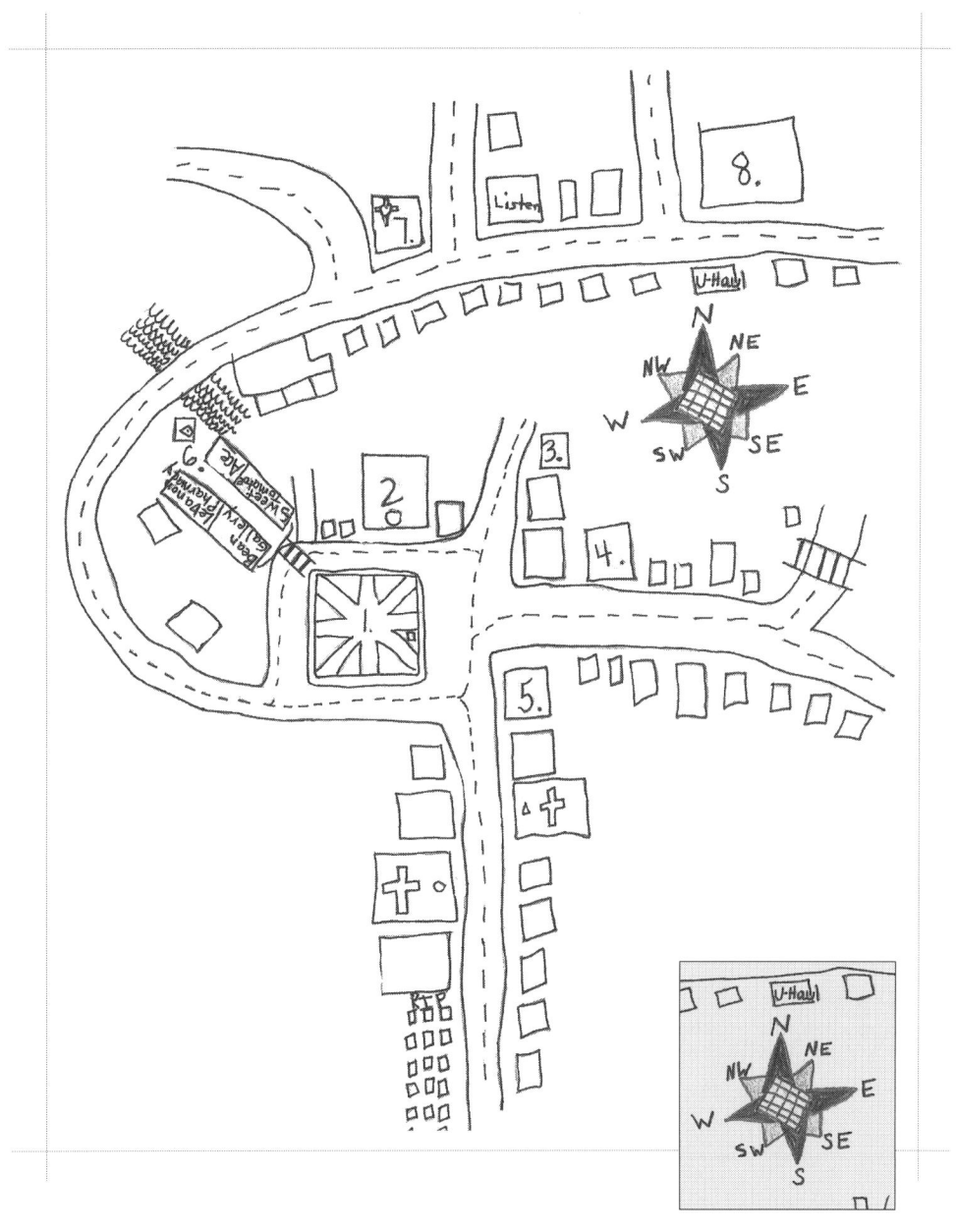

'... take a look before you start and see the place with the big heart.'

COLBURN PARK QUEST

28 RUNNEMEDE SCHOOL QUEST

LEBANON NH

To get there:
This Quest starts at Colburn Park, the park on the downtown Lebanon green.

Take a tour of Lebanon's architectural scenes
   With just a short walk from the Lebanon Green.

Old white paint covers my walls,
   I have green shutters thin and tall.
   I am an old and simple shrine,
   A fish adorns this roof of mine.
   My twelve-over-twelve windows are simple and few,
   Four columns in front will welcome you.
   Near my top, four goblets made of stone,
   Sit by the bell—all on their own.

I have arched doors and twenty-over-twenty windows,
   And a big flag that moves when the wind blows.
   On my top is a silver dome
   and a clock that tells you what time to go home.

I've got weapons on my roof, cannonballs on my lawn,
   I celebrate memories of soldiers who are gone.
   A Roman arch on my porch and words in my wall,
   A soldier in front who stands proud and tall.

Corinthian columns you will see.
   V for a U, could it be?
   A rainy day with nothing to do:
   Somewhere in here, there's something for you.

I have a painted roof with a cross on top,
   In my shutters is a bell that goes Bing, Bang, Bong!
   A Gothic style you will see,
   On a Sunday it may be.

I've got scalloped shingles on my second floor,
   At School Street you'll find me at number one-four.
   I'm fancied up, painted in pink and green,
   Look a little bit closer—something odd can be seen!

Standing in front and looking at me,
   Among others is a lesson in geometry.
   A triangular roof slopes towards my floor,

LEBANON NH
CONTINUED

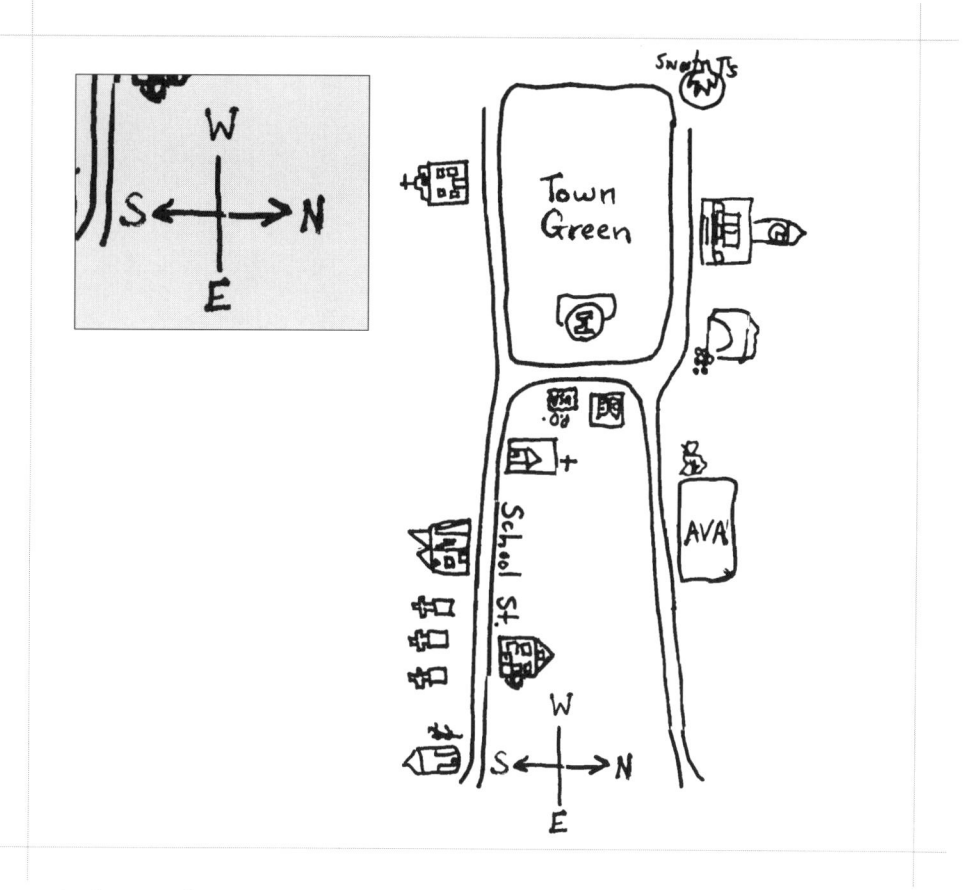

And at my front is a rectangular red door.
    Through many square windows look into me,
    And find a color mosaic transparency.

Georgian in style with vines to entice,
    Walk through these doors for some legal advice!

Victorian, Victorian, how beautiful art thee,
    Salmon is the color, green is the tree.
    Walk south of the green to a little store,
    Look across the street, you need look no more!

Made of marble in some sort of sense,
    I also have a white picket fence.
    Inside, painted arches up to the sky, rectangular stones,
    A broken chalice is nearby.
    At the far end, resting on a log, there is a book,
    Much destruction you'll see if you look.

Beyond the right turn the grass is green all around,
    And you cannot hear a sound.
    You're near the end, you've made it this far.
    Find Freeman, Smith and Hoyt—
    The box is near where you are!

Look for the box in the crook of a tree.
    Then our riddle you've solved, most successfully!

LYME
NH

PINNACLE HILL QUEST
29

To get there:

From the Lyme Green on Route 10, take Dorchester Road east. Go about 1.8 miles past the Alden Inn through Lyme Center to Acorn Hill Road. Make a left onto Acorn Hill and go about 2 miles to the junction of Hardscrabble Road. Continue about 100 feet further and look for the old dirt road on the left, where the Quest begins. Park alongside the road. Please note that the driveway on the left at the intersection of Hardscrabble is private property—please do not use this driveway for parking.

1. On this old dirt road, don't take a car.
    It's not safe. It's dangerous by far.

2. The trail is rocky and may be wet.
    I'd say hiking boots are the best bet.

3. Pass a yellow house on this trail.
    Keep going, and you will not fail.

4. At the fork in the road, don't go right.
    Just keep walking with all your might.

5. Unfinished road work you will pass by.
    Keeping straight is the route to try.

6. Open fields ahead and a pretty view
    Are just waiting to greet you.

7. Close to the woods you should keep
    Walking up but not too steep.

8. When you see two logs on a dirt pile
    Go right around them and walk up a rocky aisle.

9. Soon you'll pass more than one apple tree.
    Then you'll see an old chimney.

10. Facing the chimney's right front edge,
    Walk fifty-eight steps to the west.
    But take care not to fall off the ledge.
    The hiding place is . . . Have you guessed?

LYME NH
CONTINUED

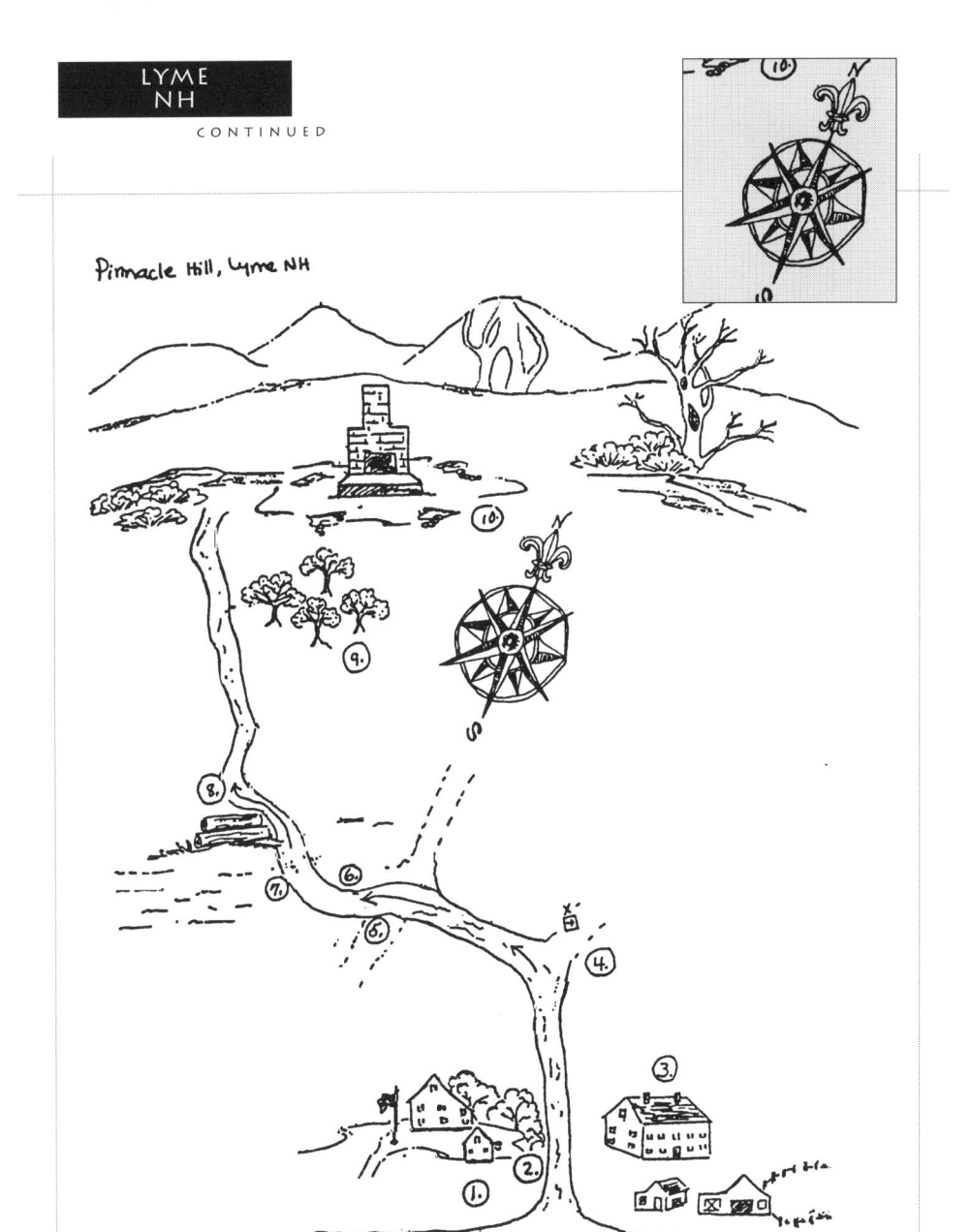

Pinnacle Hill, Lyme NH

Do you need some help or a clue?
 Well, three steps is about four feet.
 I hope that is helpful for you.
 Soon you and our hidden box shall meet.

PINNACLE HILL QUEST

30 LYME SHEEP QUEST

LYME NH

To get there: From the Lyme green travel east to Lyme Center. Pass through Lyme Center and travel 1 mile to the fork (and the Dartmouth Skiway). Fork left on Dorchester Road. Continue 2.4 miles to the parking area on the right, a hundred yards beyond the Beal Cemetery.

Welcome friends to Cole Hill. Listen closely, if you will,
   And afterwards try your best to find the treasure of our
      Lyme Sheep Quest.
   As the wires running above the road cross from left to right hand
      Look for the brown sign indicating you're in "Green Woodland."

Then find a clearing trimmed of trees, where apple blossoms catch
      the breeze,
   Lyme's Beal Tavern—surrounded by trees—was built by James Beal
      here in the 1790s.
   Beneath a great stump with outstretched arms
   You can see the cellar hole of the Beal Family Farm.

With this fine cellar hole at your back don't lurch
   But walk straight ahead to the pure white birch.
      Go further past, a sound you'll hear. Water is near—there's
         nothing to fear!
      Cross the brook, then veer to the right. A newly planted orchard
         will come in sight.

After the three pine trees bear right. Watch out that the bugs don't bite!
      Into the woods and on both sides you'll see stone walls not too wide.
      Past the wall that isn't too tall stands a group of trees that
         aren't so small.
      Keep going uphill, it isn't too steep; you may go slow but you need
         not creep.

Follow 'til you find a six-trunked tree, such a sight did your eyes ever see?
   As the trail flattens out, look around. A tree inside an old gate you
      have found!
   The big oak stands between the walls. How long did it take to grow
      so tall?
   The trail now twists, winds, between trees: steepness behind,
      the rest is a breeze.

Follow the birches beside the trail. They're on the left side, looking
      like a rail.
   Look to your left, look to your right, until you see an old sheep
      wall of medium height.
   Through the stone wall gate notice the property boundary in red.
   The past comes alive and it lies just ahead.

LYME NH
CONTINUED

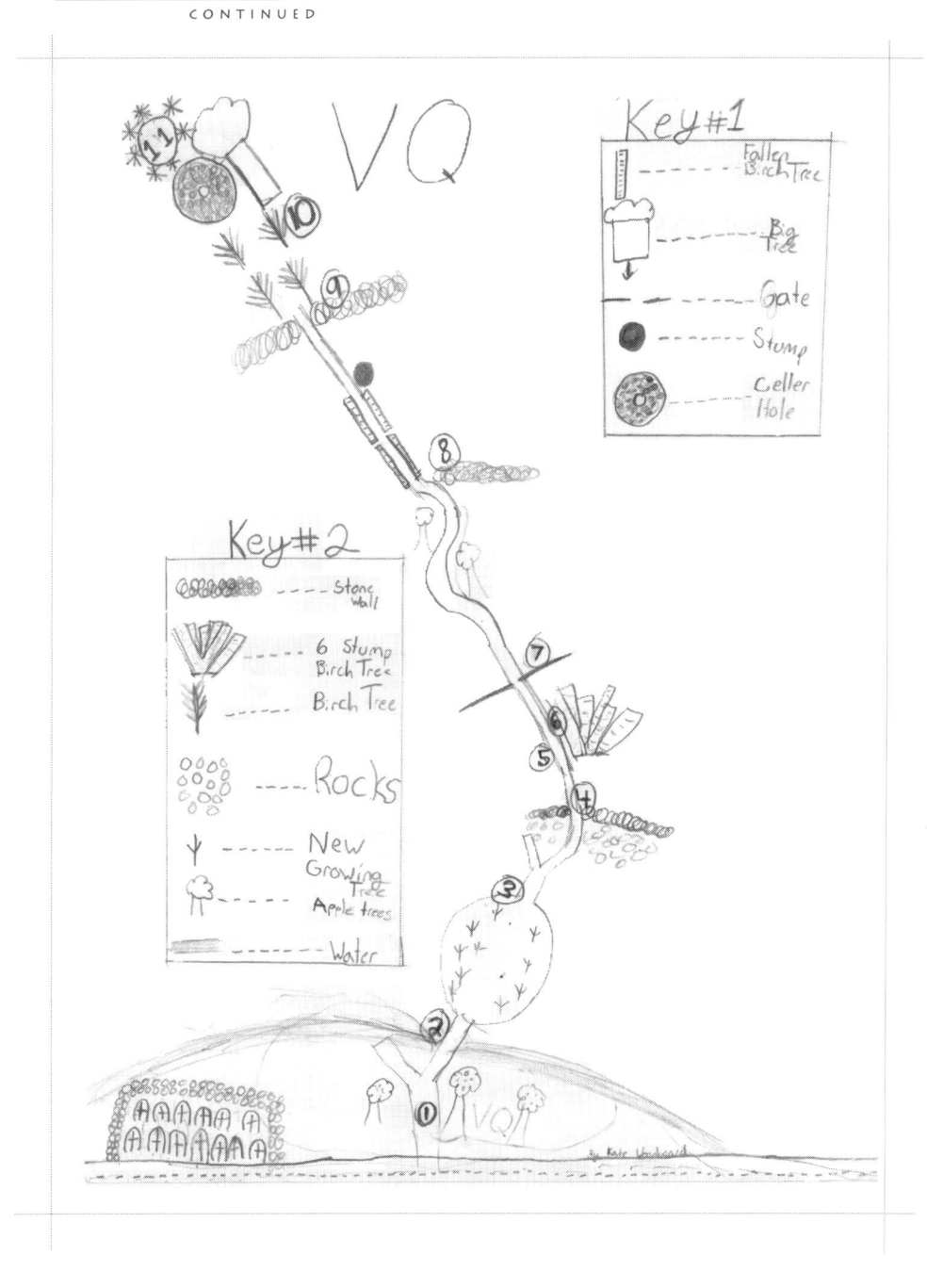

A closer look to your right . . . soon another stone wall comes in sight!
   A right angle you will spy, follow the wall but only with your eye.
   Soon (at one o'clock) you'll see a cellar hole with a huge birch tree,
   And rocks piled high . . . oh what can it be? A cellar hole from
     the 1840's!

On this, Cole Hill, there used to be a home.
   A farm, and sheep too . . . but now they are all gone.
   All that's left are walls, trees, and memories.

Our journey near over, you've completed this test.
   In the cellar hole find the treasure of our Lyme Sheep Quest.

LYME SHEEP QUEST

HAY 31 REFUGE QUEST

NEWBURY NH

To get there:
Take I-89 south to Exit 12. Take a right off the exit ramp. Make an immediate left onto Route 103A and follow it for 5.6 miles to The Fells. The Fells will be on your right. Park just inside the gate. There is an admission charge to The Fells. Check in at the office for Quest corrections.

1. Horse and buggy through the gates
   But now you bring your car.
   As you start the Quest today
   This is where you are: ___ ___ ___ (___) ___ ___ ___   ___ ___ (___)

2. Behind the gatehouse, lovely blooms
   For you to buy and carry.
   Read the sign that marks the spot,
   Then off on your Quest be merry:

   ___ ___ ___ ___ ___   ___ ___ ___ (___) ___

3. Before the house, a field of shrubs
   And food for birds and people.
   When guests were here in older times
   They got these muffins at the table:

   ___ ___ ___ ___ (___) ___ ___ (___) ___

4. Trickling water splashing down,
   Takes a secret passage underground.
   Then comes again to run and flow,
   Into the (___) ___ ___ ___   ___ ___ ___ ___ (___) ___ it does go.

5. The perennial border is fragrant in bloom,
   Here gardeners labor and carefully groom.
   Count the steps that descend through the wall,
   If you count (___) ___ ___ ___ ___, you've got them all!

6. This maple was planted by President Roosevelt,
   Teddy visited here in 1902.
   In the forest edge, almost within reach
   Are younger species of B ___ ___ (___) ___ and B ___ ___ (___) ___.

7. Off in the woods it's quiet and shady,
   Benches to seat the gentleman and lady.
   Gaze in the pool then see your reflection,
   Then follow the path in a westerly

   ___ ___ ___ ___ (___) ___ (___) ___ ___.

NEWBURY NH
CONTINUED

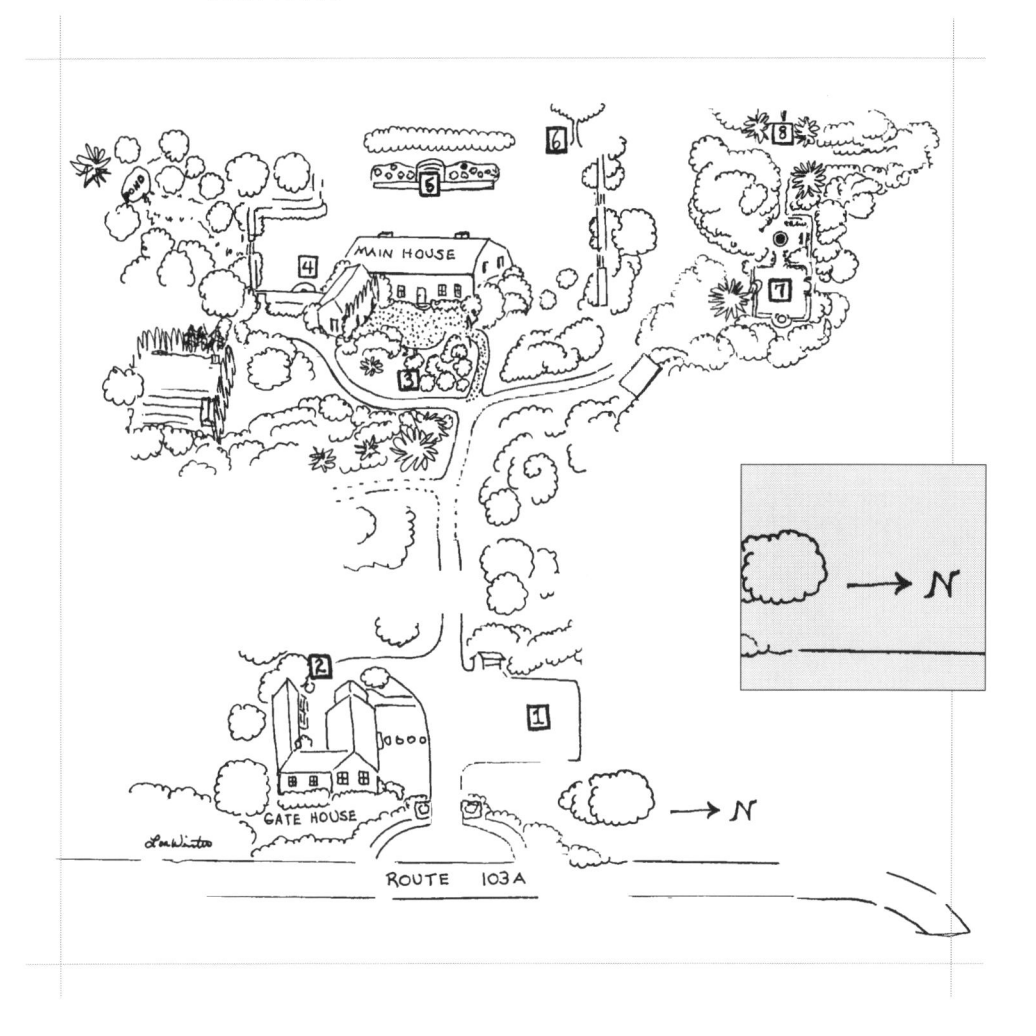

8   A pedestal stands without any head,
    The carved collarbones are all that remain
    Of this God of the woodland.
    What was his Greek name? ___ ___ (___)

9   From each of your answers, the circled letters are key.
    Unscramble that jumble, and two new words you will see.
    (A clue for those who need some aid:
    It's what the moonstruck mason laid.)

    ___ ___ ___ ___ ___   ___ ___ ___ ___ ___ ___ ___ ___

HAY REFUGE QUEST

32
SARGENT/HAYES FARM QUEST

NEW LONDON NH

To get there:

This Quest begins at the bottom of North Pleasant Street in New London. Take Exit 12 off I-89 North or South. Take Newport Road east into New London. Remain on this road, which becomes Main Street. After passing the fire station on your left, turn left on North Pleasant Street at a yellow blinking light. Follow North Pleasant down the hill to the base, where you will cross a small bridge over a brook. The road becomes Lakeshore Drive at this point. Park in the parking area on your right immediately after the bridge. Your Quest begins here!

1. Of the "pioneer" marker take note
    Between pasture and road
    Beginning in the wooded glen
    A trail sign is found within.

2. Follow needled path between
    moss-grown stumps and rock wall seen
    Bearing left at the three-trunked pine
    "Coco's Path" you shall find.

3. At the rocky crossing, look right if you choose;
    frogs and salamanders breed in this springtime pool.
    Cross old stone wall to brook and clearing
    Splashing water is what you're hearing.

4. Crossing the stream to sandy cover,
    find there a mossy border.
    Cobble shore, sand and gravel,
    Rolled by Great Brook, onward you travel.

5. Stand still there and look for a mighty birch (yellow).
    Brook forks ahead, to the right you follow
    Toward a pool deep where fish try to hide.
    Continue along brook, white blaze ahead, trail to your right.

6. Your Quest continues along this wooded trail
    under hemlocks tall but not frail.
    When small, these trees grew in the shade
    Of other trees, long to rest laid.

7. Stand by water, corner wall of rock up across the brook;
    An up and down sawmill was the form it once took,
    Herbert Hayes in the deep pool scrubbed;
    "Grandpa's Bathtub" it was dubbed.

NEW LONDON NH
CONTINUED

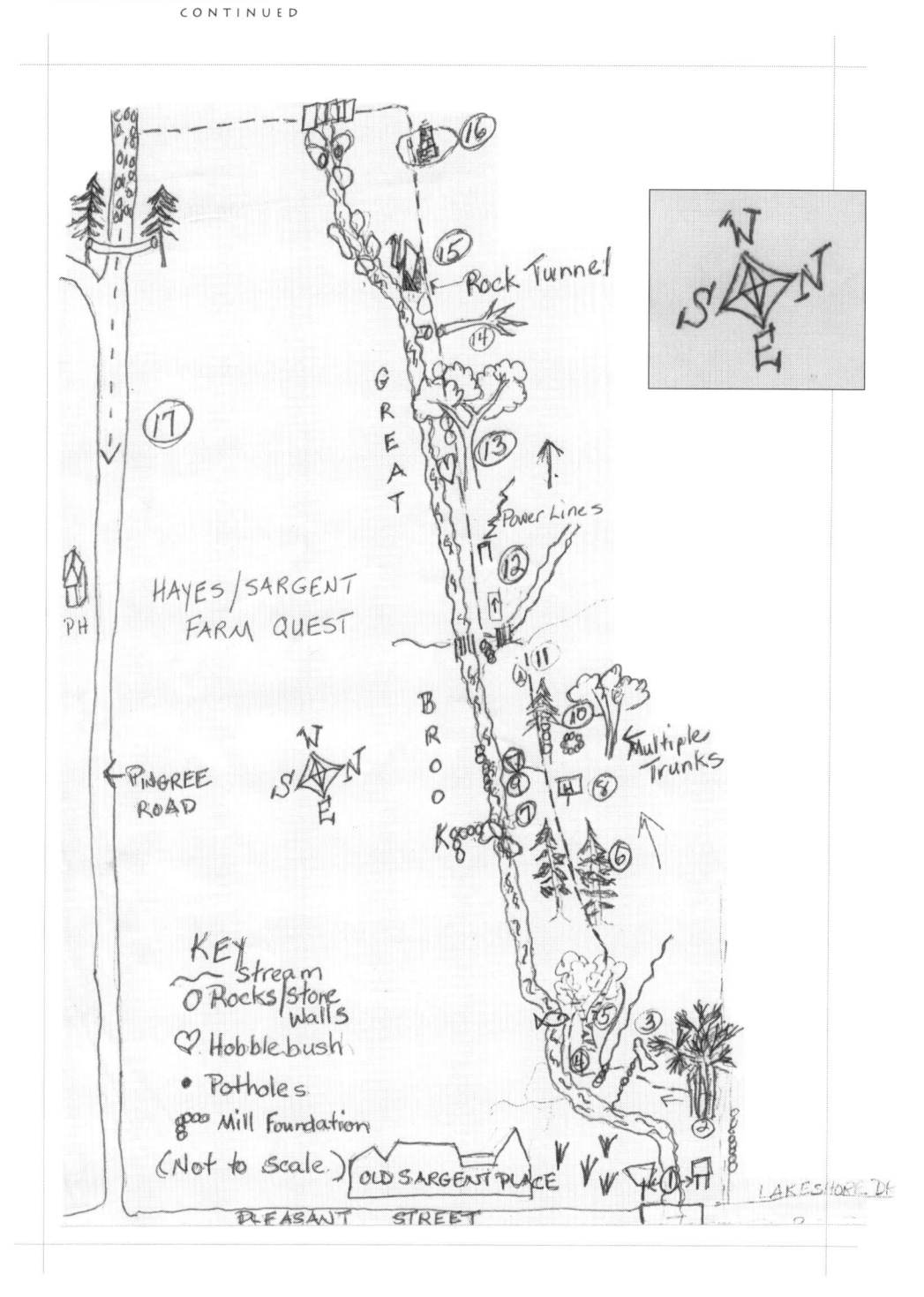

8   You've walked Sargent farmland (owned over 100 years' time),
    now come along to the "Hayes Farm" sign.
    Owned by the Pingrees six generations ago,
    Daughter married Hayes, still she loved this land so.

9   A wall of stone confines the brook,
    years of toil and labor, clearing land, it took.
    You'll find multiple-trunked trees—a sign
    That this was cleared pasture, nineteenth-century time.

SARGENT/HAYES FARM QUEST

NEW LONDON NH
CONTINUED

Note: Triangular rock juts out into brook. A bridge once crossed here.

10. Blazes move away from brook.
    Above, tree types change, take a look.
    By a long brook wall, for three orange blazes you are searching,
    To their right, find a stone-circled spring.

Note: A squatter who once lived on the land would take water from here when the brook was frozen.

11. Orange blaze on rock ahead,
    to the stream you are led.
    Crossing bridge or stepping stones
    Walk ahead to trail sign, showing where to roam.

12. Follow where the trail sign leads,
    trail right to "Lower Cascades."
    Over crossed roots, under power lines you'll go,
    After the lines, woods again you will know.

13. Smooth beech trees, maple, and hemlock surround
    over stream bed, keep your feet on the ground.
    See the big heart-shaped leaves of hobblebush;
    Ahead, the trail is rocky, hear Great Brook's whoosh.

14. Through a felled tree's gate
    along the trail you'll find Quest's fate.
    Past a large pile of rocks, up a hill,
    Cascades up ahead, Great Brook's water spills.

15. A glacial boulder to your left, ahead water falls,
    Find a tunnel of rock through which many hikers have crawled.
    This rock is of a specific type—
    Kinsman Quartz Monzonite.

16. This was a Colby College site many years ago
    with trails, a bridge, and a fireplace also.
    If you stand on the bridge and the brook is low
    below water spins out a natural pothole.

17. Cross the bridge, take a left on this old road,
    follow it out to Pingree Road, continue along, straight as told.
    Stop when you come to the Pingree-Hayes farmstead
    Unravel this riddle and to the Quest Box you'll be led.

    Facing the Pingree-Hayes farmstead:
        What took years of toil and labor along Great Brook to create?
        If you've paid attention, you know the answer, mate!
        It's right there, and behind,
        That the Quest box you will find.

NEW LONDON NH

WOLF TREE QUEST 33

To get there:

This Quest begins at the bottom of North Pleasant Street in New London. Take Exit 12 off I-89 north or south. Take Newport Road east into New London. Remain on this road, which becomes Main Street. After passing the fire station on your left, turn left on North Pleasant Street at a yellow blinking light. Follow North Pleasant down the hill to the base, where you will cross a small bridge over a brook. The road becomes Lakeshore Drive at this point. Park in the parking area on your right immediately after the bridge. The Quest begins across the street at the trailhead.

'Follow **orange blazes** *into the woods ...'*

1. Follow sky river above and pine needly road beneath
    Surrounded by trees—hemlock, birch, and beech.
    Wolf Tree is the trail on which you will stay;
    Uphill and ahead your Quest does lay.

2. Cleared pasture was this land end of nineteenth century.
    If you had been here then you'd see naught a tree!
    You can read this land that early farmers held dear:
    Multiple-trunked trees are clues this land was clear.

3. Walking on up at the first hill's crest
    you'll see boulders large both to the right and left.
    An old stone wall is found along the curve
    Stay on the wide path as to the right you swerve.

4. A "Webb Trail" sign to your right is on display.
    Go straight beyond it or you'll be led astray.
    Move to a warm clearing beneath power lines
    From cool beneath hemlocks, maples, and pines.

5. Rocky road between stone walls winds;
    up this hill your Quest climbs.
    Benjamin Bunker farmed this land for a reason.
    The south-facing hill meant a long growing season.

6. Benjamin Bunker carried up the hill, it is said,
    two hundred pounds of cornmeal for his family to be fed.
    In the late eighteenth century he had the will
    To cut, clear, and farm on this rocky hill.

7. On your left, a white birch marks much more than a space—
    It is in the foundation of the "Old Bunker Place."
    During WWII this foundation held a tower
    From which volunteers watched for planes by the hour.

NEW LONDON NH
CONTINUED

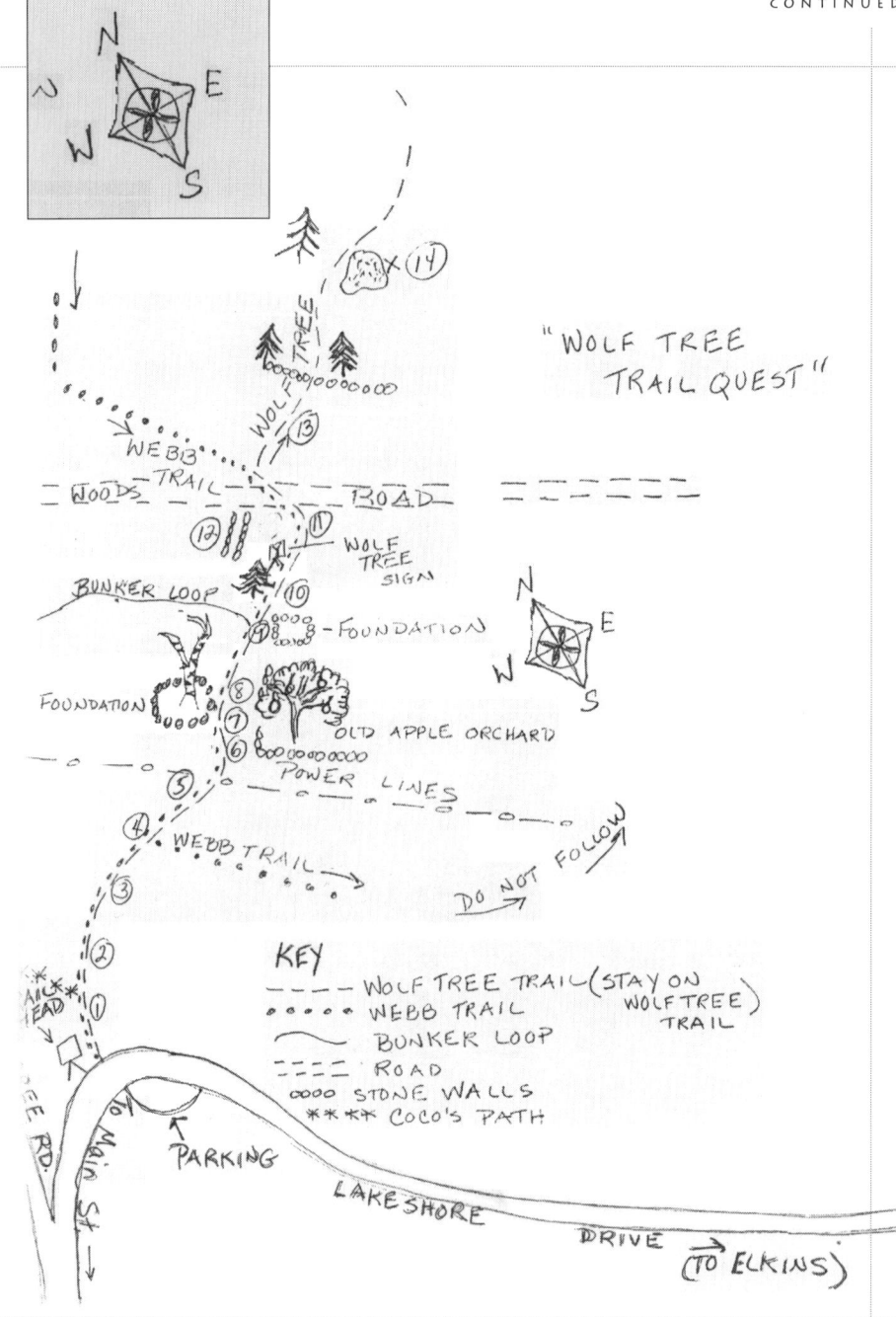

"WOLF TREE TRAIL QUEST"

KEY
- - - - WOLF TREE TRAIL (STAY ON WOLF TREE TRAIL)
ooooo WEBB TRAIL
~~~~ BUNKER LOOP
==== ROAD
oooo STONE WALLS
**** COCO'S PATH

NEW LONDON NH
CONTINUED

8   Follow orange blazes into the woods straight ahead
      as along this hilltop farm Quest you are led.
      On you left you'll see the "Bunker Loop" sign
      Across the trail on your right a second foundation you will find.

9   Once cleared pasture on your right
      go straight on as the trail gets tight.
      Friendly balsam firs on the left abound:
      "Shake their hands" and a magical scent surrounds.

10   A "Wolf Tree" sign will explain
      the nature of this great trail's name.
      Further on, find a logging road.
      Take a left and do as you're told.

11   You'll be taking a right on "Wolf Tree."
      From the trail across the road you'll see
      Stone walls, side by side, these provide a clue:
      Between these, farmers' cattle were driven through.

12   Bear right on "Wolf Tree," through glen of moss and evergreen.
      Orange blazes follow, fallen trees you'll walk between.
      Continue on and over a stone wall you will go,
      The trail winds up and on awhile—keep on steady and slow.

13   The last glacier rocked and rolled this boulder
      standing here much taller than your shoulder.
      Lichens are a clue that here air is so clean—
      Now circle the rock to find box in-between.

34 THE ELM STREET QUEST

To get there:
Take I-91 to Exit 13. Travel west into downtown Norwich. Park at the bandstand gazebo on the Norwich Green across from Elm Street.

The spirit of Norwich we think you will see
   As you follow our town through its long history.
Where you are now standing the white church was here.
The bells in the church are by Paul Revere.
Go to the street named after some trees.
Most of them died of a nasty disease.
As you walk up that street you will see something strange.
Houses set sideways just for a change.
(Why do you think they are sideways?)
When you get to Blood Brook the house down the hill
Is the oldest in Norwich—Jacob Burton's sawmill.
(What made the mill run?)
1765—Jacob and family came to this town
To build us some mills and to cut the trees down.
For the next 130 years this place now so still
Had factories, a tannery, a dam, and grist mill.
Now go up the hill and breathe through your mouth
'Til you see an odd scarecrow in a field to the south.
Turn right at the road. Walk to a pine tree by the flowers,
Look to the right, you will see Baker Tower.
Walk 40 paces to a bench near a dead tree.
What made the holes in the tree that you see?
Go downhill to a brown house, cross the street to a bump.
You have just found the old Norwich ski jump.
Down goes the road 'til you again cross Blood Brook.
Elisha Burton's grist mill was by the brick house if you look.
(*Hint:* Look upstream over the east bank to see some of the
   old stone foundation.)
At three signs you turn left to a door in a stone wall.
Guess who was put there when the ground froze in the fall.
Next to the door is a shed that is fine.
There is a hearse kept in here from about 1859.
Turn back and continue until you see beehives 1, 2, 3, 4 and 5.
Find our friend Jacob Burton (Hint: He's no longer alive.)
(*Another Hint:* Look for a flat slab in the ground.)
Back on the street find a huge old brick remnant.
Once called "7 Nation's House," it was built as a tenement.
(How can you tell it was an apartment building?)
Cross the street through an alley to see some tom foolery.
At the porch with the rockers is Norwich's own microbrewery.
Stand on the porch and turn northwest to see

NORWICH VT
CONTINUED

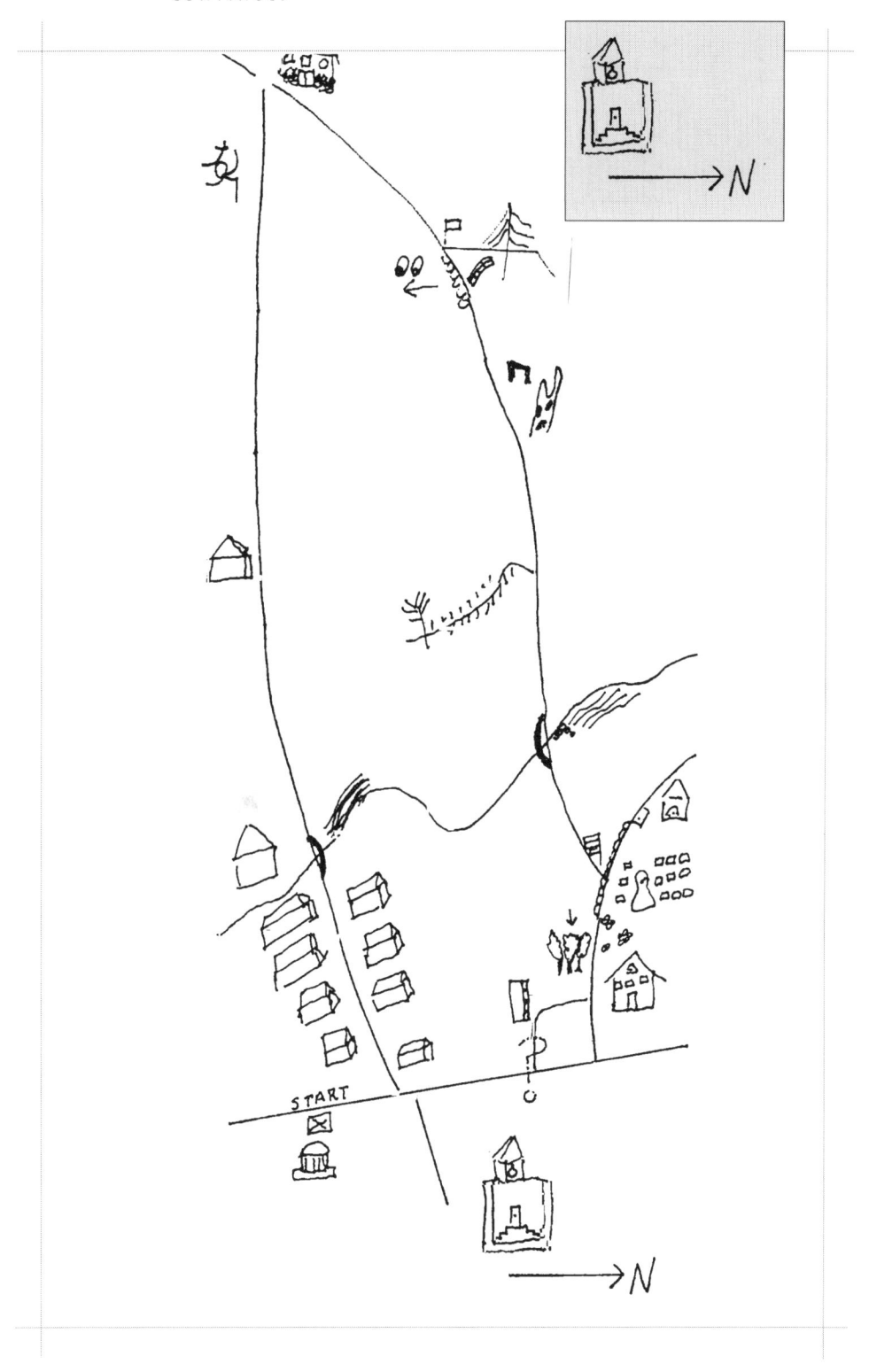

A really, truly, living elm tree.
(*Hint:* It is the middle one with the delicate leaves.)
If you find Norwich's Victorian inn
You are close to the treasure—so let's begin.
Two doors up high connected the Inn and the old town hall.
Your box is in the latter, near bird houses sold upon a wall.

THE ELM STREET LOOP QUEST

35
GILE MOUNTAIN HAWK AND HAIKU QUEST

NORWICH VT

*'Uphill.
The thermals
Lift off the land
in columns.
The hawks rise with them.'*

To get there:
Get off I-89 at Exit 13. This is the Hanover/Norwich exit. Go west toward Norwich. Pass Dan and Whit's store and continue for approximately 1/2 mile. Take a left onto Turnpike Road. In 2.6 miles, the paved road turns to dirt. In 5.3 miles you will see a sign on the right: Gile Mountain Trail and Parking. Follow the detailed map on page 77 to get there.

Wood sign names this place
    And the trail meanders right:
    Proceed, eyes open.

Tiny turkey tails
    Like little fuzzy brown ears
    Mark stump on the left.

See tree tops snipped off,
    White birches doubled over:
    Signs of ice and wind.

Trail turns to the right—
    Not a conifer in sight—
    At two blazes blue.

Stop at tiny bridge:
    Sensitive fern spore cases,
    Each spore a new life.

Turn up hill. Look up
    For a three-crotched tree and see
    Where a hawk might be.[1]

Wires marching south.
    Kestrel perch on them waiting
    For the grasshoppers.

Steeper. Trees again.
    Hawks migrate above these trees—
    Come in fall and see!

Uphill. The thermals
    Lift off the land in columns.
    The hawks rise with them.

---

1. Hawks can't weave nests but can lay sticks down. They need a sturdy place like a three-crotched tree.

NORWICH VT
CONTINUED

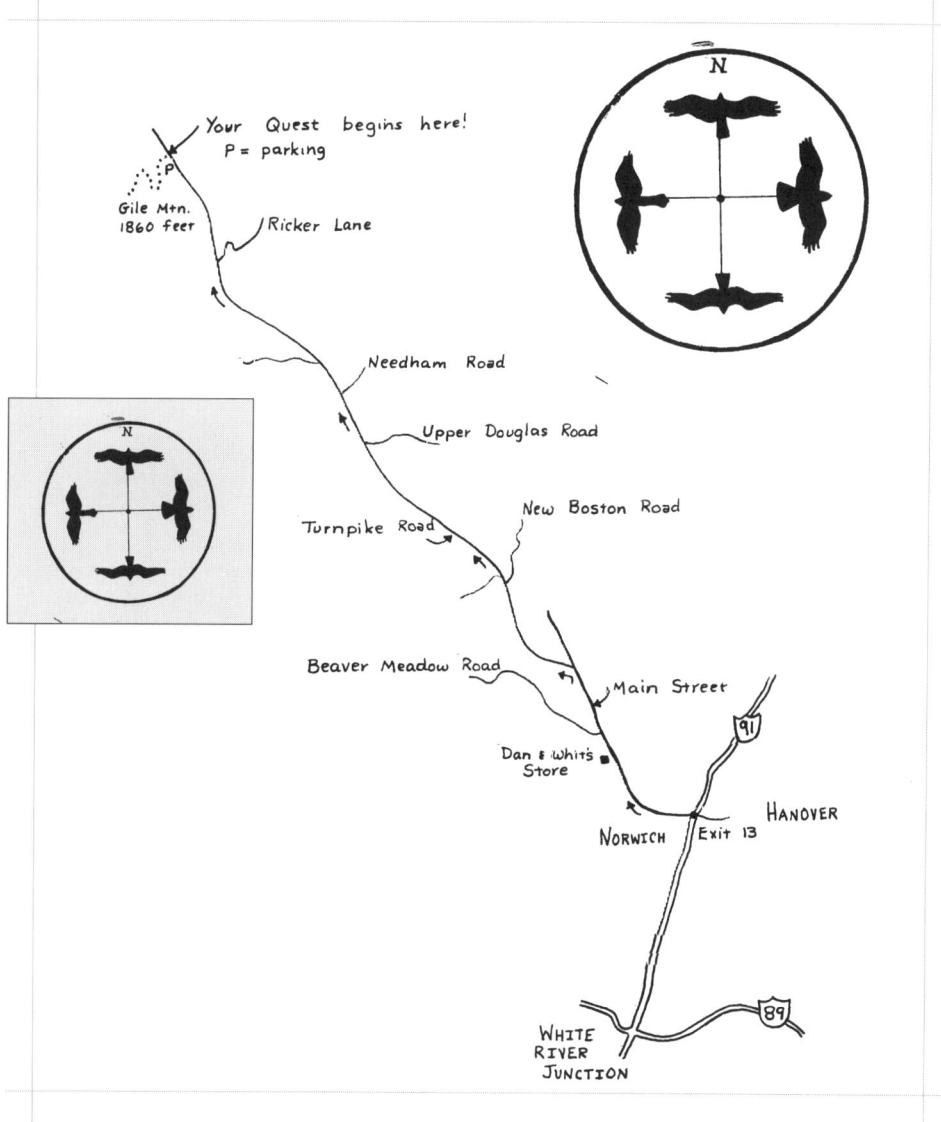

Look: ice storm central.
    Sheared trees and blown-down branches—
    The storm left its tracks.

An empty shelter
    Waits for you rain, sleet, or snow.
    Thank you, volunteers!

Climb up the tower
    For seven stories of view,
    Migrating hawks, too.

And for your treasure:

North from tower: spruce.
    Within find a standing snag.
    Behind, sugar can.

GILE MOUNTAIN HAWK AND HAIKU QUEST

GRAND CANYON OF NORWICH QUEST

To get there:
This Quest is on the Bill Ballard Trail, which is located on the west (left) side of Beaver Meadow Road about 4 miles from the Norwich Inn in the center of Norwich. *Please bring a compass.*

As you go on the Quest, I hope you will see
    Forest disturbances, there are more than just three.
    Clues of blowdown, logging, or fire you may find
    Because our forests are changing all the time.

Walk north up the road after parking your car.
    Turn on the trail to the left and not very far.

Leave ruins of pond and foundation of mill,
    Then cross the bridge and walk up the hill.
    Pick up needles. They'll be on the ground.
    Needles together in twos and fives will be found.
    The twos are red pine, with rough scaly bark.
    Were these trees planted in rows in woods so dark?

A red oak up ahead has a story to tell.
    The four trunks grew after its ancestor was felled.
    So pass #6. Look left after 100 feet more,
    then imagine the diameter of this tree's original core.
    To calculate: *Note the center of each trunk.*
    Connect them in an imaginary circle near the ground.

Cross the stream at #7 and on the right you will find
    a "pit and mound" that will boggle your mind.
    The mound was made from decomposing roots and debris
    and the pit shows where a tree used to be.
    So if you find a pit right next to a mound,
    then evidence of a very old blowdown you have found.
    The tree fell to the southwest so it was a
    northeasterly wind that blew the tree down.

On the left after 15, a poplar was scarred long ago.
    Was the basal scar from fire or log skidding? Can we know?
    Note that a collection of leaves on an uphill side
    provides the fuel for a fire to thrive.

Stop to look at the rock walls in the canyon nearby.
    Continue left on the trail and cross where a bridge of stone lies.
    Bearing from a multi-trunked birch near a pit and mound,
    go 230 degrees to a multi-trunked tree. Here, the box will be found.

NORWICH VT
CONTINUED

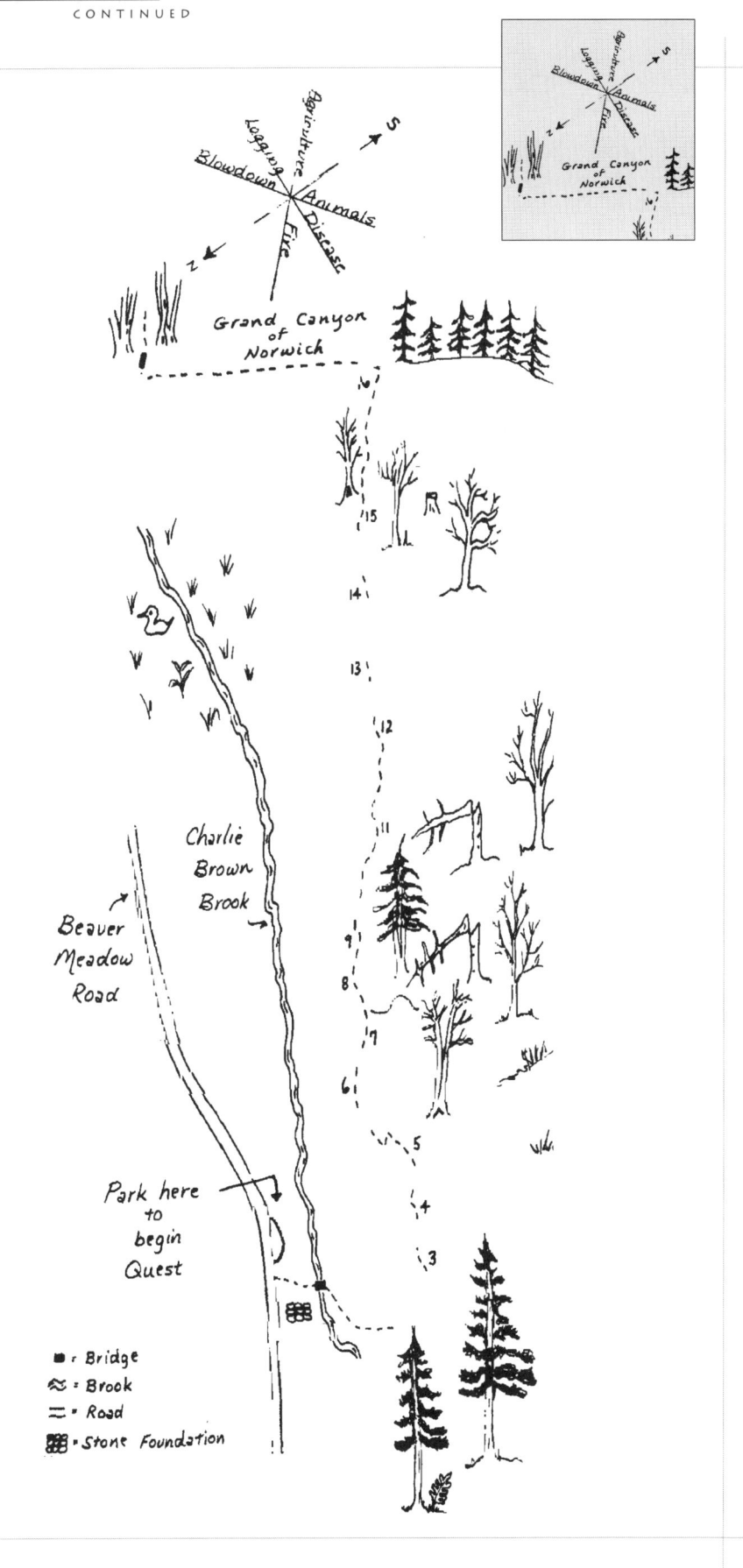

GRAND CANYON OF NORWICH QUEST

37 MONTSHIRE QUEST

NORWICH VT

To get there:

Get off I-91 at Exit 13. Head east toward Hanover. Very quickly you will turn south at your first opportunity. Follow the signs into the Museum's parking lot. The Quest begins inside the museum. Please note: The Montshire Museum and property is open from 10 to 5 daily. Admission is charged for non-members: Adults $5.50, Children $4.50, Children under 3 free.

Begin your Montshire Quest with a trip up the stairs,
   A visit up the tower as you lose all your cares.
   Take a look around and enjoy the view.
   Can you spot the Connecticut River and the Ledyard Bridge, too?
   Make sure you turn and see all around,
   Over the railroad tracks and down to the ground.

Back down the stairs to the bridge through the door
   (but first check out the notes written on the white board).
   Walk cross the bridge, and up to the woods.
   Take a break at the end and read some of the goods.
   Follow the trail, into the Northwoods you head,
   Look closely down as you carefully tread.

> 'Trillium grow here, when the season is right, as well as ferns and lichen ...'

Take a right at the **T** and walk the trail toward the road.
   Head through where the hemlock trees grow.
   What do you notice as you crouch to the ground?
   Do you hear anything around making a sound?
   Trillium grow here, when the season is right,
   As well as ferns and lichen and plants that don't love the light.

Head to the left once the road you have crossed.
   Don't give up hope, for you are not lost!
   Listen for the sound of a bird or you may just miss her,
   Or in the winter look for the tracks of a fisher.
   A red squirrel may be scampering with nuts he is keeping,
   While a fox up the hill in her den may be sleeping.

NORWICH VT
CONTINUED

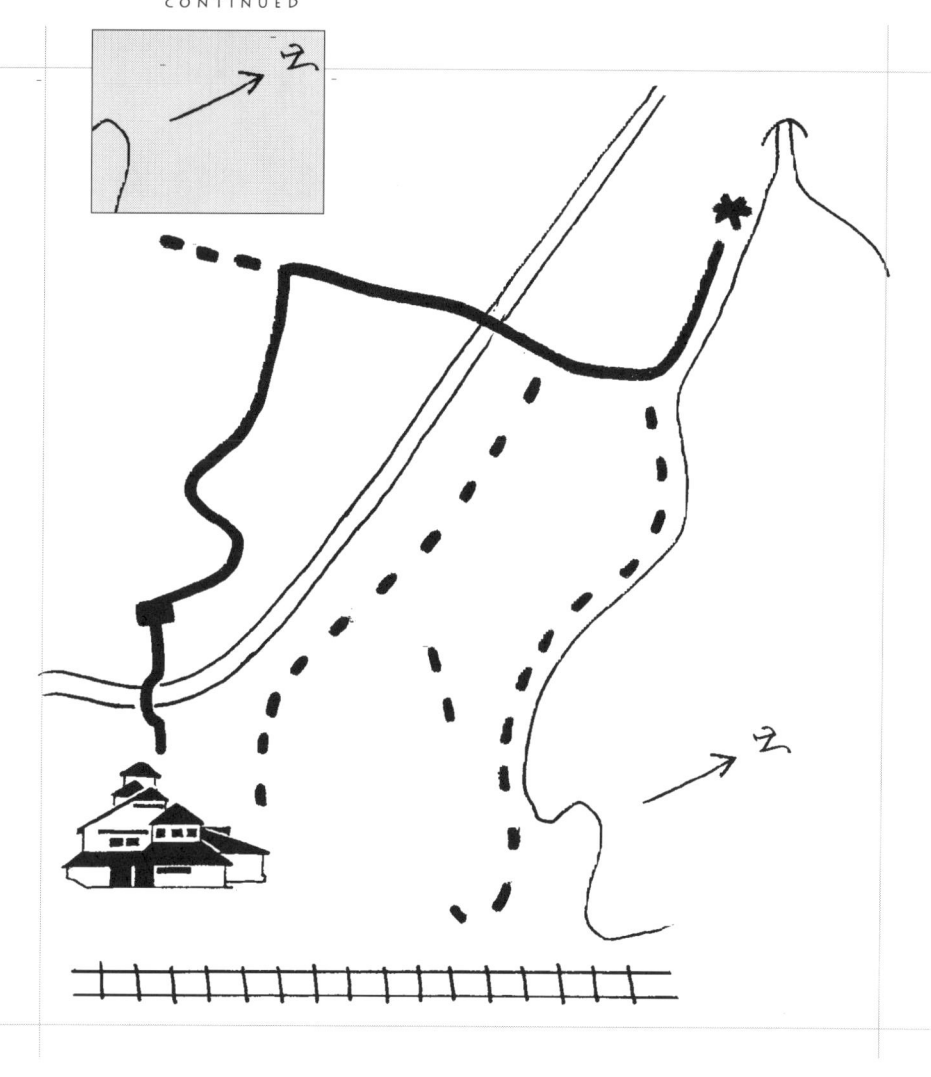

At the hill bottom take a left to the overlook.
    Observe all around you from the turn you just took.
    Go till you see a waterfall of a brook that once was called Bloody.
    When the water is low the lagoon may look muddy.
    See the arched railroad bridge all made of stone,
    Or if you are lucky a duck in a group or alone.

The platform is this Quest's final destination,
    So look in the box attached at this station.
    Look down in the bottom for the stamp you might need.
    Congratulations on following this lead!
    There is much more to do besides playing this game,
    So return to the loop or go back the way you came.

BOAT LANDING QUEST

ORFORD NH

To get there:
Take Route 10 south from the Orford/Fairlee bridge and pass 25A on the left. Park in the firehouse lot on the left just past 25A. The boat landing is across the street.

Park your car near the Orford firehouse,
   but don't block the way of the fire trucks.
   Bring a writing tool—that's cool.

Go to the baseball field and find the scoreboard.
   Look at Visitor and find the second letter: ___
   Look at Home and find the first letter: ___

Go to the street, but don't cross yet.
   Look for the first letter on the speed limit sign: ___

Now cross the street and don't watch your feet.
   Look for a sign that's quite fine.
   It's in front of an old church, but there is no birch.

Go to the sign that says "Boat Landing Road."
   Look at the second word and find the fourth letter: ___

Start to walk down Boat Landing Road.
   Peek through trees on the right at a yellow house.
   It is very old—1799.
   Don't look for a letter. That's better.
   Keep going.

You've had a long walk. Now rest and talk.
   Then take the first letter of this town's name: ___

Straight ahead to the wooden signboard.
   If you had a boat you could say "All aboard."
   Take the 10th letter of the name of this river: ___

Take a walk toward the dock.
   Look for a sign that says "Boat Landing only."
   Find the seventh letter of the third word in the
   "White part" of the sign: ___

ORFORD
NH
CONTINUED

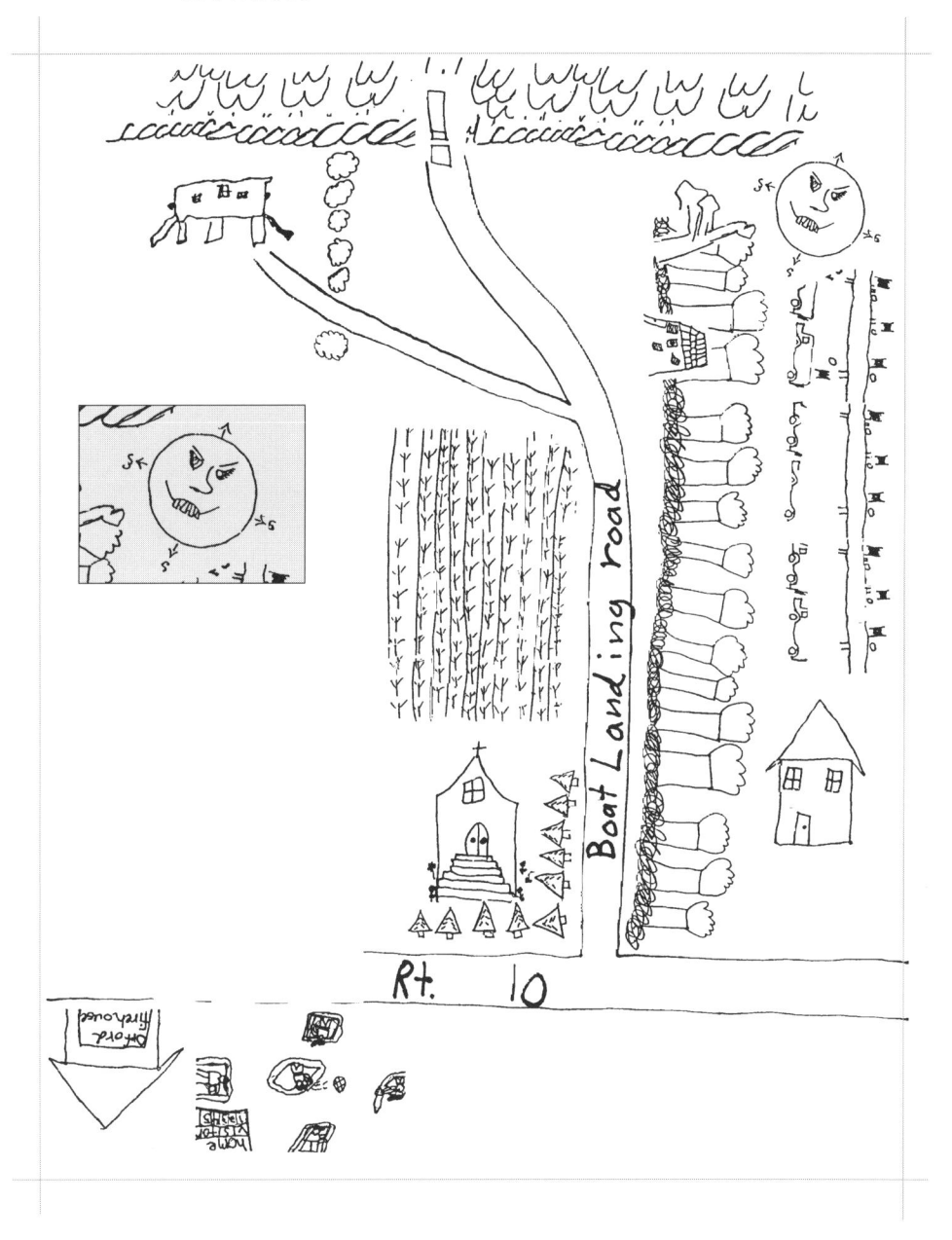

You have all the letters. You can unscramble them now.
 Here's a clue. It's a compound word that starts with B and ends with E.

B _ _ _ _ _ _ _ E

Look to the right at just your height.
 And there it will be—hanging on a tree.

BOAT LANDING QUEST 83

ORFORD BRICK QUEST 39

ORFORD NH

To get there:
Take I-91 to the Fairlee/Orford exit (Exit 15). Follow signs to New Hampshire. After crossing Samuel Morey Bridge, turn south on Route 10 to 25A. Turn left (east) on 25A, and then drive a few hundred yards to the school parking lot on your left. The Quest starts at the flagpole!

With your back to the school
   And your nose to the river
   Make toward the academy
   Like an arrow from a quiver.

Made of bricks in 1851
   And three stories high
   Its old white bell tower
   Points toward the sky.

With this view in front of you
   Turn 180 degrees
   And head down through the trees.
   At the octagon do what it tells you!
   Turn left on 10—
   You are on your way again!

With this view in front of you
   You are at "Ye Old School House."
   Used from 1829 to 1886—
   It's now quiet as a mouse.
   Carefully cross to wheels and deals,
   Turn right, jump and click your heels.
   Go north on 10—
   You're on your way again!

"1847" will be on your left
   Then six poles you shall pass
   'Til you're at John Mann's
   and his house built to last.

Pass 1829 and 1824.
   And then pass two more.
   Now a nice pair you'll see
   Built of fired clay 'round 1830.

Here is one of two
   That is now in your view:

With the two
   In front of you
   Cross toward "the Ridge"
   (With your back to the bridge).

ORFORD NH
CONTINUED

Turn left to Wilcox
    And a line of five rocks.
    Pass on through
    With cooked stone *under* you.

"Follow the fired brick road,
    Follow the fired brick road."

Straight through the stones
    (Bypassing "Six Chimneys")
    Then northbound along
    A straight row of trees.

Past church, post office,
    Eight columns and then . . .
    Twelve stones standing on end.
    Find 1840, and your Quest
    Is near over, my friend!

Once the Unitarian Church
    Stood so tall.
    Now the very same building
    Is the Masonic Hall!

Now think of all that
    You've heard and seen.
    Think hard . . . Do you think
    You might guess our theme?

All these things made out of brick?
    Ah yes, that is our trick!

For our starting place—
    Behind Rivendell Academy—
    Was the site of John Mann's
    Brick yard, you see.

In operation from
    1770 to 1907 right there,
    It turned out more bricks
    Each and every year.

Bricks for houses, for chimneys . . .
    For nice walkways beneath the trees!

Now just 'round to the north
    Of this building standing tall
    You will find made of wood
    A retaining wall.
    Secreted in a small gap in the wall
    You'll find our treasure box—
    Hope you've learned AND had a ball!

ORFORD BRICK QUEST

FLAT ROCK QUEST 40

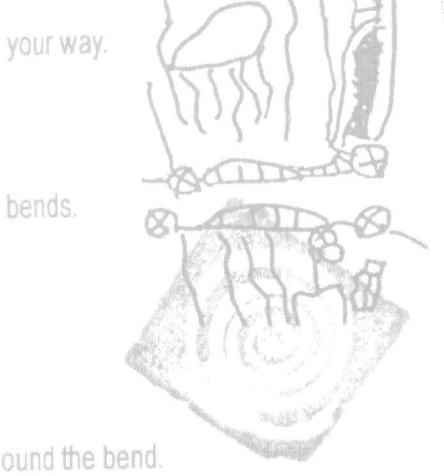

ORFORD
NH

To get there:
From Route 10 in Orford, take 25A for about 4 miles to Quintown Road. Take a right onto Quintown Road and go almost exactly 1 mile. Parking is on the left. The road widens out just a bit to allow for parking.

1. Start where you park.

2. Go to the big boulder
   Beware it's colder.

3. Go to the pool
   and you'll be cool.

4. Go to the bank
   and don't get spanked.

5. Go to the upper edge
   of Flat Rock.
   Don't slip and take a dip.

6. Go to the culvert and
   try not to take a slide ride.

7. Go to the middle
   of Flat Rock, Doc.

8. Go to the steps
   but don't get wet.

9. Go back to the bank—
   duck your shoulder
   so you don't hit the boulder.
   Under those rocks
   you'll find the box.

ORFORD NH
CONTINUED

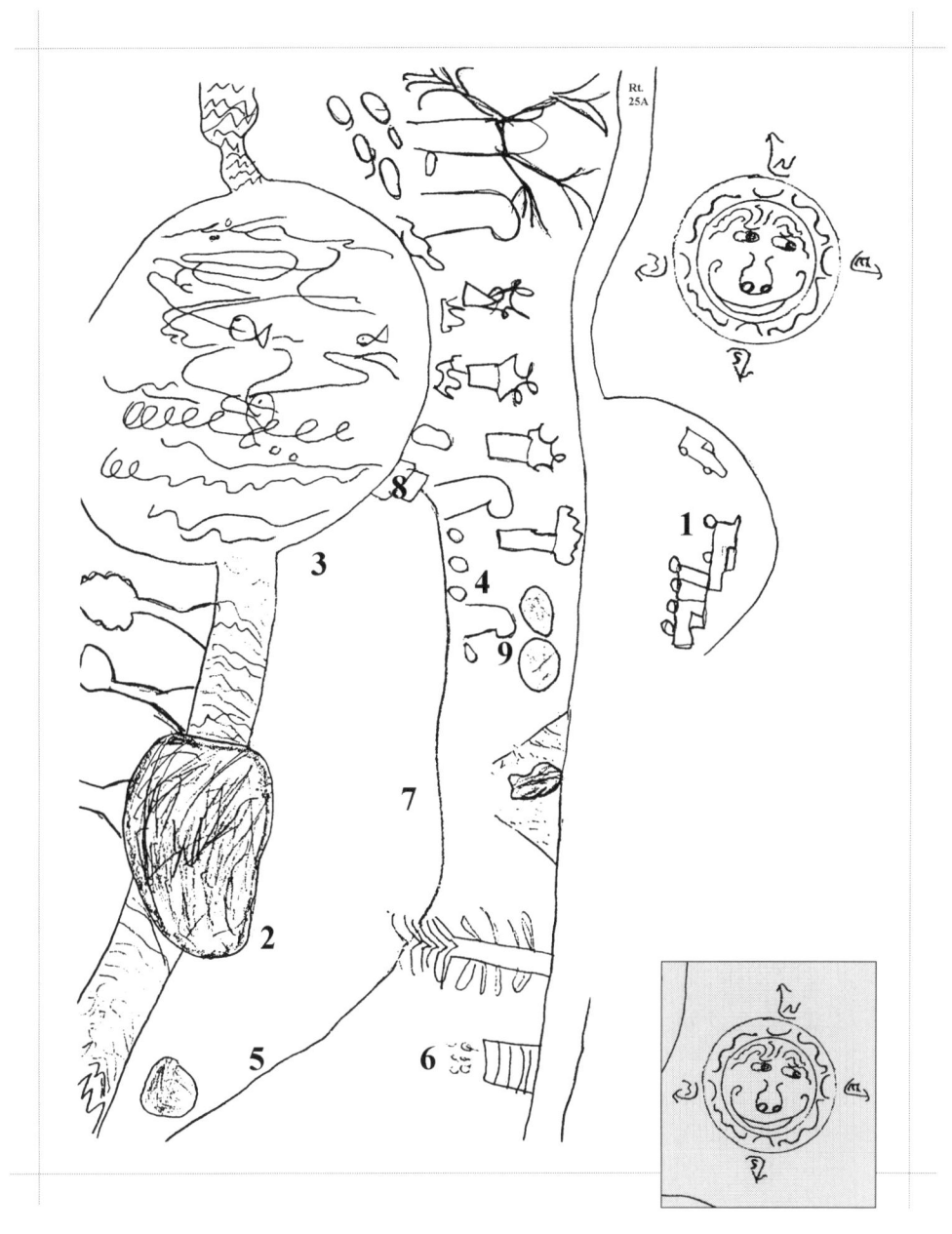

'Don't slip

and take a dip'

FLAT ROCK QUEST 87

41
INDIAN POND QUEST

ORFORD NH

To get there:

Take Route 10 south from the Fairlee/Orford bridge and take a right onto 25A. Pass the Rivendell Academy School on the left and go about 2.3 miles to the Orfordville General Store. Turn left onto Dame Hill Road. Go about 1.9 miles to Indian Pond Road. Turn left and go 2.7 mile to Indian Pond Boat and Beach parking on the right.

1. Start at me,
    I am a tree.

2. I am a sign,
    I tell the time.

3. I am barbed wire,
    And I'm not on fire.

4. I am gray,
    I keep cars away.

5. Leeches are near,
    But do not fear.

6. I am a forked tree,
    But I don't have bees.

7. I am strong,
    And I am long.

8. I will stop your car,
    But I'll lead you far.

9. Go 29 steps to the west,
    And look for the turtle nest.

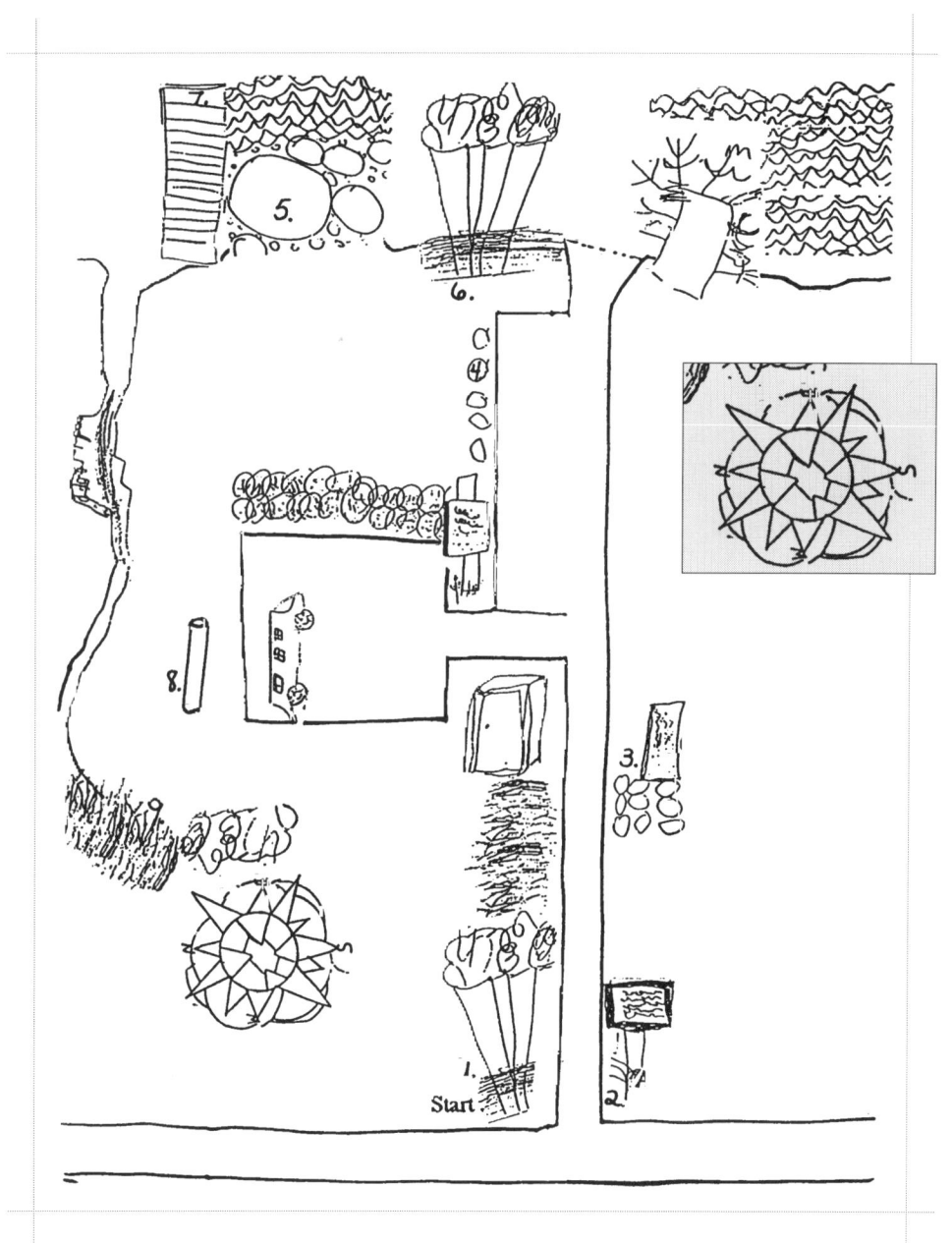

ORFORD NH
CONTINUED

'Go 29 steps to the west,
And look for the turtle nest.'

INDIAN POND QUEST

FRENCH'S LEDGES QUEST 42

PLAINFIELD NH

To get there:

Take Route 120 about 3.5 miles south of Lebanon and make a right onto Main Street in Meriden. Make a left in about 1 mile and cross the covered bridge. Proceed to the fork of Colby, Ladieu, and Columbus Jordan Road. Go left onto Columbus Jordan. Go almost 2 miles to a pull-off. The trail will be on your left.

There's a sign
   you can find
     on the tree
       near the trail.

Be polite; there could be a bee
   in the tipped-over tree.

Follow the white marks on the trees.
   Climb up the rocks on your hands and knees.
   Get to the top and feel the breeze.

When you get to the top annoy the fox.
   Slide down the rocks, then find the box.

Get to the tippy top, then stop.
   Point to the school and the radio tower.
   Follow your faces and go twelve paces (or more).
   It's hard to find 'cause
   it's under a pine.
   Look for a log that fell down on the ground.
   Under the rock the box will be found.

PLAINFIELD NH
CONTINUED

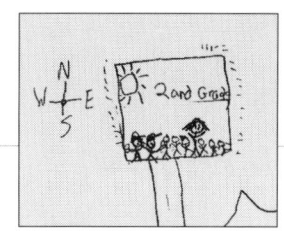

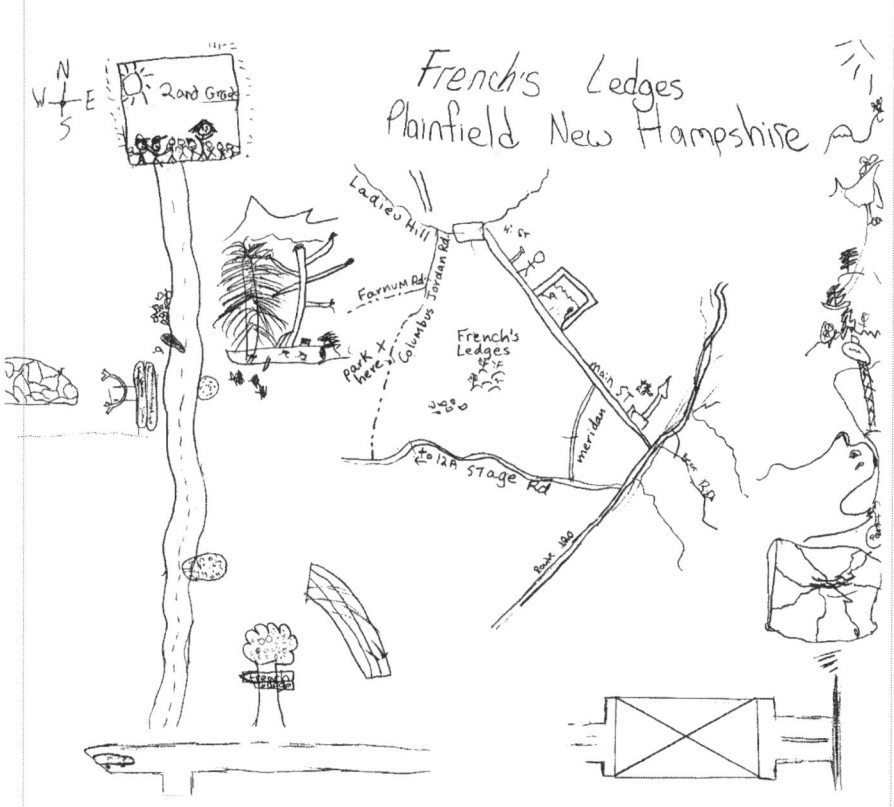

FRENCH'S LEDGES QUEST

43 PLAINFIELD VILLAGE QUEST

PLAINFIELD NH

To get there:
This Quest begins at the Plainfield Cemetery. It is located about 7 miles south of Lebanon on the east side of Route 12A. It is just south of Stage Road and about ¼ mile north of Plainfield Village and Daniels Road.

The view of Ascutney looks the best
   when you're facing the southwest.
   Go into town toward the gray building where kids were taught.
   Now it's a place where antiques are bought.
   It used to be in a shed behind the town hall
   and firemen leave there when they get a call.
   Continue south to the brick building and that's how it looks
   #1088 is its location. It has lots of books.
   It's a brick building where lightning hit the steeple
   in 1948 and scared all the people.
   South some more, go to the raspberry and pink store:
   buying things is what it's for.

Now arrange to go to the grange.
   Cross the street where a hurricane blew in 1938.
   That's why the windows are bricked in. Don't be late!
   Go northeast to where Maxfield Parrish's back drop must hang
   (Open Sunday afternoons in summer.)
   and have an old town meeting with the selectmen and gang.
   Go to the clubhouse where the Mothers' and Daughters' met.
   Rugs were woven and historical artifacts are set.
   Kingsbury tavern is up on the hill.
   If you run into Aunt Ester's ghost, you might get a chill.
   Now for the final place on your map,
   go to the place where the spirits take a nap.
   Lastly, look along the wall made of rocks near the hitching post.
   Don't worry, you won't find a ghost . . .
   You'll find the box.

PLAINFIELD NH
CONTINUED

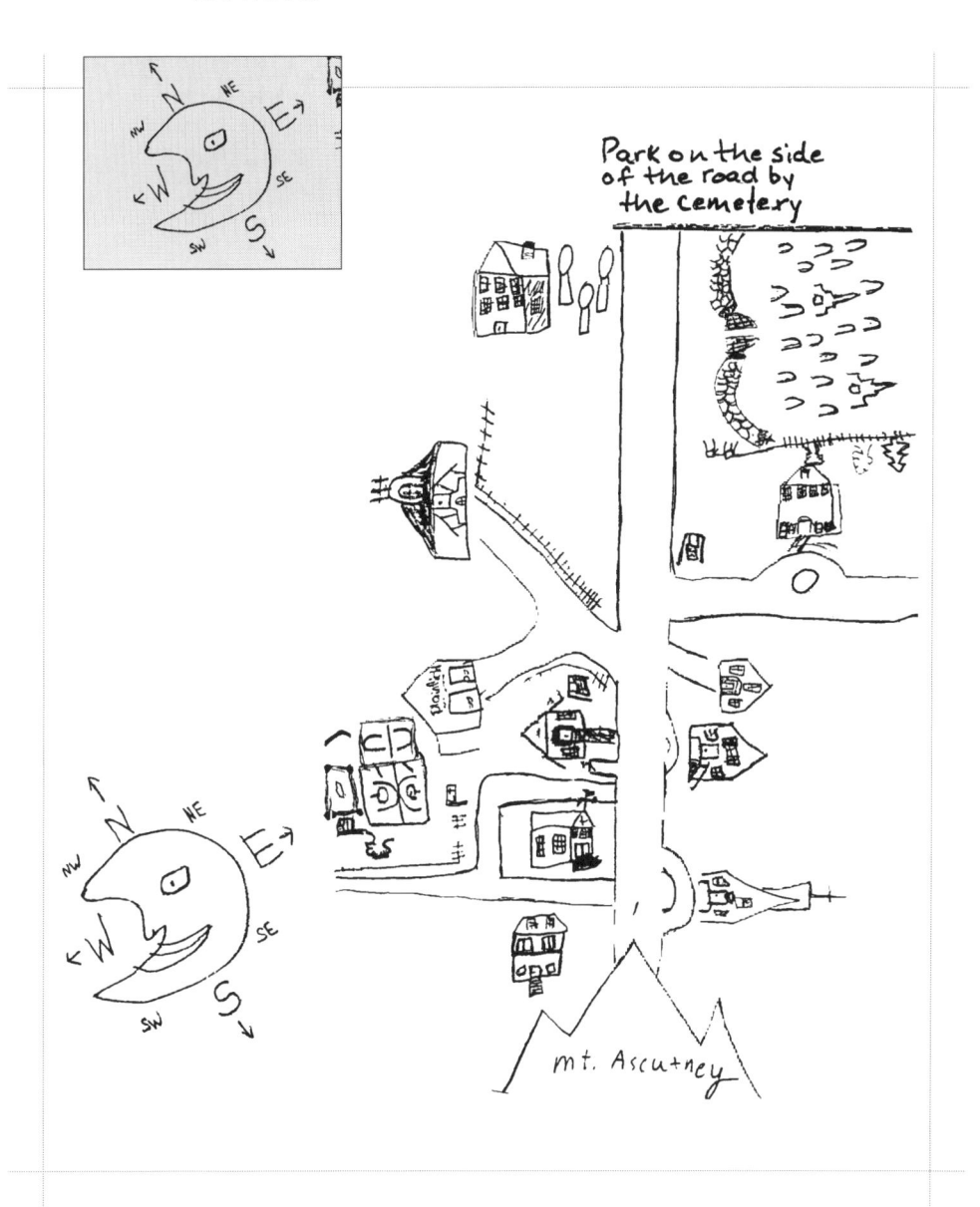

Park on the side of the road by the cemetery

mt. Ascutney

PLAINFIELD VILLAGE QUEST

QUECHEE VT

OLD QUECHEE CEMETERY QUEST 44

To get there:

This Quest begins at the gazebo on the Quechee green. Take I-89 north from White River Junction to Exit 1. Travel west on Route 4 for about 3.2 miles to the blinking light of Quechee Village. Take a right and cross the covered bridge. Go left at the junction. After .2 mile, take a left at the Deli sign and park by the green.

Start at the Quechee Village green gazebo.

Down the hill, go opposite of right, you must follow a watery sight.
    Down where the water flows, that is where you must go.
    Follow the sign that says "Dam Ahead," yes you did hear what I said.
    Be careful as you walk this little stone wall, because we don't
      want you to fall.
    Up ahead you'll find a bridge and the water will go over a ridge.
    Hey look! It's Simon Pearce glass, go up and around where the cars pass.
    Take a right and walk until the Dentist sign is in sight.
    Walk down all the stairs, make sure you don't fall; you will
      see a waterfall.
    Head toward the covered bridge, go up however many steps there are.
    Go over the bridge, enjoy the view, cross the street, you have to!
    Walk back over this side, we hope you are enjoying this ride.

'You will see a yellow house on the corner,
          cross the street,
                you're GETTING WARMER'

    Go past the parking lot, look all around, there you will see three trees
      in the ground.
    You will see a yellow house on the corner, cross the street, you're
      getting warmer!
    Be careful as you cross the street or you will be dead meat!
    Walk to the stairs, don't forget to get in pairs.
    Go down seven steps and you will find people who have gone to rest.
    Go not that long and find a place that says "Strong." (These eleven
      have gone to heaven.)
    From "Evelyn T.," go diagonally, find two graves that look the same, see?
    Look straight at the yellow house. Take a left to see the big green tree,
    Let's see how many paces it would be.
    Find the lonely grave hidden under the tree, can you read the name?
      It's hard to see.
    Look ahead at "Porter," take as many steps as a quarter.
    Turn left to where we just came in, you're almost near the ultimate win.
    Go toward the stairs and past a little star, now you are not very far.
    Stand by the star and stand very tall, now go check out the wall.

QUECHEE VT
CONTINUED

OLD QUECHEE CEMETERY QUEST

OTTAUQUECHEE QUEST 45

QUECHEE VT

To get there:
This Quest begins at the small parking lot on the south (village) side of the Quechee Village bridge. To get there, take I-89 north from White River Junction to Exit 1. Take Route 4 west for about 3.2 miles to the blinking light of Quechee Village. Take a right and cross the covered bridge. The parking lot will be on your right.

Head east on foot (stone wall on left and river on right)
    Until the red octagon is in sight.
    Left is the direction you should go
    Pass the gravestones row by row.

Don't go too far, look over your left shoulder
    It's a wall of stone, not a boulder.
    The door in the wall of stone
    Goes to the great unknown.

Do not enter, you must beware
    Walk left past the door with care.
    Stroll to the top of the knoll you shall see
    Letters galore from A to Z.

From the white post left to twin pines it's fifty-three steps
    Watch out for gravestones or you'll fall in their depths.
    Face the southwest bench from twin pines
    Take as many steps as four dimes.

Find the nearest stone cross
    Look up close—do you see any moss?

From here, place each foot on the ground 20 times
    toward a red stone with a bus.
    You're getting close. (Nothing rhymes.)
    From here, follow the road to a baseball game of sorts
    Look for a stone shaped like the field used in that sport.

Face the stone front and turn 90 degrees to the right
    and you will see an interesting sight.
    You've found the jagged stone with the symbol of wealth
    The next place you'll go you'll read of a child's health.

Walk back from whence you came until you see
    a stone black as night
    Read the words of Ralph Waldo Emerson,
    a man who could write.

Football is a game where if you get stopped
    You might just have to _ _ _ _ a lot.
    Veering leftish, fill in this blank
    But don't go too far and up onto the bank.

VALLEY QUEST · 2001

QUECHEE VT
CONTINUED

Follow stones in a line that's straight
   That's it! You're doing great.
   Find the stone of Mr. and Mrs. Banagan, then turn right
   if you see Allice L. you're doing all right.

Turn left and walk sixteen steps, look for the "father" stone
   It looks quite unlike a throne.
   Veer left toward the high road then prepare for a thrill
   Between the pine and maple, climb the grassy bank hill.

Go up to the wire fence and turn to your right
   You're doing very well, the treasure is almost in sight.
   See a stump straight ahead with many circular places
   Roll or walk down the hill, about twenty-five paces.

In the stump you'll find our box
   some magical trolls protect it from a curious fox.
   The trolls live in those stone culverts
   and one of their perks . . .

. . . is to play on the playground
   Or pitch from the mound.
   Open the box and find the treasure
   Now it is time for more simple pleasure.

Please don't disturb the trolls in their homes
   But relax in our playground after your roam.
   We hope you enjoyed our little Quest
   We hope you rank it as one of the best!

OTTAUQUECHEE QUEST

QUECHEE GORGE QUEST

QUECHEE VT

To get there:

This Quest begins at the parking lot for Quechee Gorge Gift Shop and Ott Dog. It is located just east of Quechee Gorge off Route 4 and about .8 mile east from the blinking light of Quechee Village.

Begin your Quest at John W. Storrs,
    Consulting Engineer.
    He helped to build a bridge right here.

Walk down the stairs, and under the bridge.
    About 150 feet past the red diamond
    Walk over the mossy root ridge.

Eleven steps AFTER this ridge
    Turn left, bushwhack, & then cross over
    A fallen tree bridge.

(If you are not a dare devil
    It is fine for you to
    Walk on the "lower level.")

Climb up the steep, small knoll and stop
    When you reach the hole-y pine
    That no longer has a top.

From there head uphill towards 2 o'clock.
    When you reach the crest of the knoll
    There please stop.

Next, follow the gully down to the right
    (You may not want to attempt this
    If you are Questing at night.)

QUECHEE
VT
CONTINUED

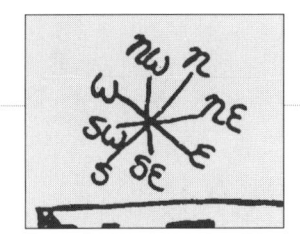

A long rotting log on your right side
    Points just to the right
    Of where the treasure box hides.

Look down to a fat chopped-off log—it's a chunk.
    Behind it is our box—
    You've shown real spunk!

QUECHEE GORGE QUEST   99

47 QUECHEE LIBRARY QUEST

QUECHEE VT

To get there:

Take I-89 north from White River Junction to Exit 1. Take Route 4 west for about 3.2 miles to the blinking light of Quechee Village. Take a right and cross the covered bridge. Go left at the junction. After .2 mile, take a left at the Deli sign and park by the green.

From the Quechee Village green gazebo:

Look up high for your first clue. Can you count the cupolas?
    You should see two.
    Go straight and stay on the right, where the parked cars should
      come into sight.
    Walk down the path and look to your side, you will see a stone wall
      that is not very high.
    Walk down the path until a brick building is in the way, then turn
      to your left where the cars pass everyday.

Cross across a busy street, hurry up your little feet!
    You will see a quilt store and to get out of its way, turn to the left,
      you will see a "school" some day.
    Continue on, don't go too fast. Look for the colors of stained glass.
    Look at the stairs that lead to heaven: there should be seven.
    Hey, it's a sleigh, if you look closely, you won't see any hay.
    If you look carefully, then look some more, count the diamonds,
      you should see four.
    Come to a winding brick path on the right. Take a tour, for the flowers
      are a beautiful sight.

This building beside you is not very old, in it a lot of stories are told.
    Go down Willard Road, then take a right, look for the shed
      that is white — (adjoining the library)
    it is not very high in height. Look inside for your prize
      to come into sight!

QUECHEE VT
CONTINUED

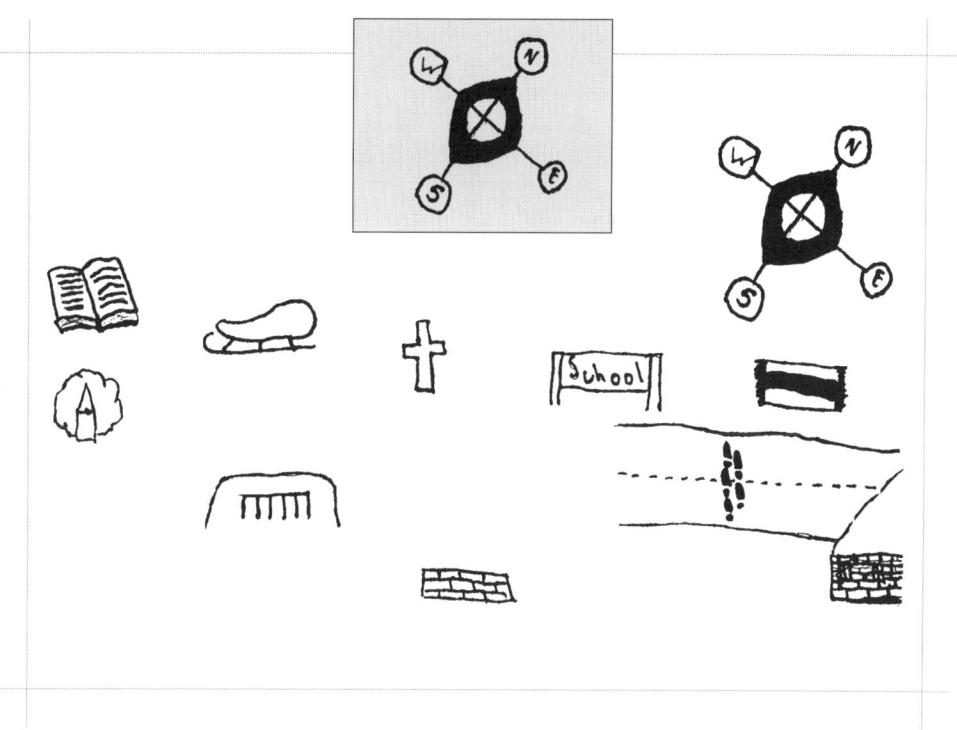

'Look for the colors of
stained glass.

Look at the stairs that lead to
heaven.

QUECHEE LIBRARY QUEST   101

48 SIMON PEARCE WATERFALL QUEST

QUECHEE VT

To get there:
Take I-89 north from White River Junction to Exit 1. Take Route 4 west for about 3.2 miles to the blinking light of Quechee Village. Take a right and cross the covered bridge. Go left at the junction. After .2 mile, take a left at the Deli sign and park by the green.

Start at the Quechee Village green gazebo

Start at the gazebo and go thirty-two paces northeast.
   If you're lost, make a call.
   Over the trees you'll see a sight
   Where people go to pray at night.
   Go towards this place but bear to the right.
   From here take the small gravel road, not the Main.
   Look to the right and see a weathervane.
   Go down a hill, past a stone wall.
   Don't go on it for fear you might fall.
   Pass the white fence, look to your right.
   Two granite posts in olden days were familiar sights.
   Go up the hill, pass the brown building,
   Which is still used to house the town's children.
   Stay to the right,
   You'll see a deadly sight.
   Continue on even when the path turns black.
   Go down the path, look to your right.
   Here are some numbers at a very high height.
   Keep going straight. Look to your right
   And you will see a yellow sight.
   Cross the busy street,
   But don't trip on your feet!
   Go right. Look for the blue "candy canes"
   Left of the two busy lanes.
   You'll see some bars on the ground. This is not a jail.
   Keep going, cross on over, and you shall not fail.
   Down the stairs where a sort of green plant grows.
   Be careful, it's near an overflow!
   Look by this plant, near the ground,
   For this is where IT is found!!

'Look

QUECHEE VT
CONTINUED

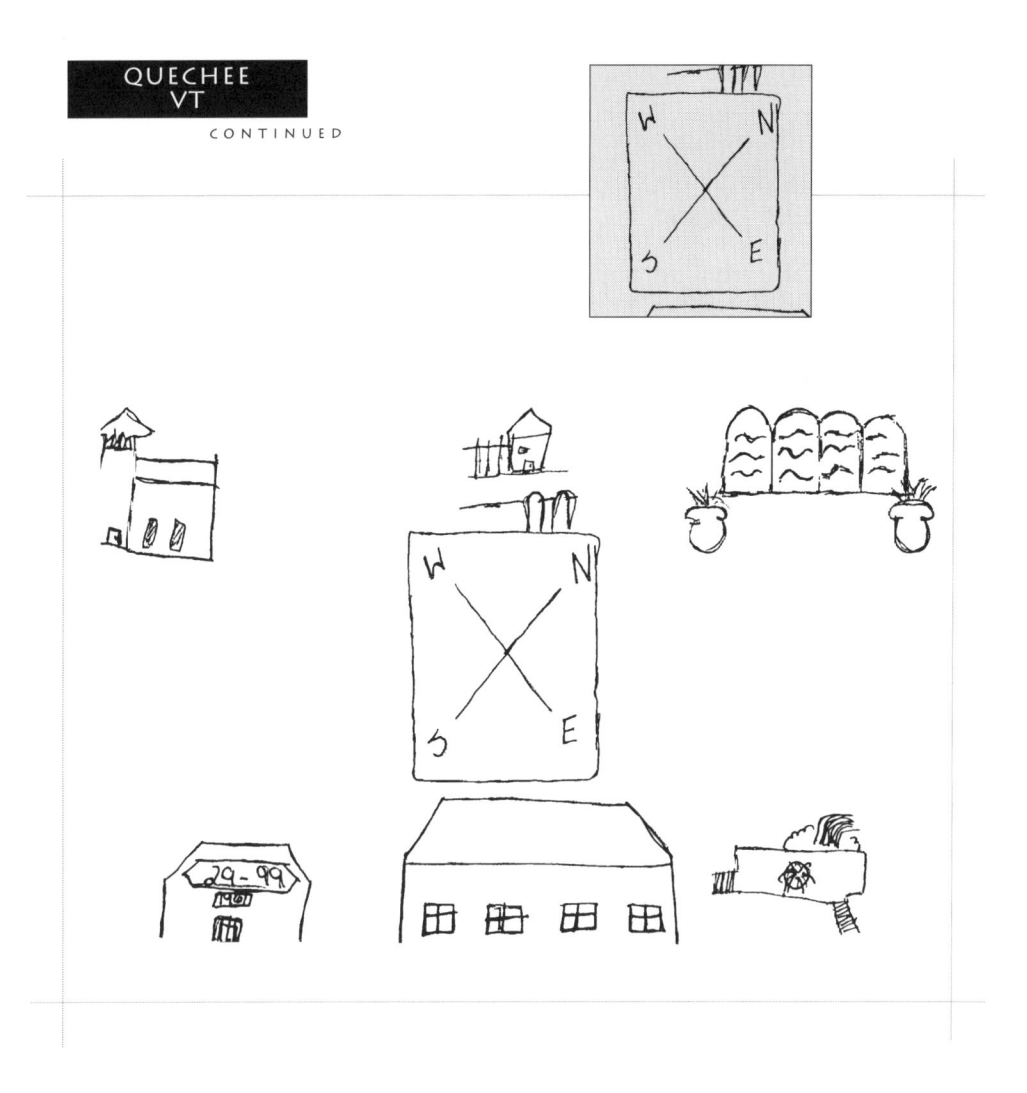

for the blue "candy canes"

Left of the two busy lanes.'

SIMON PEARCE WATERFALL QUEST

49 ROCKINGHAM MEETING HOUSE QUEST

ROCKINGHAM VT

To get there:
Take I-91 to Exit 6. Travel west on Route 103 about 1 mile until you see the Rockingham Meeting House sign on your right. Turn left and then the meeting house will be on your right, about .3 miles in, at the top of a steep driveway.

A pace is every other step.

Start at the most prominent house of white,
　its colonial architecture is quite a sight.
　The building went up in 1787,
　the folks in back are now in heaven.
　As you travel through the Quest you will
　collect clues that will lead you to our box at the end.

Go west from the meeting house;
　look for the Divoll monument near the gate.
　One of them suffered a terrible fate.
　His birth and death months have the same second letter,
　you will need that for the final clue: ___

Go a little north of west and walk twenty paces,
　turn right and go thirty more.
　The Eldridge grave is what you're looking for.
　This grave has a tree engraved on its back; on its front are names.
　How many are not dead as of the year 2000?
　That number is part of your clue: ___

Travel southeast and look up to the grave with the books
　that cannot be read. As you face the open books,
　the name is what you're looking for; use the last
　of the first and the first of the last, these
　will help you in your clue: ___ ___

Go east to a little old grave by the open gate.
　Amy Kibby is underneath, her age was
　98 when she died. In the fifth line use
　the sixth, seventh, ninth, tenth, and eleventh letters,
　they are in spaces 5, 6, 8, 9, 10: ___ ___ ___ ___ ___

Go east past the grave that's flat in the ground, to the
　mound with stone underneath, we don't
　know what is was used for, but it has
　a wooden shelf inside and latches on
　the door, like the box you will find at
　at the end of your quest.

104　　VALLEY QUEST · 2001

ROCKINGHAM VT
CONTINUED

Go southwest on the other side of
the meeting house, next to the road.
It is the waiting room for the dead, under
ground. Check out what its made
of. It will help you when you look for the box.

Go east to the little house of
white, inside is an old hearse for
the dead to ride in.

If you followed the clues correctly and
filled in the blanks, then you now know
where to go to find the box. You have
now reached the end of your quest, now
you can go home and rest.

Final clue:

___ paces ___ ___ ___ ___ ___ from h___ ___ ___ se.
From clue # 3   4 4 2 5 5   5 5 5

ROCKINGHAM MEETING HOUSE QUEST   105

50 KIDDER BROOK QUEST

SPRINGFIELD NH

To get there:
From I-89 take Exit 12 and head east toward New London. Take a quick left onto Little Sunapee Road. Bear right at the fork on Little Sunapee Road. Bear right again onto 114. Turn left on Twin Lake Village Road. The parking area is on the right after you cross a little bridge over the brook. Note the stone bridge just beyond the parking lot.

1. Embark upon your Quest,
   Stones arc over the stream.
   Scramble up sundry ___ ___ ___ ___ ___ steps
   Before you run out of steam.

2. When you're cold and you tire
   Come down by the stream
   And warm up by the ___ ___ ___ ___ ___ ___ ___ ___.

3. Then turn to the left
   And you shall see
   25 feet long
   And 10 feet tall
   A boulder ___ ___ ___ ___.

4. You come down to the Sandy Beach.
   There's plenty of moss and rocks.
   You can bask in the shade and wade.
   Don't forget to take off your ___ ___ ___ ___ ___.

5. As you approach the power line
   notice a pile of sticks and mud.
   ___ ___ ___ ___ ___ ___ ___ made this with their big teeth.
   Have you seen them eat? I wish I could.

6. There's a fork in the trail . . .
   Which way do you go?
   The blazes are white
   And they lead to the ___ ___ ___ ___ ___.

7. Traverse above a stone wall
   20 meters along the path
   turn left and climb on top of the boulder
   Don't go too far, or you'll fall in with a ___ ___ ___ ___ ___ ___ .

VALLEY QUEST · 2001

SPRINGFIELD NH
CONTINUED

8. Three hundred ancient rocks stand
    the remnants of a hand-made ___ ___ ___.
    Imagine almost 200 years ago
    A farm with a millpond spread out below.

9. White blazes lead 100 meters northeast.
    Where did this come from, this road to travel?
    Across the road, overgrown with trees
    A sandpit provided sand and ___ ___ ___ ___ ___ ___.

10. Turn left, walk 200 paces
    to a grassy path signed with red.
    Proceed upward if you dare
    But you will not find the treasure there!

11. Follow the road to the echo dome
    Walk its circumference to a little known
    Black circle with a heavy ___ ___ ___ ___ ___ ___.
    Put your mouth near it and let out a scream.

12. Pond number one has many creatures
    each with its own unique, special features.
    Flowing ___ ___ ___ ___ ___ down a cement drain
    Wrecking the weeds that come again.

13. To the left of pond number two
    You will see a bridge of land
    Follow it straight along, my friend,
    For there you will find your Quest's ___ ___ ___.

KIDDER BROOK QUEST

51
McDANIEL'S MARSH QUEST

SPRINGFIELD NH

To get there:

Take I-89 to Exit 17 and head east on Route 4. Bear right (south) onto Route 4A. Follow it past Shaker Village and Enfield Center (7 miles) to Bog Road. Turn right onto Bog Road and continue about 5 miles until the road merges with George Hill Road. The marsh will be right in front of you.

Park the car and come on out!
 When you get here, there's no doubt.

McDaniel's Marsh says the sign.
 If you fish, then drop a line.

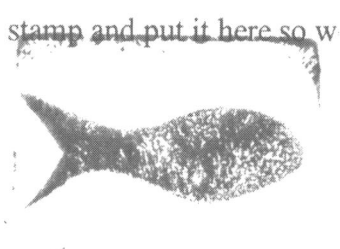

Treasure hunting is why we came,
 so let's get on with this game.

Back to George Hill, this time on feet,
 across the bridge, slow and sweet.

Our distance will not be too far,
 so don't worry about your car.

Don't complain about the upcoming rise.
 Take a left toward your surprise.

Orange blazes on the trees—
 follow them, if you please.

Not too far and left toward the dam,
 our path is further than if we swam.

The field of green gives a different view.
 What can you see that is new?

You're real close to finishing your search.
 The treasure is hidden in a pile of birch.

Best of luck with these rhyming clues.
 Please record in my book all of your views.

Birds, bees, fishes, trees:
  So many things that you will see
  If you linger here, quietly.

108 VALLEY QUEST · 2001

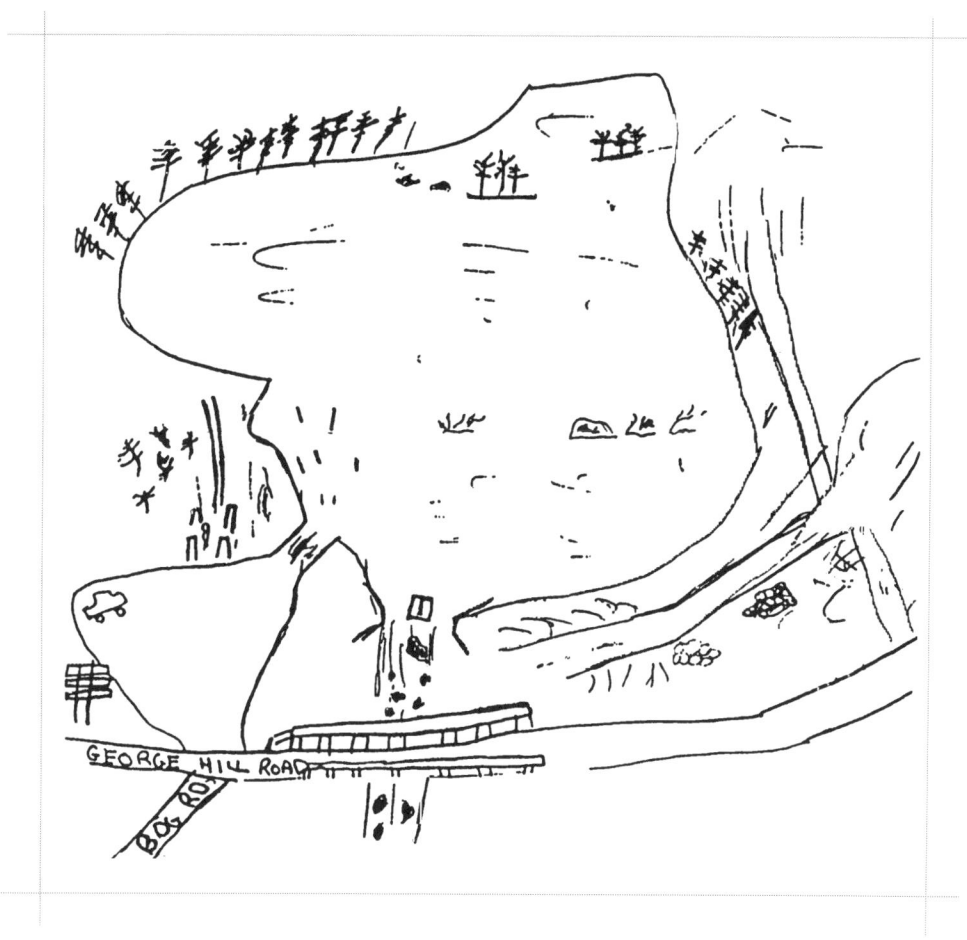

SPRINGFIELD NH
CONTINUED

'Birds, bees, fishes, trees:
So many things that you will see
if you linger here, quietly.'

McDANIEL'S MARSH QUEST

52
NORTH SPRINGFIELD BOG QUEST

SPRINGFIELD VT

To get there:

Take I-91 to Exit 7. Head west and go through Springfield on Route 11 to Riverside Middle School. It will be on the right. Take a right onto Fairgrounds Road and go 1.9 miles. Beyond the recycling center on the right, turn left into the sand pit area and park. Look for the small green Bog sign on the left. You may wish to bring a compass.

Walk with your back to the sign.
   Walk to the post in a straight line.
   @ 110 degrees[1]

Walk down the wood path
   with the greatest of ease,
   'til you see on your left
   a lying dead tree.
   @ 200 degrees

Turn to the right, so the forest you face,
   And walk straight ahead
   to the peninsula base.
   @ 246 degrees

With the water on your right
   you'll march
   Until you reach
   the bending tree arch.
   @ 245 degrees

Stand under the arch
   and stroll to the trees
   That have grown from one trunk,
   so they're twin Siamese.
   @ 200 degrees

Stop here and look
   around until you sight
   And walk to the birch
   that is all white.
   @ 260 degrees

1. For compass enthusiasts: The degree numbers show the direction you should head for each verse.

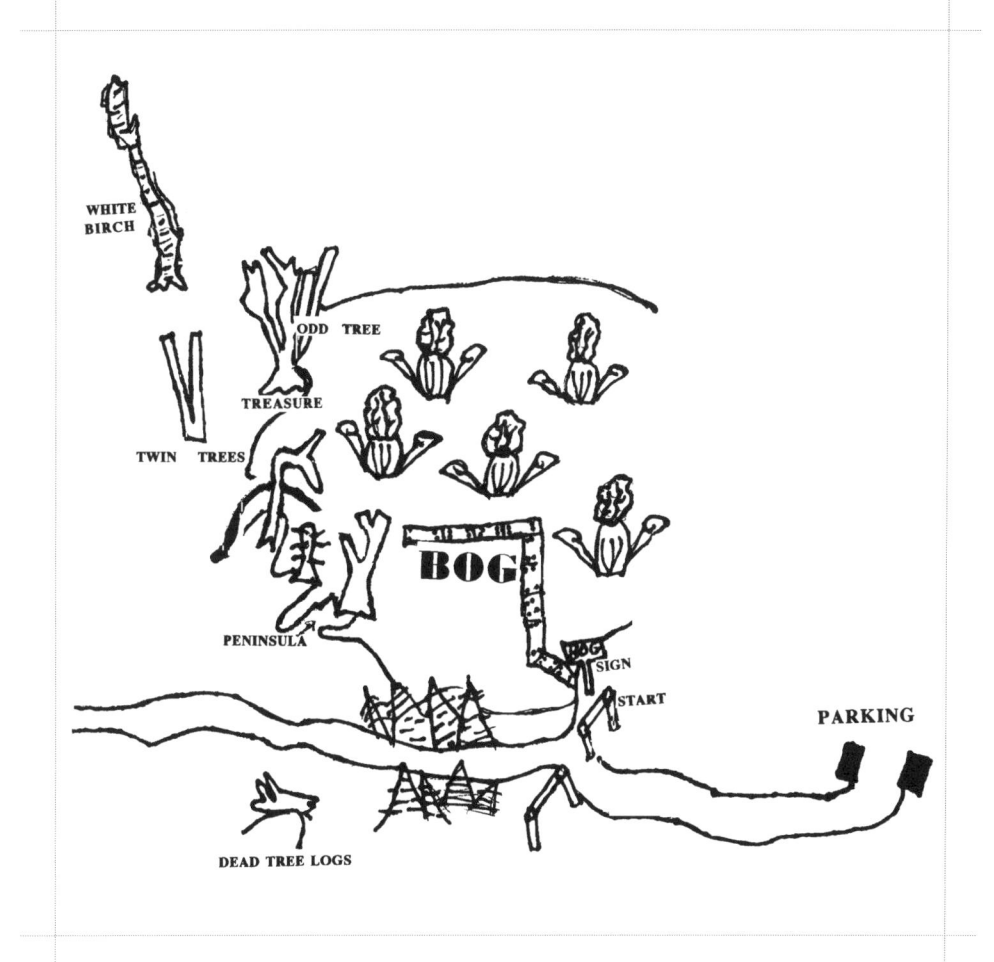

Look to the bog
   and see with your eyes
   the big tree by the water.
   It holds our prize.
   @ 20 degrees

Look on the trunk
   for the woodpecker hole.
   Reach inside.
   It contains your goal.

So now you're finished.
   You're done. You're through.
   And you still have time
   to explore the bog, too![2]

2. This bog is a fragile, protected ecosystem. The insectivorous pitcher plants are an endangered species. Please respect this special environment. Thank you.

SPRINGFIELD VT

53. SPRINGWEATHER QUEST A

To get there:

From the junction of Route 11 and Route 106 in Springfield, continue north on Route 106 for approximately 1.8 miles. Turn right onto Reservoir Road, and go 1.5 miles to the left turn into the parking lot for the reservoir. You may wish to bring a compass, to follow the orientation clues indicated in parenthesis.

Start with the signs, to begin with our rhymes
  Go down the trail faster than a snail.
  (46 degrees)

Stay to the left, being careful not to step on the roots,
  You'll wish you had your hiking boots.
  (270 degrees)

To the left will be a great big tree,
  It's falling apart as you will see.

Continue along the left path,
  Until you face the stream's wrath.
  (130 degrees)

Now cross the bubbling brook,
  Go up the hill and take a look.
  (280 degrees)

Keeping the stream on your right,
  Go to the field's light.

Go straight past the B3 post,
  For in the end, you'll have a reason to boast.
  (220 degrees)

At the B10 post, go right,
  The sun will be shining bright.
  (264 degrees)

At about 30 paces take the first right-side trail that you see,
  You've gone too far if you pass a short, round, bushy tree.
  (350 degrees)

Go right at the top of the hill,
  Keep the twin white birches at your right if you will.
  (50 degrees)

If you're going the right way, on the right you'll pass a fence,
  Continue along the trail using your common sense.

SPRINGFIELD VT
CONTINUED

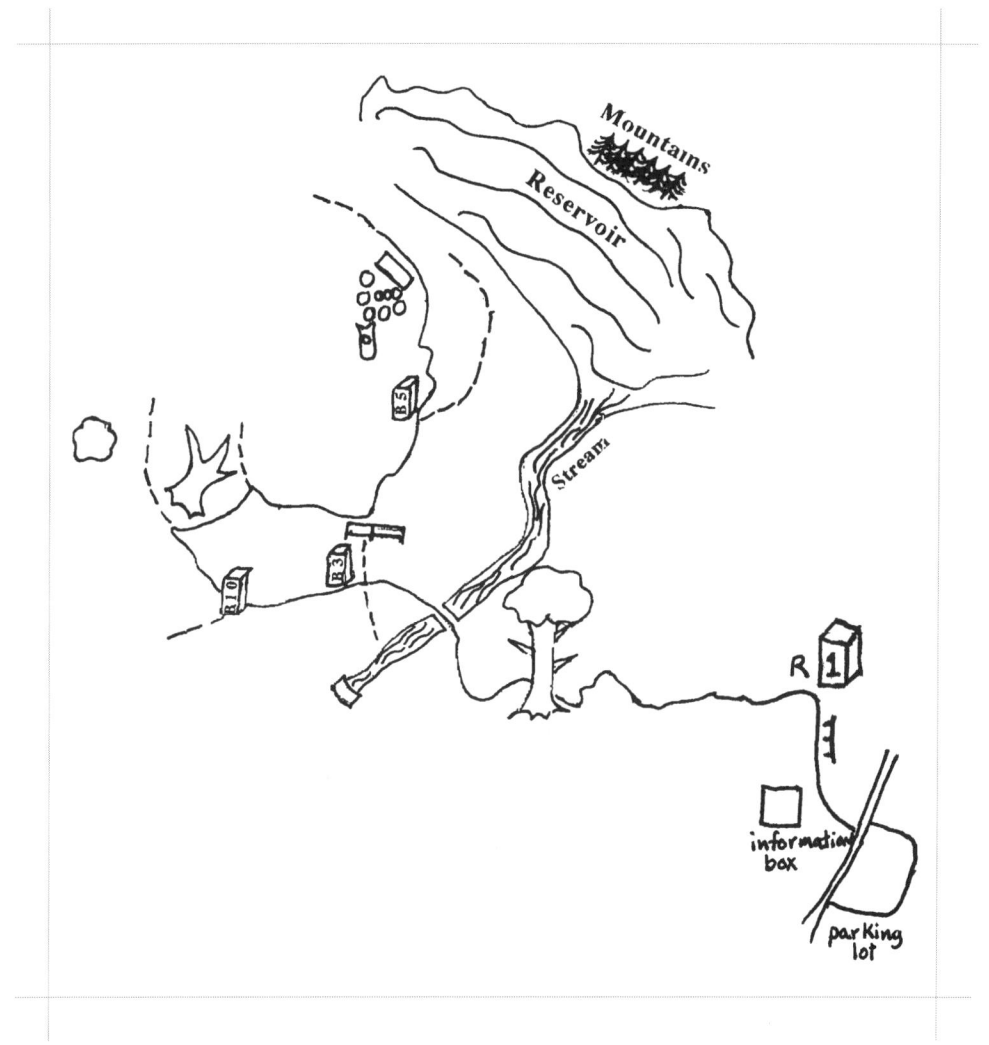

Take a left at B5,
   You're sure to see trees with ended lives.
   (278 degrees)

Follow the path right on through,
   In the end you'll have quite a view.

Soon we'll tell you what to do,
   But sit and look at the glorious view.

Turn around, and go straight past the triplet trees,
   Now, look on the ground behind the middle, big pine tree,
   The treasure is what you should see.
   (159 degrees)

With your foot on the treasure, and your back to the tree,
   You will spot a woodpecker's hole in a nearby tree.

SPRINGWEATHER QUEST A

54
SPRINGWEATHER QUEST B

To get there:

From the junction of Route 11 and Route 106 in Springfield, continue north on Route 106 for approximately 1.8 miles. Turn right onto Reservoir Road, and go 1.5 miles to the left turn into the parking lot for the reservoir. You may wish to bring a compass to help you follow the orientation clues.

Start in the information area. Follow the railing to marker #1.
   Take the red trail, your Quest has just begun.

Walk the plank to marker R2,
   I'd take the right if I were you.

At marker R4 *don't* bear right,
   Or you might go out of sight.

Follow the path to marker R5,
   Don't take a left-hand dive.

Go around the corner to the bench with a view.
   I'd go slowly if I were you.

To continue your outdoor thrill,
   Walk on to the top of the hill.

Don't turn into pine-tree heaven,
   Stay to the left of marker R7.

Go past the bench to the left of pine-tree heaven's gate,
   Proceed through the clearing to marker R8.

Stand on the left of marker R8,
   Head to the bench where you can wait.
   (350 degrees)

Follow the trail to marker R9,
   Stay on the green trail and you'll be just fine.

Watch out for the mighty fall if you please,
   And go by the branch that weaves between two trees.

Follow the trail around the ravine,
   And continue to the bench where a view can be seen.

SPRINGFIELD VT
CONTINUED

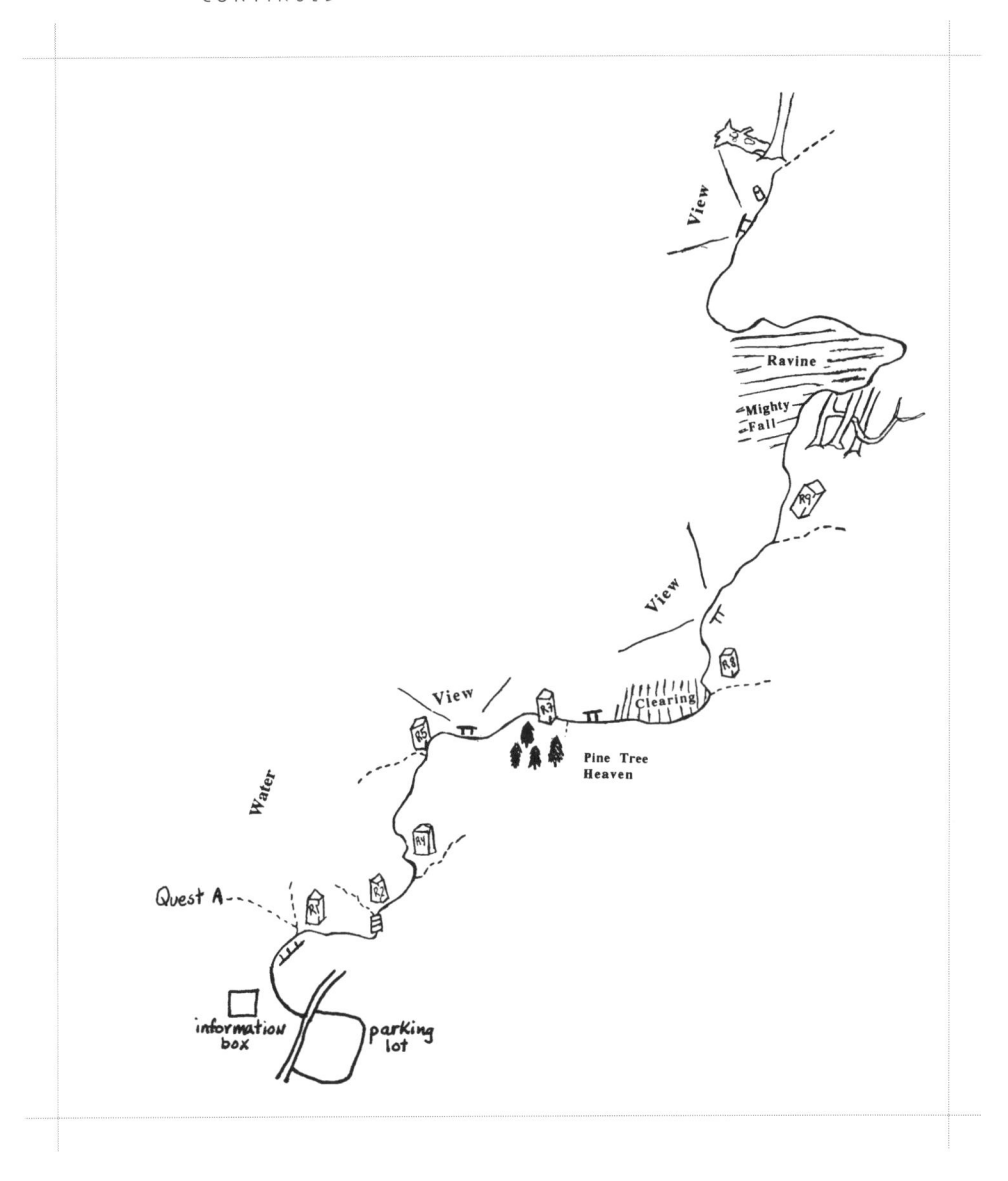

Facing the water, find the man-made stump with the bluish-green hat,
   About 34 degrees to the right from where you sat.

To find the treasure if you please,
   Put your toes to the stump, and face 8 degrees.

Search near the moss on the decomposing tree,
   The prize is there for you to see.

If you found the treasure—now you're done.
   We hope you had a bit of fun!

'pine-tree heaven'

SPRINGWEATHER QUEST B

55
SUNAPEE HARBOR QUEST

SUNAPEE NH

To get there:
Take I-89 south to Exit 12A. Make a right onto Route 11. Follow the signs toward Sunapee for about 2 miles. Take a left at the sign and yellow flashing light into Sunapee Harbor. Park near one of the public parks on either side of Main Street.

At the tan Inn Knowlton, upon the hill,
   on the paved road's edge, stand so still.
   Look to the wall and its majestic rock,
   here is where you begin your walk.

Crossing Garnet and Main on a ladder of white,
   lean over green rails; water shimmers with light.
   Relax and take some time to see,
   Sunapee Harbor of large Lake Sunapee.

A right turn you make,
   on your left is the lake.
   Cross ahead to the dam, and if you are able,
   stand by the building that once was a stable.

See the lake join a river so sweet.
   Sugar River it's called; again cross the street.
   Stand over water and find a stick white
   used to measure the lake's water height.

Class A lake on your left, follow the walk
   'tween buildings and boats where folks often talk.
   When you reach the boat ramp, south you shall cross
   to a park where there is much grass and some moss.

Walk to where sand and soil join a wall,
   careful now, don't you fall!
   As you admire the beauty of this lake,
   there are choices we each make
   to keep the water clean and clear.
   It is a treasure we hold dear.

Go north and cross Main to the cottage Woodbine.
   Straight ahead now, a road you will find,
   called "River," which is aptly named.
   Follow this now to the source of its fame.

SUNAPEE NH
CONTINUED

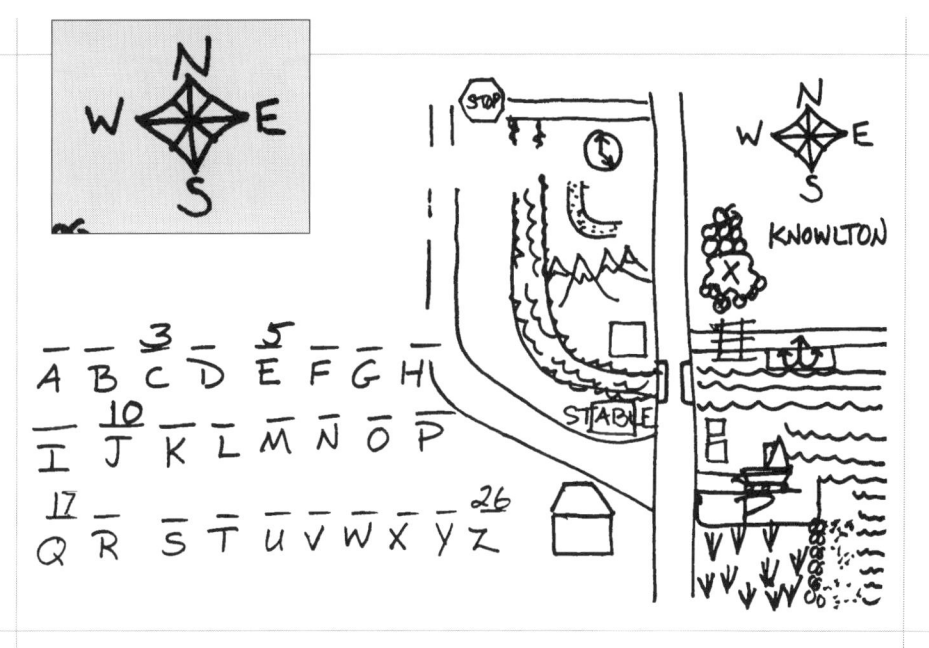

Which way do you think the water is moving?
Pick up a leaf fallen and set it to cruising.
    Following now as your leaf floats along,
        go ahead, loosen up, just burst into song!

Across the river, see clock and tower,
    you've been moving along by your own power.
    A large white birch by the river grows,
    on this side of the river, stop, stretch your toes.

Along the Sugar River, we take tests,
    to make sure the water is at its best.
    Conductivity, turbidity, pH are a few,
    Samples like these give water-quality clues.

At the stop, take a turn east.
    Cross over the river and, last, but not least,
    south, tight 'tween clock tower and river,
    'til a building you find.
    Unscramble letters 1, 12, 16, 19;
    they'll be on its sign.

Now you'll take a different tack,
    head due west around the back.
    Climb up wood with zeal and zest.
    Look underneath. You've completed your Quest!

SUNAPEE HARBOR QUEST

56
HOUGHTON HILL QUEST

THETFORD VT

To get there:

Get off I-91 at Exit 14. This is the Lyme/Thetford exit. Go toward Thetford. At the top of the hill, take a right onto Houghton Hill Road. Continue 1.5 miles on this road until you see a small pond on the left. Shortly there will be a small, rocky pull-off on the right. The pull-off has room for only 1 or 2 cars. The trail begins on the opposite side of the road.

Go up the road 50 feet or so after parking your car.
You'll find a trail on the left. It is not far.
You'll immediately see a couple of uprooted trees
And gravel for a short way. These are two keys.

First, look for a tree with light gray, smooth bark
Most other trees will have bark that is dark.
Look for the veins that transport materials in the leaves
At the end of each vein, how many teeth are there, please?
Write the number here: ___

At the end of each of these beech leaves is a drip tip
So the rain can run off and not get stuck there; that's hip.

Continue on the trail till a hemlock tree you find.
Its needles are green, even in wintertime.
Each needle is really a short, thin leaf, you see.
To help the tree shed snow and not lose water is key.
On the underside, how many white lines can you find?
Put the number here, if you don't mind: ___

Get hiking uphill. Past ferns and oak trees you'll go.
Once the trail flattens some, look on the right, and go slow.
Look for small trees with many trunks. Trees here were cut at one time.
Sprouts came up around each tree stump. Look for three different kinds.

a. First, a tree is cut.
b. A stump is left.
c.
d. They grow and become a multiple trunked tree.

Sprouts grow from the base of the stump. The stump rots.

118   VALLEY QUEST · 2001

THETFORD VT
CONTINUED

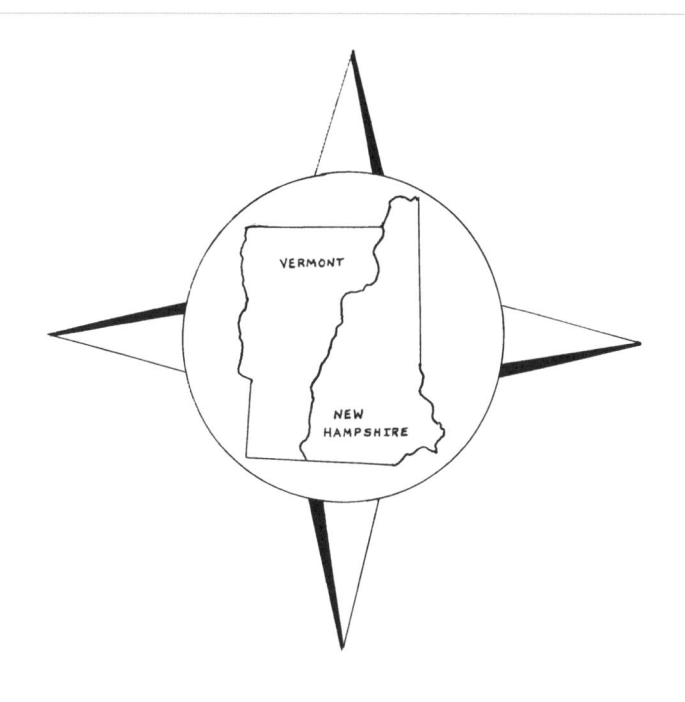

Before long, the trail levels again. See quartz rock that is white
   It's in the trail. A small, grassy meadow is on the right.
   Two oaks on the left with rough bark stand tall
   Count the number of roots on the oak on the right; that's all.
   Write your number here: ___

Continue uphill until two connected sawed-off stumps are in sight
   Past it on the same side is a small sapling with green bark and
      stripes white.
   It is called striped maple, with lobes on its leaves.
   Count the number of lobes, but don't "Go Ask Jeeves."
   Write your number here: ___

Grouse and deer find the leaves, twigs, and buds to be good.
   Since moose do as well, the tree's
   nicknamed "Moosewood."

HOUGHTON HILL QUEST

THETFORD VT
CONTINUED

As you walk along don't miss the large tree off trail on the left
   in the shade.
  It is a beautiful old sugar maple, from whose sap maple syrup is made.
  You'll come to a "T." Take a left onto the wide trail.
  Go up a rise and down a little dip. Do not fail:
  A pine tree with long, thin needles must be found.
  Count the number of needles in one bunch, loosely wound.
  Write the number of needles in a bunch here: _____

Several hundred years ago, this area was covered with 100 to 200 foot
   tall pines,
  The King of England said the largest (over 24 inches in diameter)
   "are mine"
  To be used for ship masts for his Royal Navy.

Continue and look right. How long are the thorns on the sapling
   that you find,
  1, 2, or 4 inches? Check several thorns, if you don't mind.
  Write your number here: ___

Hawthorns oft made hedges between fields in a line.
  Its leaf has a distinctive and jagged outline.

Keep walking. There's a flat rock on the left for you to sit.
  Mosses and reindeer lichens carpet the area quite a bit.
  Look for triangular, broad-leaved ferns.
  A field of these gives excellent shelter to small animals, one learns.
  Each plant divides into nearly equal parts.
  How many parts? (Just to check your smarts.)
  Write the number here: ___

Reindeer Lichen

Before you go further, and to continue the fun
  You must add all your numbers together to make one.
  Total of all your numbers = ___ minus 1 = ___

Soon as you continue a view will be on the right.
  Leave the main trail. Go left up the rocks for east, west, and
    south sights.

Look for a quartz vein, a line of white rock pointing to trees whose
   bark peels.
  Carefully, go to the closest one. The treasure is close to your heels.

From this birch, in a 16-foot radius circle all around,
  You should look for a cut stump, which soon must be found.
  The trunk had sprouted, and the sprouts got cut too.
  The number of cut sprout trunks matches your answer.
    The treasure is in view!

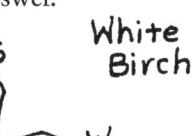

White Birch

(Don't give up. You'll know when you find it.)

VALLEY QUEST · 2001

THETFORD VT

LONESOME PINE QUEST

57

To get there:

Take Route 113 into Thetford Center. At the foot of Thetford Hill, turn onto Buzzell Bridge road and proceed toward the Union Village Recreation Area. Travel .4 miles and then park in the large lot on your left. Your Quest begins there.

Walk to your west for a quarter mile along the peaceful country road.
  For the east branch of the Ompomp. may be good for a toad!
  After awhile look for "Mystery Trail" signs to the right
  Then follow my lead with all of your might.
  Look at the signs that speak of the past.
  We are on our way, on this Quest at last!
  The mystery clues do abound—they just need to be found.
  Whether it is human history or giving nature a chance.
  This Quest will do part of the loop, so look deep and give more than a glance.
  Before the bridge with buds alternate and red-brown
  Look for an American basswood, the wood-carvers' tree
  It has heart-shaped leaves, and coppice wood
  (four big stump sprouts) for you to see.
  Let's cross the river. Be sure to notice its sparkle and quiver.
  Kingbird may be chief, but it is the blue jay who cries "thief, thief."[1]
  At the fork we will bear right, and look for the red oaks, sturdy with might.
  Having flat-topped ridges and salmon-colored grooves in the bark,
  The leaves are big and pointy. Acorns are clues to this tree in the park.
  You will pass hemlock, with needles so tiny and green.
  Maybe a red squirrel will chatter—begging to be seen.
  Thriving in soil so poor, this one reproduces by spore,
  It likes lots of sun: find this fern for fun!
  It can be up to 3 feet high, and has three branching parts the same.
  With fronds widest at the base it is bracken by name.
  From the days of yore, an old town road you roam
  Look for a few fence posts made of stone.
  The quacking and peeping you may hear,
    may be frog's music reaching your ear.[2]

---

1. During the late spring and summer, the blue jay's diet includes baby birds and eggs. In no way, however, are they a threat to the survival of other songbirds. They are a principal planter of acorns.
2. Spring peepers can be heard here from late April until early June.

Bear right at the fork for treasures are near. What could they be?
   Look and see!
Can you hear the "laugh" of a robin?[3] Or the "wrock" of a raven?[4]
Both of these birds inhabit this haven.
Follow the path and you shall see a specimen from days of olde—
If only this lofty white pine's stories could be told!
Be they natural or human, mysteries and wonders are abundant.
Just how was the old stone farm gatepost relevant?
There are old cellar holes, a silo pad, foundations.
Being a history sleuth you will have many investigations.
Now find yourself nearing the pond's soft edge
Graced with alders, with cattails and sedge.
Listen for the bubbly song sparrow's "Madge. Madge, please
   put on the teakettle" song.[5]
Or the "wichity, wichity, wichity" of the common yellowthroat
   (a warbler). You can't go wrong![6]
Dragonflies dart and zoom. Do the milkweed dance and spin?
We have a wetland with lots of room—and wood duck boxes
   ready to go in.
Look close, for there may be a painted turtle, heron—even a
   migrating green-wing teal.

'Can you hear the "laugh" of a robin?'

Were it me that was here, Aye, I'd surely give a squeal!
Butterflies do flutter and yearn, and have nary a care.
Tree swallows bank and turn—the acrobats of the air.
Can you find a berm built of twigs, sticks, and mud?
Keep an eye and ear for the beaver, which whacks his tail with
   a thud.

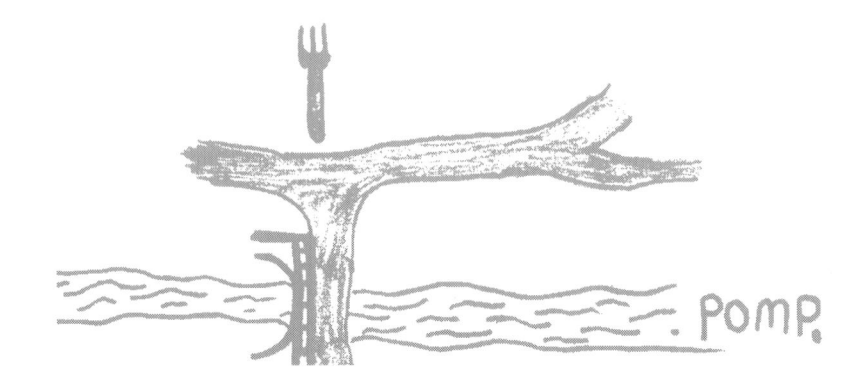

3. Robin arrives in late March, has two nesting cycles, and departs by fall.
4. Ravens enjoy this setting year-round.
5. Season: Late March through October.
6. Season: May through July.

THETFORD VT
CONTINUED

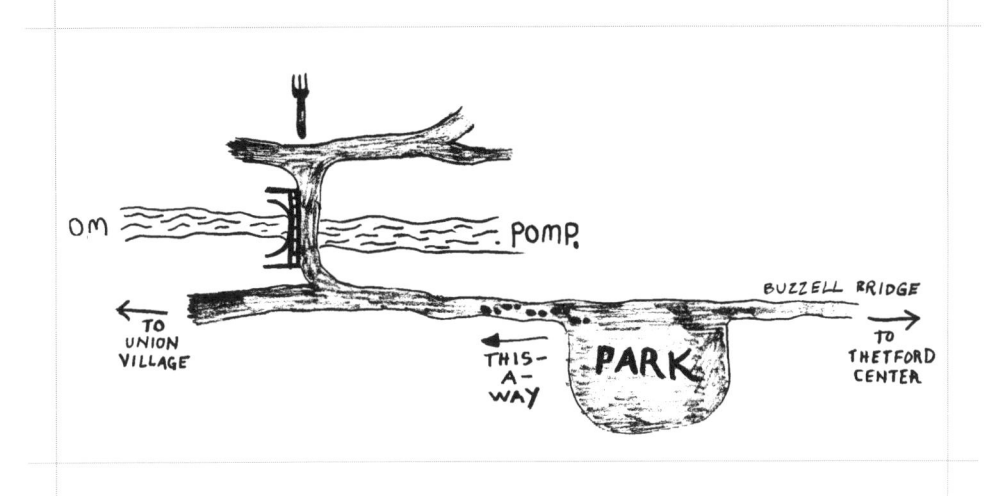

Ah . . . there is so much more to this story,
Like the hillside in fall in all its glory.
So many mysteries waiting to be solved
In a place so far away from the maddening crowd.
Let the peace feel its way in . . . 'cause there's so little that is loud.

"'Or the wrock' of a Raven?'"

Spring, summer, fall—which time is the best?
Come again and again, and experience the rest.
And for the last mystery: Find your treasure chest.

Remember how you looked for the "Lonesome Pine."
Make your way there and the last clue you will find.
From pine make your way 20 feet
To a stump and a log where the bugs and birds eat.

LONESOME PINE QUEST

MOVING HOUSES QUEST

THETFORD VT

58

To get there:

Get off I-91 at Exit 14. This is the Lyme/Thetford exit. Go toward Thetford Hill. At the top of the hill, turn south on Academy Road. Travel .3 miles to Thetford Academy and park. Your Quest begins here.

Park your car in the lot or on the road,
    Then head "up" Academy toward the church—but leave your load.

Third on your right, you'll see the Grange Hall.
    They started a new foundation Y2K in the fall.

Shuffle further and on your left you'll see
    Goddard Hall. Keep walking and don't say "Gee."

You'll come to a white double house on the left.
    This house has two chimneys and no less.

By now the church is in plain sight.
    There is no need to stop or fight.
    The church lies across the street now,
    But it was in the middle of the green before 1830 . . . Wow!

Jog along farther until Library Road.
    You'll pass the green on your right but it may not be mowed.

On the left is a small tan house, the old library place,
    You can keep walking but don't show your face.

Go to the green mailbox on the library front
    And get yourself ready for the final hunt.

In front of you there is a door.
    But, alas, there are so many more.

Look at all the doors you see—
    And above one of them you just may find me!

THETFORD VT
CONTINUED

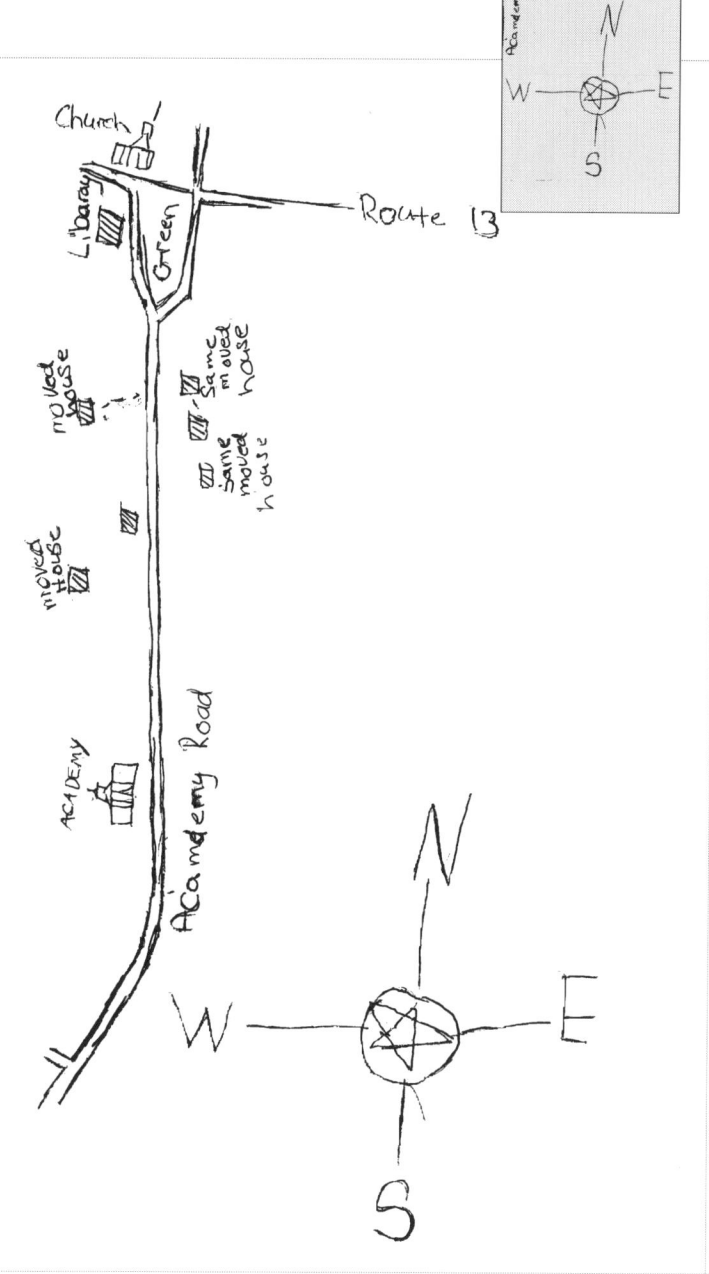

Hand-drawn map showing Academy Road running north-south, with Church, Library, and Green at the north end near Route 13. Along Academy Road are labeled "moved house" markers and "same moved house" pairs, with the Academy at the south end. Compass roses show N/S/E/W orientation.

I hiked with my daughters on the Monday before school started. It was a sunny, cool day and we shared lots of ideas along...

MOVING HOUSES QUEST 125

THETFORD VT

PEABODY LIBRARY QUEST 59

To get there:

Travel north or south on I-91 or Route 5 to the town of Thetford. Travel west on Route 113 over Thetford Hill, down through Thetford Center, and up to Post Mills. Coming into the village, the Peabody Library is on the right, after the store, the old village school, and the "odd fellows" hall. Please note that the Peabody Library has limited hours: Tuesday 5 to 8 p.m. and Wednesday 2 to 8 p.m.

Go on this Quest and
   You will see and learn
   About George Peabody
   At every turn.

The journey meanders
   From clue-to-clue
   So find the white rectangle
   That appears in front of you.

Please remember
   To put every clue back—
   Or this Quest will get thrown
   Quite out of whack!!

Before we start
   I repeat this Quest's rules:
   NO RUNNING
   And GENTLY remove all the clues.
   And please put them back
   GENTLY too.

And now here at long last is your first clue:

What is gigantic, has six legs, and drawers?
   Look in its far "mouth."

[*Note:* This is your first clue . . . It will lead you to other clues hidden around the library.]

THETFORD VT
CONTINUED

'So find

the white rectangle

that appears

in front of you'

PEABODY LIBRARY QUEST

60 THETFORD CANOE QUEST

THETFORD VT

To get there:
Take I-91 to Exit 14. Go down the hill on Route 113 to Route. 5. Take a left onto Route 5 and go about 2 miles north to Bridge Road. Take a right onto Bridge Road to the boat launch. You need a canoe or a kayak for this Quest.

Welcome to North Thetford,
   we're glad you are here.
   Now put your boat in the water,
   to the south you will steer.

Now look behind you for a view to the past.
   This old covered bridge
   was not meant to last.

On your trip down river keep your senses sharp.
   Birds and beavers, on your Quest, may take part.

Now it's time to paddle forward.
   You'll know you're on track
   if you see a brown house with a big red barn out back.

Off to the right old white pines stand straight.
   Back in the 1800s good ship masts these did make.

This river tells stories of floods every spring.
   Can you see signs of erosion exposing roots and fallen limbs?

Paddle on voyagers, though your muscles must ache.
   When you see a white house you'll soon know your fate.

Just past the white house
   there is an old barn.
   Now carefully look for a rock ledge
   on the bank of this farm.

On the opposite shore
   you'll spy a picnic table.
   Paddle over, park,
   and climb up there if you're able.

Welcome to the campsite,
   you're almost through.
   Better check the mailbox,
   there might be something for you!

THETFORD VT
CONTINUED

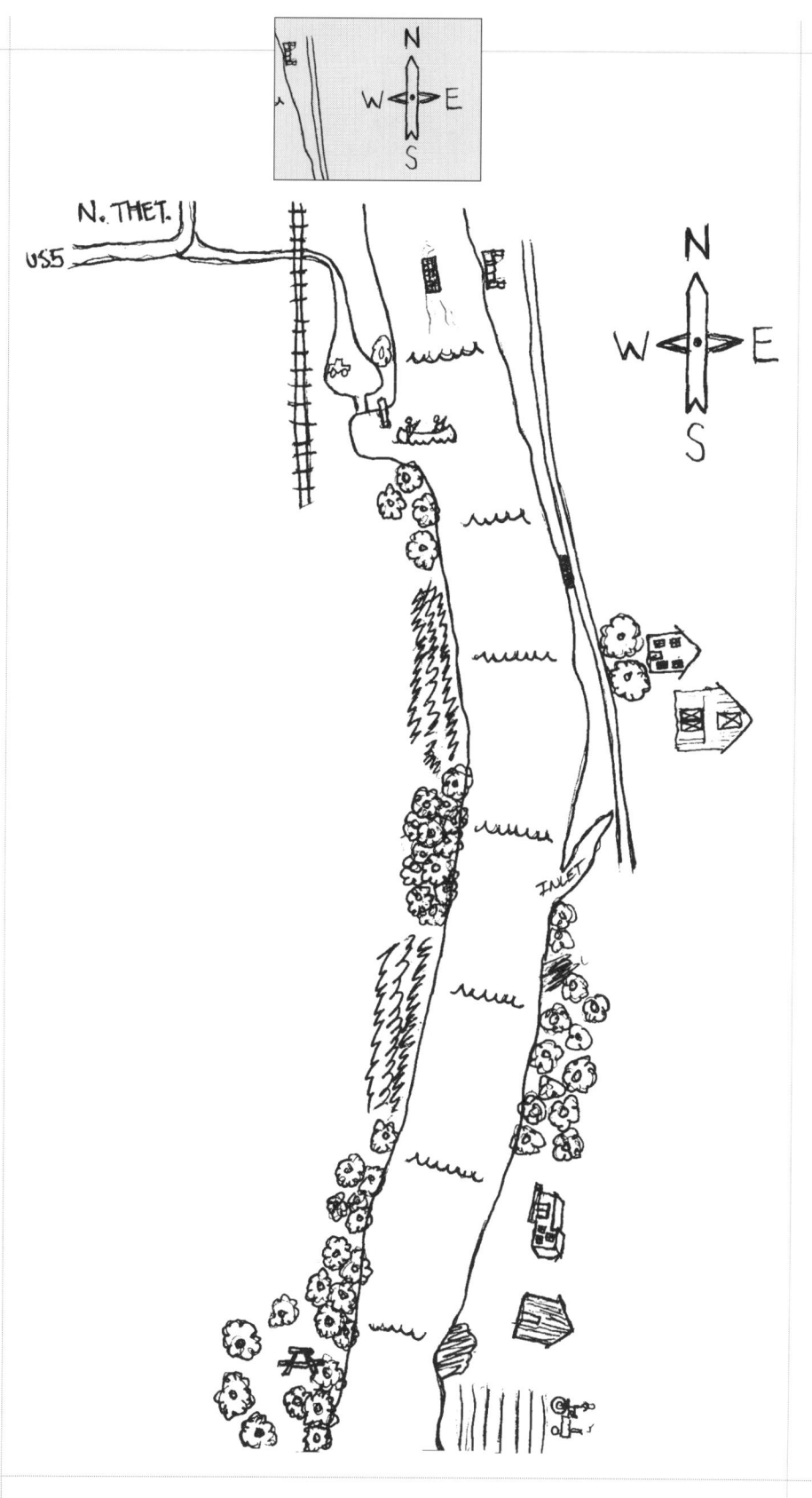

THETFORD CANOE QUEST 129

UNION VILLAGE QUEST

THETFORD VT

61

To get there:

Travel north (from Norwich) or south (from East Thetford) on Route 5 to the village of Pompanoosuc. Turn west on Route 132. Take 132 to Academy Road. Fork right onto Academy, and travel slowly through Union Village. Do not cross the covered bridge, but stay straight until you reach the Union Village Dam gate. Your quest begins there.

Named for the confluence of two rivers on the map you will see
   They are the east and west Ompompanoosuc—though branches they be.
   From Route 132, please drive on through.
   Norwich and Thetford this lumber lays astride—
   Look for this structure spanning the Ompomp. so wide.
   It's got water down near to its feet,
   With beams, a roof, and history not to be beat.
   Just a bit further north to go . . . but please, please, do drive slow.
   Warmer you are getting—and this Quest you shall find
   When you leave all the buildings of the village behind:
   A simple place full of nature's glory,
   It is here that we begin unfolding our story.

Park and then walk between gates of brick.
   Yes, I'll tell you that's the first trick!
   Grey and imposing (even when covered in white)
   This looming mass up ahead's quite a prominent site.
   Walk past the spot where you find material found on Cape Cod a lot.
   Two trees stand ahead mighty and tall. One is stately—losing leaves in fall.
   The other has needles bundled in five, 10 feet around, and very much alive.

Now follow your ear—listening for something that runs all year.
   It is the staff of life, and a cure to all strife.
   They call it magi, l'eau, agua, wasser, pani, and wet.
   One source is big and one is small. The nearer is the best find for all.
   It is cool and clear, so follow it uphill toward its source, my dear!
   North the "Drinking Gourd" will guide: ah but it is *west* that we shall stride.

Birds abound—if only they be found.
   The sputter of Fisher the king: listen for rattle and ring.
   "Potato chips, potato chips" the goldfinches do say
   At last you are off on your way.
   Least resistance is best. Mowed it is at first on this Quest.
   Pass picnic areas with purpose and with thrill
   And enter into the wood by the last table and grill.

Trees of cherry, oak, and basswood
   A stone find of history is a clue for the good.
   The original did plan the water to span.
   Made of stones laid up dry a carriage home it would fly.

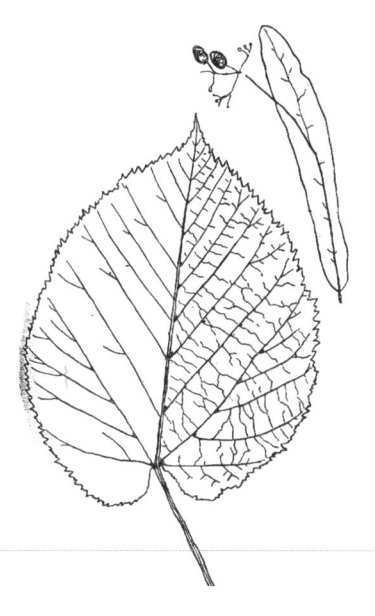

They be marginal and wood, oak and Christmas the fern
   Be careful! Watch your step at each little turn.
   Though perhaps a little shady and dark
   Where we are headed is surely no lark.
   Now listen for song, for surely we will not be long
   Be it vireo, robin, tanager, or thrush, oh hush, hush, hush.
   Here, flowers do abound—through all seasons can be found.

Ah, 'tis forest quiet and frail—for now you are certainly hot on the trail.
   Though temperature be cool keep your eyes open for the jewel.
   Voila! Eureka! The treasure brings such pleasure.

The pool is so cool. Now box you must find!
   Cylindrical with moss, on ground found behind.
   Too far it is not. Good luck finding the spot!
   A place to respect—
   Now take some time to pause and reflect.

VERSHIRE VT

COPPERFIELD TOWN QUEST
62

To get there:
Travel on Route 5, I-91, or Route 110 to Route 113. Take 113 into downtown West Fairlee. At the crossroads, turn west onto Beanville Road (also called South Vershire Road). Travel along the brook, and after 1.4 miles you will come to a pull-off on the left. Your Quest starts here.

This Quest begins after you park,
   Turn left and head north in order to embark.

Please follow the road carefully—
   Because of cars that you might see.

On both sides are cellar holes.
   These were dug by people, not by moles.

One thousand people lived here
   One hundred and twenty years ago.
   They had a big coal smelter
   And small houses built in rows.

The holes, you see, were houses
   Inhabited by people—also by mouses.

One hole a church, another a store,
   Mr. Ely's mansion and many more.

Pass four telephone poles
   Then take twenty paces
   And turn left to the cellar hole
   With your smiling faces.

Take a look but don't go in
   Then back to road and left again!

Pass one more pole.
   Then look for a path
   by a cellar hole.

It's near an old sign
   have faith—you'll do fine!

On the downward path is
   a cluster of birches
   (Something often found
   On Valley Quest searches).

Thos. Pascoe, Capt. Mine
R. W. Barrett, Capt, Dressing House
Mine opened 1853

VERSHIRE VT
CONTINUED

VERMONT COPPER MINING COMPANY

Smith Ely, Pres!
W. H. Long, Treas & Supt
D. F. Long, Ass't Supt
Thos. Pascoe, Capt. Mine
R. W. Barrett, Capt. Dressing House
Mine opened 1853
Smelting Furnace 450 Feet in lenght
erected in 1867 & 1876 under the
Superintendence of W. H. Long
Depth of Mine 1500 Feet. Angle 25° pitch

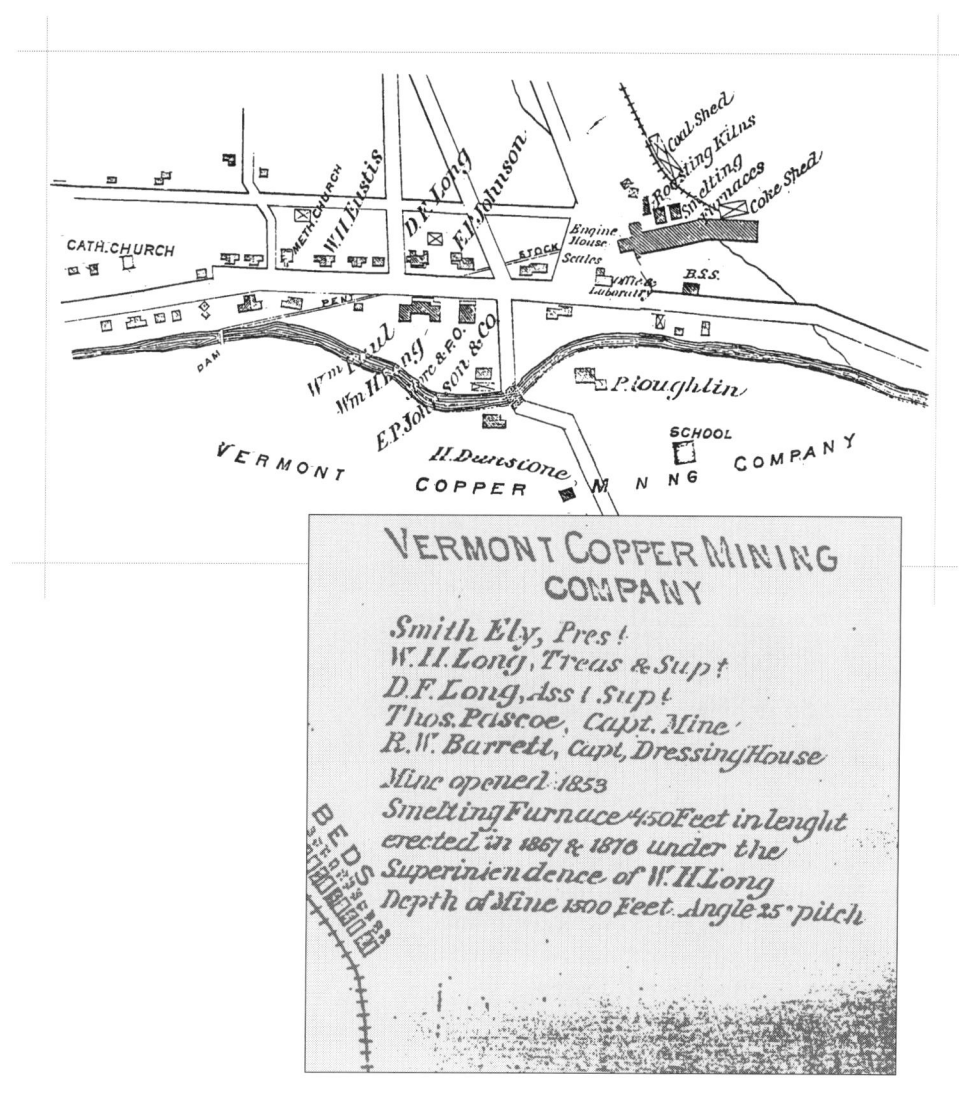

You might see traces of
   A beaver or an otter—
   Giving you a clue
   That you are near to water.

After you have seen our
   Splendid, rushing waterfall
   Turn back uphill and proceed to
   The corner of the "great wall."

Now slowly north along the wall
   Eyes open for our box (which is small).

Beneath a tall balsam fir tree
   The wall continues—don't you see?
   Look in the gaps between the rocks
   And if luck would have it, you'll find our box!

COPPERFIELD TOWN QUEST

VERSHIRE VT

VERSHIRE VILLAGE QUEST 63

To get there:
Travel north or south on I-91 or Route 5 to the town of Thetford. Travel west on Route 113 through Post Mills and West Fairlee to Vershire. Shortly after the town offices, turn on Vershire Center Road, and park in the lot immediately on your left.

Welcome to the Town Center.
    It's the best spot in town but please do not enter.
    We play games and shows are given here—
    The building was moved, but its first spot is near.

Go out the driveway and head toward the road
    On the right is some water where you might find a toad.
    Go right and head to Route 113.
    We love our town. It is clean and green.

Turn right and see the big white house
    Which was left to us by the family Orr.
    Continue on to the Town Clerk's office
    Where you pay your taxes and much more.

Cross over the BRIDGE to a big stone bench and hike left up the hill, inch by inch.

Back in the '60's, the Town Hall stood on this spot.
    The town had to tear it down—nothing is left on the lot.
    The old Town Hall was a school as well
    Stop in the Clerk's office to see the old bell.

Walk straight on, keep going, don't stop.
    Travel along with a skip and a hop.
    On your left, up a hill, see a church nice and neat.
    It once burned down, but once again people come to meet.

VERSHIRE VT
CONTINUED

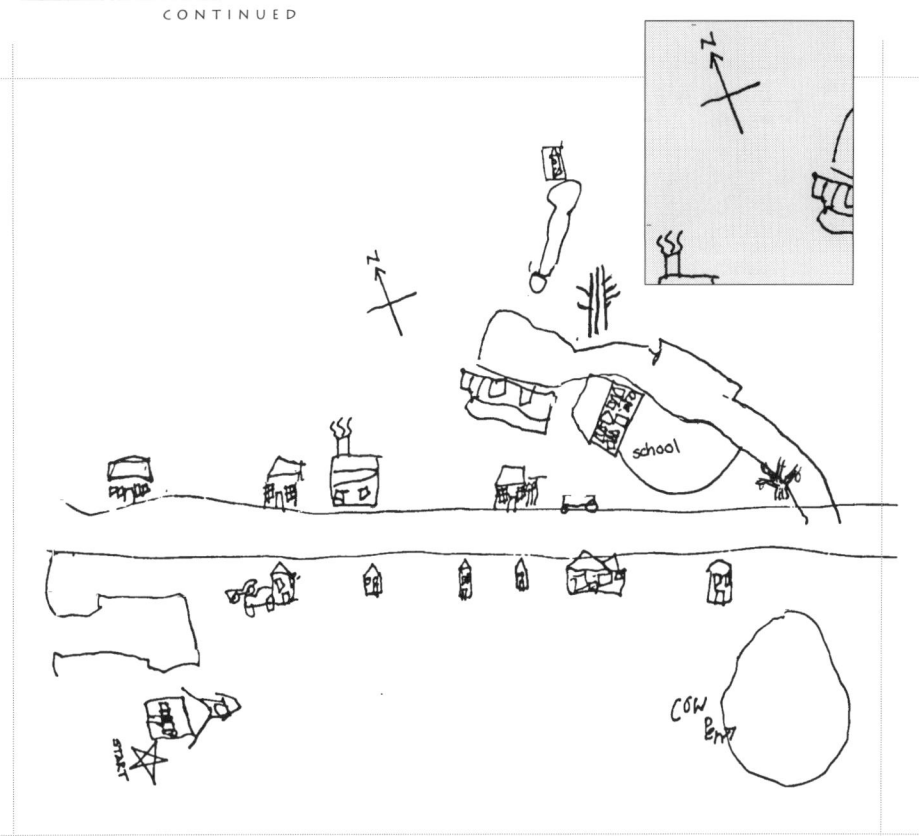

Keep going straight on 113.
    You might hear a dog who thinks he's mean.
    The road you're walking used to be made of dirt
    But now that it is paved wear shoes and a shirt.

Walk on for a while, passing houses and cows.
    Listen! The brook . . . the sound of it . . . WOW.
    Walk on to a green sign and turn left up the drive
    Here is the place where kids learned nine times five.

The old school burned down, an unlucky fire.
    The brick part stayed up, higher and higher.
    The inside came down with a thumpety-thood!
    And now the building's rebuilt with bunches of wood.

Walk up the hill past the school to the lonely trees.
    Then look for a trail to the right if you please.
    Cross over the bridge to a big stone bench
    And hike left up the hill, inch by inch.

At the top of the field, after taking a rest
    Head left up the path to where the view is the best.
    Walk to the spot were you see school's chimney
    Then turn to the small house found upon popple tree.

64
FALL MOUNTAIN QUEST

WALPOLE NH

To get there:

Just north of downtown Bellows Falls, cross the bridge from Route 5 in Bellows Falls to North Walpole. The sign shows arrows to Route 12. Cross the bridge and bear right at the light on the other side. Take the third left onto Main Street (right beside the large Route 12 sign). Take the first right onto Mountain View Road. This right is at the bottom of the hill by North Walpole Elementary School. Follow Mountain View Road as it curves right, then left, then go 0.5 mile to the end where there are parking spaces. You will see a metal gate. Do not drive up through the gate. This is where the Quest begins. Note: *If you decide to follow this Quest from mid-October through December know this is a popular mountain for hunting. Please wear bright orange clothing if you decide to hike during hunting season.*

Remember a pace is every time your right foot lands, or in other words: "two steps make a pace."

From the parking lot, go over the large boulders and up the hill and through the power lines. Coming up the trail, you need to turn right. There is a pond there (40 yards long). Walk along the stone wall until you come to a break in the wall where the water flows through. That is the dam. This pond may have been used as a fire pond or for agriculture. Your next clue is only a little ways away.

Head up the trail that was an old carriage road to a great lookout. After about 100 paces, look to the north side of the trail for white birch and oak trees and to the west side for pines, birches, hemlocks, and oak trees. Now, your eyes should be on the ground looking for a bare rock with white and narrow quartz veins. This is called Bethlehem Gneiss and is about 400 million years old. It's from a volcano that originally formed in the Atlantic Ocean. This bedrock was pushed up to the surface for just one purpose, to help make Fall Mountain! Keep going up the trail.

Start looking for a triple-trunk tree north of the trail. It's about 50 to 75 feet tall and it's a northern red oak standing on the small ridge. It was formed from one big tree that was cut down and it sprouted these trees. Around the tree are plenty of ferns, red maples, and white birches.

In this long stretch of land, keep an eye out, if you dare; for squirrels, deer, partridge, and . . .
Watch for the black bears. In the last four to five years, they've made a comeback.

As you head up the trail, you should also see lots of stumps on the right and these are a sign of recent logging. When you get to a level spot toward the top of the mountain where the trail splits in two, take the right trail through the power lines. Look down the mountain toward Bellows Falls. As you look at the Green Mountains across the Connecticut River Valley, you can see Okemo, the skiing resort.

WALPOLE NH
CONTINUED

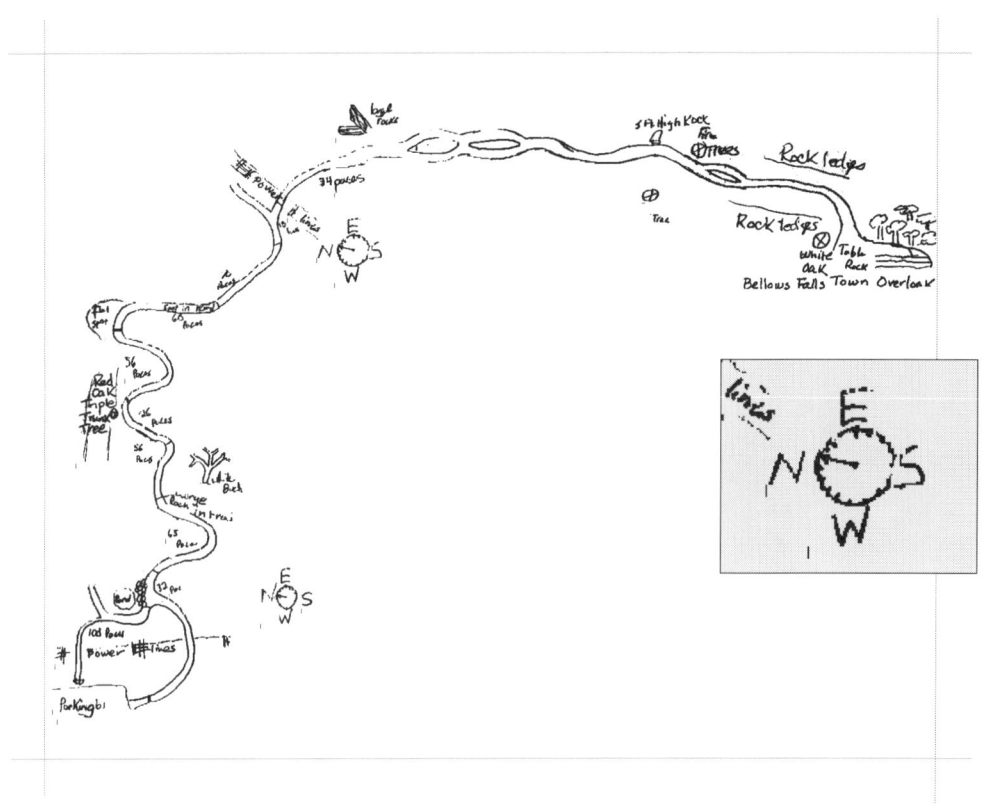

Keep on the trail. Soon, you will see some large rocks on the left (to the east) of the trail. The large rocks are hardened schist from the middle of the ocean that were originally sand and granite. When the continents collided 400 million years ago these were also pushed up to the surface. Off you go to your next site.

Keep going up the trail until you get to the 3-foot-tall rock standing on its edge on the left (or east) side of the trail. Look around. There are some trees that were not logged. They were burned! They survived the railroad fires. Since the railroad company opened in 1849, there have been forest fires on Fall Mountain. The sparks used to fly off the coal train and start uncontrollable fires. The rattlesnakes that were on Fall Mountain have been eliminated or extirpated from being hunted and from the fires.

Keep on the trail heading south until it opens up to a beautiful view to the west and the town of Bellows Falls below. You will find a large white oak tree. It is about 10 feet away from the cliff. You made it to the top, also known as Table Rock! In a local myth, John Kilburn, the supposed first white settler of Walpole, pushed the Indians off Table Rock. Also, upon this spot, 1,200 feet above town, there once stood a pavilion in the mid-1800s for guests of the Island House in Bellows Falls. Go five paces to the south from the white oak whose trunk is 15 inches across! Over the rocks, you will go through rain, sleet, and snow. Now turn east and walk another five paces or so into the woods where you might see black and red as well as more white oak. These are also signs of the fires of the recent past.

Have fun looking for the box tucked in the rocks close by!

FALL MOUNTAIN QUEST   137

65

WARREN NH

THE MOOSILAUKE HISTORICAL QUEST

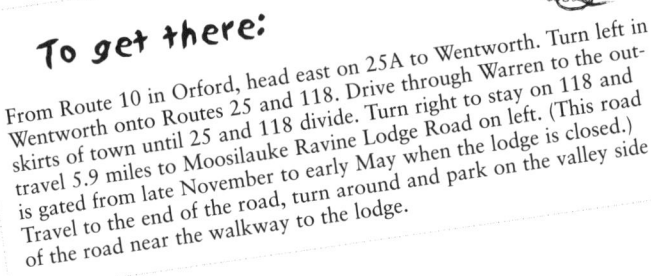

Homeschoolers from Enfield - ages 2, 4, and 8

To get there:

From Route 10 in Orford, head east on 25A to Wentworth. Turn left in Wentworth onto Routes 25 and 118. Drive through Warren to the outskirts of town until 25 and 118 divide. Turn right to stay on 118 and travel 5.9 miles to Moosilauke Ravine Lodge Road on left. (This road is gated from late November to early May when the lodge is closed.) Travel to the end of the road, turn around and park on the valley side of the road near the walkway to the lodge.

This quest has been created in honor of J. Willcox Brown, class of 1937, who served as Graduate Manager of the Dartmouth Outing Club from 1937 to 1939 during the time when the Ravine Lodge was built. Will has been a charter member and guiding light of the Moosilauke Advisory Committee since its inception in 1974. One of Will's greatest delights is giving the historical tour of the Ravine Lodge and its environs. To honor his enthusiasm and spirit of adventure, we dedicate this quest to him.

To start off this Quest, we'd like to introduce you around
   (You should be starting at the sign where this Quest can be found)
To a man who, in these parts, is a legend more than any:
It's the incomparable C. Ross McKenney.
'Twas Ross who built this lodge and yet, even more,
'Twas Ross who cemented Dartmouth's tie to the out-of-doors.
Keep Ross's name in mind as you make your forest quest,
And while you're here, in the library, take a look at the rest
Of the names in this room, Emerson, Sayre, and Haile,
Whose contributions will come to life once you're out on the trail.
After finishing on the ground floor please ascend to the next,
For it is in this main room that we begin our forest quest.
Logs cut by hand were carefully notched
   (Supervisor McKenney's eyes, eagle-like, watched)
In 1938 as these spruce walls were built,
And Dartmouth at Moosilauke took off at full tilt.
These trees would have shattered in 1938
When a legendary hurricane struck the Granite State.
But as luck would have it, these trunks were aground,
   (Crosscut saws and axes having taken them down)
So the Lodge could be built just one year after,
And we now can witness these glorious rafters.
   (Oops—a technical note, one that Ross would have mentioned:

WARREN NH
CONTINUED

These are purlins, not rafters, because they're horizontally directioned.)
People and trees have a dubious past—
The tales of abuse are legion and vast.
But once in awhile it all comes together,
Take this room—could there be a finer endeavor?
There's another thing to mention as we get going,
It's an historical point, one well worth knowing.
You've probably wondered, "What was happening here
Back before anyone these woods came to clear?"
The fact is the opposite was really the case.
Trees arrived second—after our race,
Who lived here on the tundra and hunted the bear,
Ten thousand years back when the landscape was bare
Of all but low mosses along cold, icy creeks
(A landscape still visible on Moosi's main peak).
So the conventional wisdom, you see, had it all backwards—
Folks were here first and the trees grew up aft'wards.
But no more diversions about days long ago,
Let's get back to the present—out of doors we should go!
So you can see for yourself what the woods have to offer,
And not just what other folks may try to proffer.
Walk out through the main doors and up on a trail.
Bring tough shoes and raincoat if it looks like to hail.
We'll be gone for an hour, perhaps a wee, small bit more,

'Folks arrived
at the pace of a snail
Along the old Carriage Road
and today's Hurricane Trail'

Before the treasure you've found and this woods quest is o'er.
Ahead in the path is a low-slung shed
Made of concrete and logs, twice the size of a bed.
It's the lodge's first water source, a cistern if you will,
To store water from streams caught by dams up the hill.
But this hillside is porous, just a pile of stones
Covered by forest, like skin over bones.
So this water being fickle dodged under those dams
And down to the Baker and much further lands.
The cistern still stands here, no water now stored,
The whole thing replaced by a well deeply bored.
*First Number: How many stacked logs are there
in the wall of the cistern next to the trail?
Multiply this number by 10 and write it here:* ___
A few dozen steps further uphill you must climb,
To a road non-existent in 1939
When the Ravine Lodge was finished—that was the year—
Folks arrived and departed on a road no longer clear.
We'll give you a hint—it's the route of an old railroad
That, before long, you'll have a chance to be showed.
And even before that, folks arrived at the pace of a snail

WARREN NH
CONTINUED

Along the old Carriage Road and today's Hurricane Trail.
The road under your feet in the '40s was born
To haul timber from hollows to a mill down
    in Warren.
At that time, this hillside was covered by
    fallen-down trees,
The debris from that famous storm in the late 1930s.
But now we return to our purpose at hand—
To find treasure with each step through this Moosilauke land.
So, turn to the left, to the north you must sally,
Past the point where vehicles are asked not to dally.
Cross over some gravel and come to a shrine
Put up for a man ahead of his time,
Who saw in these woods a great place for skiing
And hiking and learning and tree-type-I.D.ing.
You're standing right now in a place he thought wonderful:
The site of the Dartmouth '52 Winter Carnival.
There wasn't much snow in yon Hanover that year.
College skiers came here, with their dates and their gear,
To race down this hillside where you stand today
(Moosi was among the first ski hills built in the U.S. of A.)
If you face up the hill and look with sharp eye,
A change in the tree type you are sure to spy.
Like an alley are birches lined up in a row,
One sign of the route of the old rope tow.

'On this route long ago horse pairs could be seen Hauling logs for the Lodge down from Jobildunk Ravine'

Second Number: The plaque lists two pairs of dates.
Add the last digit from each of these four dates, multiply
the total by 3, subtract 2, and write the number here: ___
There's still more to be seen from those old skiing days
If you turn back toward the mountain (with luck there's no haze).
Look for stripes of hardwoods, zigging left, zigging right,
On the slope below south peak, (the ridgeline's left-most height).
It was called Hell's Highway, a trail steep and great,
Cut by hand in '33, wiped out in '38
By the aforementioned hurricane that made such an impression
(Though weather folks knew it was an extra-tropical depression).
Folks in their thirst for routes wide and groomed
Forgot that straight, steep trails are bound to be doomed.
One last thing to ponder on that ridge far above:
In '33 climbed skiers in leather boots and leather gloves

WARREN NH
CONTINUED

For the first National downhill ever held in this land,
A race thought too dangerous, it now has been banned!
But back then through the woods like rushing water skiers flowed,
Around the tight turns and sharp corners of the old Carriage Road.
Continue ahead, smoothly and deft
'Til you come to a sign pointing down to the left.
Don't take this new trail—keep the one that you're on,
Until a new intersection you happen upon.
Where to go now, standing at this next junction?
Screw up your nerve, your wit and compunction
And make a hard left, almost all the way 'round,
And descend down this new road you've recently found.
(If you miss this junction two brown signs you'll soon see,
Halt where you are, take a U-turn and flee!
Back several steps, now to the right you must turn,
To continue on toward the treasure you'll earn.)
Proceed a dozen steps more and look to your right
To see a quite common yet interesting sight.
A clump of young needled trees all in a row,
What kind are these—perchance do you know?
If not, here's a technique to help you ID:
Shake hands with a branch from each type of tree.
As your fingers run along each needled bough,
One hand will say, "ooh," the other shout, "ow!"
Fir needles are friendly: friendly, fir, "f."
Spruce needles are spiky: spiky, spruce, "s."
'Twas the spruce that drew loggers up into these hills
Seeking wood to become lumber in valley sawmills.
Its wood, more than others, is strong, light, and durable
(Human thirst for such qualities is downright incurable!)
As the forest has grown back the spruce is now rare.
The reason for which is either genetic, or a scare.
The life cycle of spruce is much longer than fir,
Allowing firs to dominate early while spruces defer.
But perhaps the spruce absence is a more troubling tale:
A tree species hurt by acid rain, fog, and hail.
These both are likely causes of the sparse spruce's story,
A tree now less common than in past days of glory.
Turn away from these youngsters and down the path sail.
This road is still known as the old Go-Back trail.
On this route long ago horse pairs could be seen
Hauling logs for the Lodge down from Jobildunk Ravine.
Our path continues downward and straight through the trees,
Watch out! Heads up! Look sharp if you please!
A trail that descends from the left isn't yours.
Stay straight to avoid any undesirable detours.
Pretty soon at a fork you will want to stay left,
(Staying straight towards the river will leave you bereft.)
If you are now wondering, "Am I on the right tread?"
The clue you should walk toward is an oldish brown shed.
If ever there was a case open and shut,
It's our general aversion to a woodland clear cut

WARREN NH
CONTINUED

In which every last tree has been cut to the ground
And traces of forest life are scant to be found.
From this perspective, therefore, it may be a surprise
That this hillside was once ski trails, cleared
  many yards wide.
Spruce, fir, and pine were predominant species,
Some trunks far taller than any we now see.
But today in this place grow more birch, alder, and aspen,
Their numbers a sign that such a clear-cut did happen.
Soon along this route are three buildings in a row:
The middle one the base-station for the old rope tow.
It was here through the fifties that in fanciful flights
Folks lined up for the trip to the ridgeline's frosty heights.
The first building is the center of much investigation
Into the alpine effects of acid precipitation.
This building used to stand in a different location,
Atop the ridge at the site of the old Meteorological Station.
The third building, on the right, is called Benton bunkhouse—
Home to overnight sleepers and the occasional mouse.
Benton has replaced an old log one now gone
Named for Dartmouth alumnus Nat Emerson.
Now who was this Emerson? Perhaps you are asking?
He was Class of 1900, and he once stood here basking
In a vision of Dartmouth preserving land on this river.
He helped make it happen as a Ravine Lodge staunch giver.
This original Lodge bunkhouse stood to the left in deep shrubs,
All that's left now for the curious are a few concrete stubs.
Built after the Ravine Lodge yet fallen far before,
Emerson Bunkhouse's short life span underscores
A message that old log buildings require vigilance and care
If we are going to have something with the future to share.
From this settlement set forth, with the bunkhouse on your right,
'Til a main intersection comes quickly to sight.
To the right please descend and listen with sharp ear,
For the sound that reveals flowing water quite near.
If you're in the right place and haven't gone wrong,
A long bridge over the river you should have happened upon.
The bridges that have stood here are too many to mention,
Though a unique feature now is worthy of your attention:
The one you see today is unlike the rest—
It's the first time that iron's been put to the test.
Third Number: How many spans are there in the bridge?
How many steel beams support the main span?
Subtract the number of beams from the number
of spans and write the difference here: ___
Do not cross here on this bridge, it would be a mistake,
To the left it's the old road we beg you to take.
A dozen steps on to your right there is cribbing—
Stone-filled timbers that look like wood ribbing—
On the opposite bank; it used to carry weight
Of an old wooden bridge up until '98.
A bit further on there's an old concrete cover,
More evidence of what used to be another
Lodge water source, perhaps a dug well
Though at this point in time it's too hard to tell.

WARREN NH
CONTINUED

Back in the fifties, before the days of plastic
There crossed here a wooden pipe—it was
   really fantastic—
That brought water down and up from the Gorge Brook
   to the Lodge
In a tight-fitting and effective wooden hodgepodge.
Two dozen more yards should bring you to a clearing.
Look right toward a stone pile. Can you imagine steering
A canoe on a pond out in this swift river?
These stones cored a dam that used to stand thither
Until in '42 a spring flood came roaring
And freed the pond's water that the dam had been storing.

'Named after Ross McKenney, that teacher of woodcraft, who taught students many things, including how to draft designs for cabins such as this, where students came to play

So much for deep diving in the Asquamchumaukee—
These days it's too shallow and narrow and rocky.
Scramble out onto the dam and in your mind's eye
See a pond full of swimmers 'neath a summer blue sky.
A few timbers still hold back the gravelly till—
Peek over your shoulder, there's the Lodge up on the hill.
Now back to the trail, carry on, keeping count
For 200 feet, more or less, that's the amount
Until you come to the end of the path that's quite rough,
And you're about to step up to a road still covered by duff.
Right there in the trail, under foot, in plain sight,
There's a rock that's been blown up by a stick o' dynamite.
Back in the days when this woods road was built,
Horses pulled logs here (not quite at full tilt).
So the lumbermen blew off the top of this boulder,
To make for the horses a smooth and wide shoulder.
Feel its sharp edges with your feet or your hands,
Far too rough to be natural among river bottom sands.
In about 200 feet more this road comes to an end
In a bit of a hollow, a forested glen.
Turn left at the road's end and start up a stone stair,
And suddenly you'll find yourself in a place where
On the corner, to the right, amidst the raspberries,
Are the remains of a burned structure, look carefully if you please.

WARREN NH
CONTINUED

Named after Ross McKenney, that teacher of woodcraft,
Who taught students many things, including how to draft
Designs for cabins such as this where students came to play,
This cabin in '84 saw its last and final day.
Why it came, and why it went, is an interesting story
Full of intrigue, subterfuge, and a touch of student glory.
In '46, without permission, u-grads built this here log cabin
To protest the high fees that the Ravine Lodge staff were nabbin'.
For the next forty years, this was a low-brow student dive,
'Til the newly appointed John Rand Cabin did arrive.
(John Rand Cabin is up the ridge a quarter mile or two—
Too far away to be mentioned in this Quest's local purview.)
Now turn up the hill to observe signs from the past,
And prepare to imagine activities quite vast.
Down from above a stone roadway comes ramping,
It was here in the old days that horses came tramping
Uphill in the summer pulling railroad wheel pairs,

'A favorite activity was to ski this front lawn at night—under floodlight, and star light, it must have been a special sight'

Further up to the clearing 'midst lumbermen's stares.
These woodsmen set the wheels on a rolled iron track,
And upon these steel wheels proceeded to stack
Whole trunks of tree giants, 'specially the spruce,
And when fully loaded, they gave it a goose
Which set the whole thing rolling down, downward indeed,
Traveling with the force of gravity feed.
So the trees were transported 3.5 miles further on,
'Til meeting still more horses who hauled the trunks down to Warren.
This grade used to be among the Lodge's first driveways.
At the top, near the clearing, perchance to look sideways.
On the left you may see old logs covered by moss
That didn't measure up to the standards set by Ross,
And have lain here in the leaves now for several generations
(Don't be fooled by the newer logs from recent renovations).
Continue out into the open, the Ravine Lodge now in sight.
This open space has seen many things—activities day and night.
The first of these, a logging camp, built more than a century back,
Gave food and rest to loggers in a modest tar-paper shack.
Camp 2 it was called, for its distance from the mill,

WARREN NH
CONTINUED

(Camp 1 was back by the Carriage Road, Camp 3 further up the hill).
Though today's Lodge leach field has reworked the topography,
One last vestige of Camp 2 is still possible to see.
Those fat birches, across the road, at the field and forest marg,
Date from the Camp 2 clearing—that's why they're big and large.
After Camp 2 burned in the 1920s, Dartmouth came upon the scene
And turned the Camp's old horse stalls into a ski lodge,
   neat and clean.
From '33 to '35 Ford and Peggy Sayre here held court
'Til the good food and camaraderie were once again cut short
By a fire that leveled that first Ravine Camp and did such major harm
That the DOC retreated down to Warren and the old Spyglass Farm.
But in the winter of '37 with Will Brown now on the scene,
Along with Ross McKenney here below Jobildunk Ravine,
Work began on this Ravine Lodge—rising from the ashes,
And for that, six decades later, we can still raise up our glasses!
Keep in mind, as you stand here, that the Lodge was for winter built,
(Though the smarties, despite the furnace, never lodged here sans quilt.)
A favorite activity was to ski this front lawn at night—
Under floodlight, and star light, it must have been a special sight.
But in the late fifties as skiing took a mechanistic bent,
The Ravine Lodge for a decade into oblivion was sent
Until, thankfully, it was once again reopened,
And folks like ourselves it can lovingly now tend.
We've come to the end of our outdoor bit of quest,
Return to the Ravine Lodge by whatever route seems best.
Go in through the downstairs door, and once again take time
To meet the people and places mentioned in this questing rhyme.
At long last, here and now, it's time to find the treasure.
Whether or not you can will be a sort of measure
Of your searching skills and our writing craft—
Here's hoping that neither of us is hapless and daft!
Picture yourself arriving at the Lodge with your skis.
There's a big sign over a doorway that seeing it would please
You no end, in the fifties, for it would tell you how to go
As you prepare for a tow trip up the mountain on snow.
Standing under this sign and facing away
Walk until you get warmer, much warmer I say!
You should be facing a wall full of crazy designs
If you know Dr. Schlitz, it's his Forest of Signs.
It is here you must look, perhaps high, perhaps low,
The treasure box has been hidden quite carefully, just so.
When the box is in hand and your excitement is roiled,
Drats! You are likely to find yourself foiled
Unless with great care this Quest you've attended
And noted above the three numbers we recommended.
Open the box now with pleasure and glee—
It's as easy as the numbers one, two, and three!
Thank you for following this historical quest
If you've made it this far, you're simply the best!
Give a nod to Will Brown and all who've gone before
For helping us peer through this historical door.

WEATHERSFIELD VT

CRYSTAL CASCADE QUEST

66

To get there:
From Exit 8 off I-91, travel west on Route 131 for 3.2 miles to Cascade Falls Road. Turn right onto Cascade Falls and take an immediate left at the fork onto High Meadows Road. At the last house, bear right into the parking lot.

Ayup, it's 422 feet higha
   To the Crystal Cascade up yonda
   Lil o'er a mile from the parkin' lot heya
But shucks, don't you worry,
Halfway up there, levels off in a hurry!
Well you start up these steps of wood
Followin' the white blazes if you could
  Cross the 'lil brook then uphill you'll scramble
  Hope Lil Cascade's flowin' as o'er it you amble
Through gorge, up steps, why—there's a view
Near halfway there, rest'll be plain to you
Two ATA's (Ascutney Trail Association signs)
 Near Crystal at 1510 feet
'Neath one is a find that can't be beat
With stories about rocks and long-ago heat.

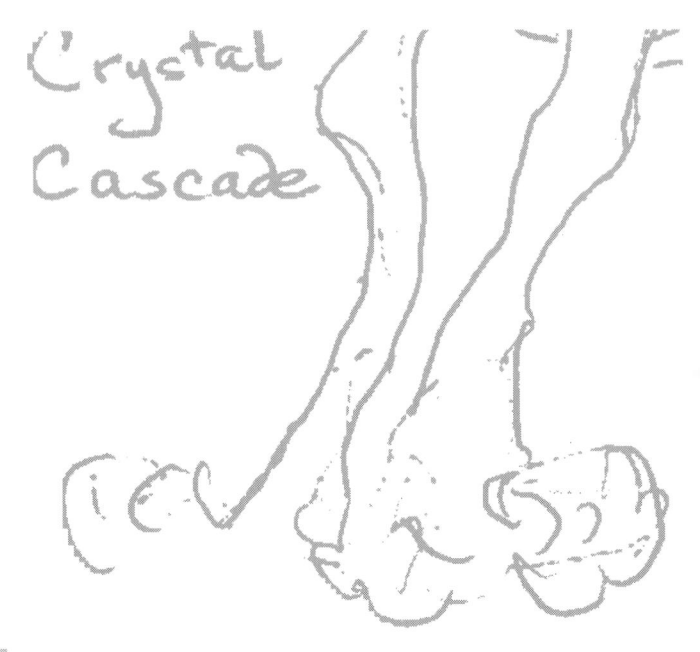

Crystal Cascade

VALLEY QUEST · 2001

WEATHERSFIELD VT
CONTINUED

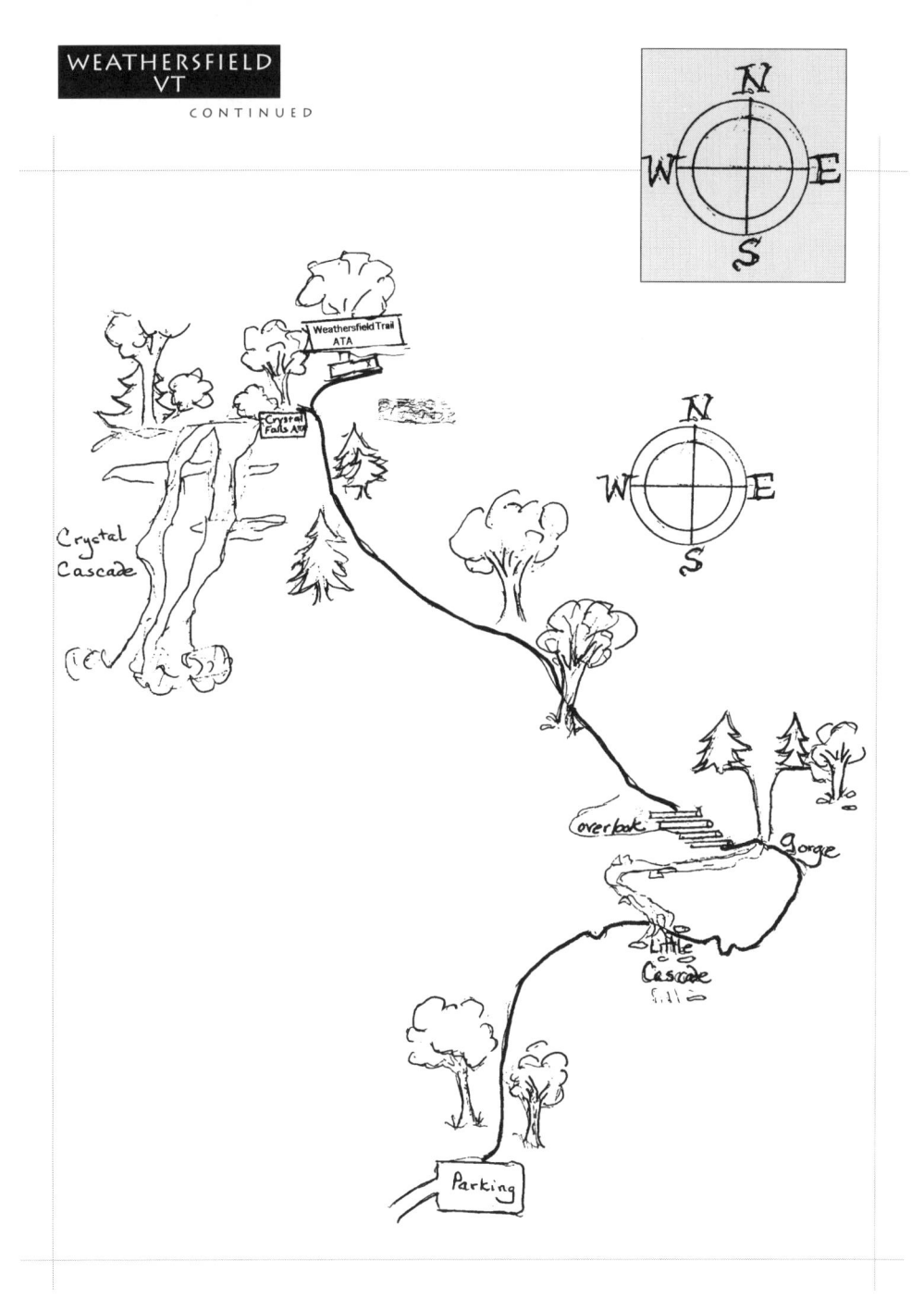

' 'Lil o'er a mile from the

parkin' lot heya'

CRYSTAL CASCADE QUEST 147

67

LINNY'S LOOP BICYCLE QUEST

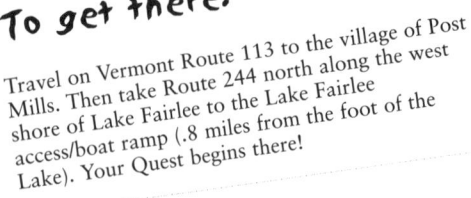

WEST FAIRLEE VT

To get there:
Travel on Vermont Route 113 to the village of Post Mills. Then take Route 244 north along the west shore of Lake Fairlee to the Lake Fairlee access/boat ramp (.8 miles from the foot of the Lake). Your Quest begins there!

Welcome to our lake! Fifty-six feet at its deepest point—and six miles around.
    Looking carefully, its seven in-flowing sources can be found.
    Today we'll explore just two—leaving the other five up to you.
    Hop on your bike and head northwest (left) to look
    At the tributary known as Middle Brook.
    At the bridge, stop and take in the view
    Of all the nutrients flowing under you.
    Nutrients, perhaps, that you cannot quite see . . .
    But what about birds, beaver or otter? What do YOU see?
    Eagles? Osprey? Muskrat lodges? Wood ducks? Painted or snapping turtles?

From the bridge find the white arrow. Take the first word
    And fill it in the space labeled #1. That is how this Quest is done!

After a right turn on Middle Brook, to your left is a camp
    And along the banks of the brook a willow alder swamp.
    Now take a ride in style . . . for at least another mile.

Next to 1003 is something with many, many windows.
    Fill that word in space #2, for that word is your next clue!
    One side of this fine structure is marked clearly with two Xs.
    The number of windows on this side goes in space #3. Really!

You'll pass a lake on your left and then the three silos of Stever's Dairy,
    Still milking and shipping milk—which makes our hearts merry.
    There is a breed of cow named upon their sweet sign.
    Fill it in space #4 and you're doing just fine.

Three miles in, watch out for the griffin!
    Upon a lawn on the right you may see him a-sittin.
    One part eagle, one part lion; lots of presence but hardly flying.
    Straight on lies a church marking West Fairlee Center
    Bear Notch Road turns left but *do not enter.*
    Stay on the main road right and straight—
    For Blood Brook Road is the name of your fate.
    Turn up to the right when this road comes in sight.
    The climb may be steep, but try and stay on your seat . . .
    It's only a half-mile climb. Breathe, relax, take your time.
    The reward comes as a long downhill without a clue . . .
    For a little while the entertainment's all up to you!

There's a peaceful resting place under some trees,
    And the top of its fence is marked clearly with these.
    Mark this symbol as word #5—then off you drive!

WEST FAIRLEE VT
CONTINUED

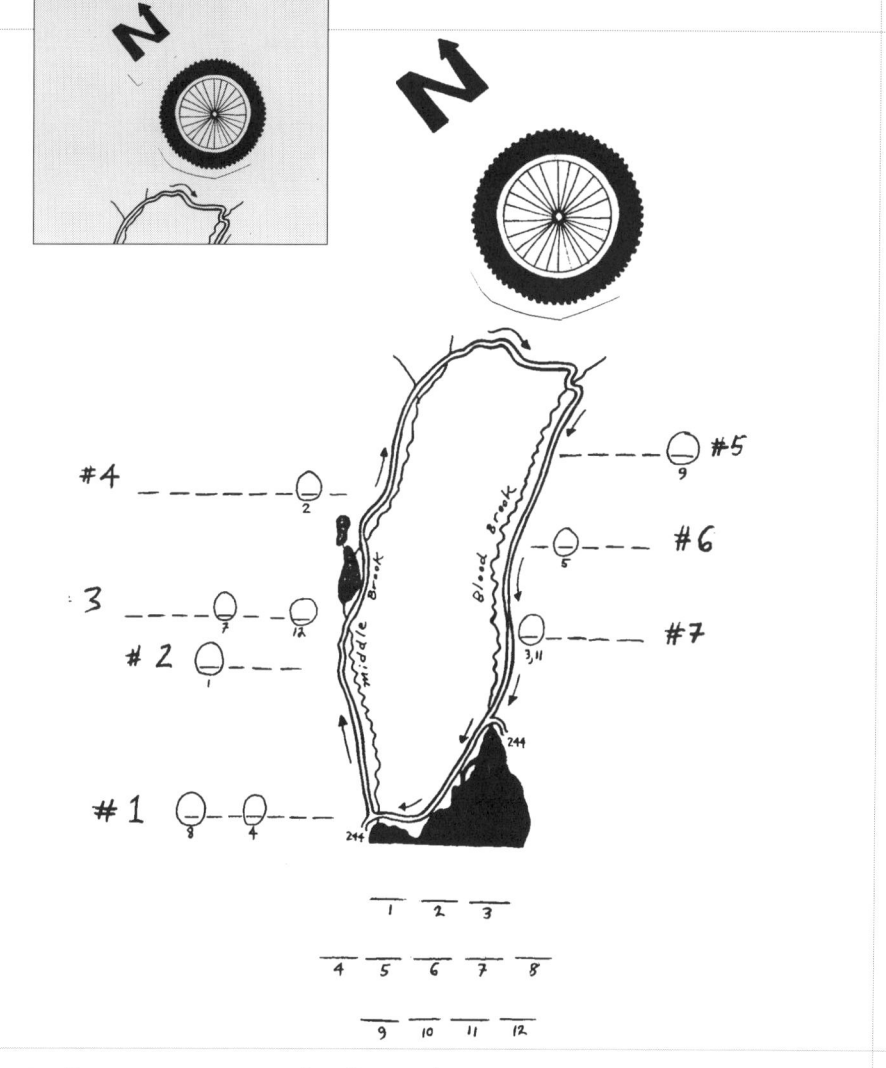

You'll pass a one-room schoolhouse from 1871
   Record the name of its number and clue #6 is done.

Take a right on Marsh Hill to see a neat old sawmill.
   Lichen has covered the rocks in its cellar
   Turning them to a quite curious color.
   The seventh word names the color you've learned.

Back to the main road and coast down to the lake
   And at the stop sign a right turn you must take.
   Here, Blood Brook flows in through a culvert
   Offering the lake rich freight for dessert:
   Rock flour, pulverized leaves, soil, and even pieces of trees.

Alas, the time has come to compute and to spell . . .
   And if you've collected all the right words you can tell
   The place the Linny Loop Treasure Box will dwell.

Missing two clues? Aye, use your eyes!
   Then bike .3 miles until you see
   The triangle where the treasure must be!

LINNY'S LOOP BICYCLE QUEST

68 BOSTON LOT QUEST

WEST LEBANON NH

To get there:

Take Route 10 about 2½ miles south of Hanover. Park at the parking area on the left for the Wilder Dam.

Look for the brown and yellow sign
   on the big brown pine.

Note the fallen tree
   where the roots are free.

Look for the "tower of power"
   which is not a flower.

Stay straight on the tree-lined path
   or you'll take a bath.

Go straight pass the gate, up the hill.
   What a thrill!

You come to a fork and what do you do?
   I'd go right if I were you!

Next, go to a place where the water is still.
   There you watch duck, fish, or swim at your will.

Cross the wooden bridge where you'll find a "group of six."
   Watch out for the ticks!

Pass three big boulders
   that don't fit in folders!

Stand with your back between two fallen birch trees.
   LOOK! and see a trunk of three.

Take about 50 paces southwest
   where under the trunks you'll end your Quest.

WEST LEBANON NH
CONTINUED

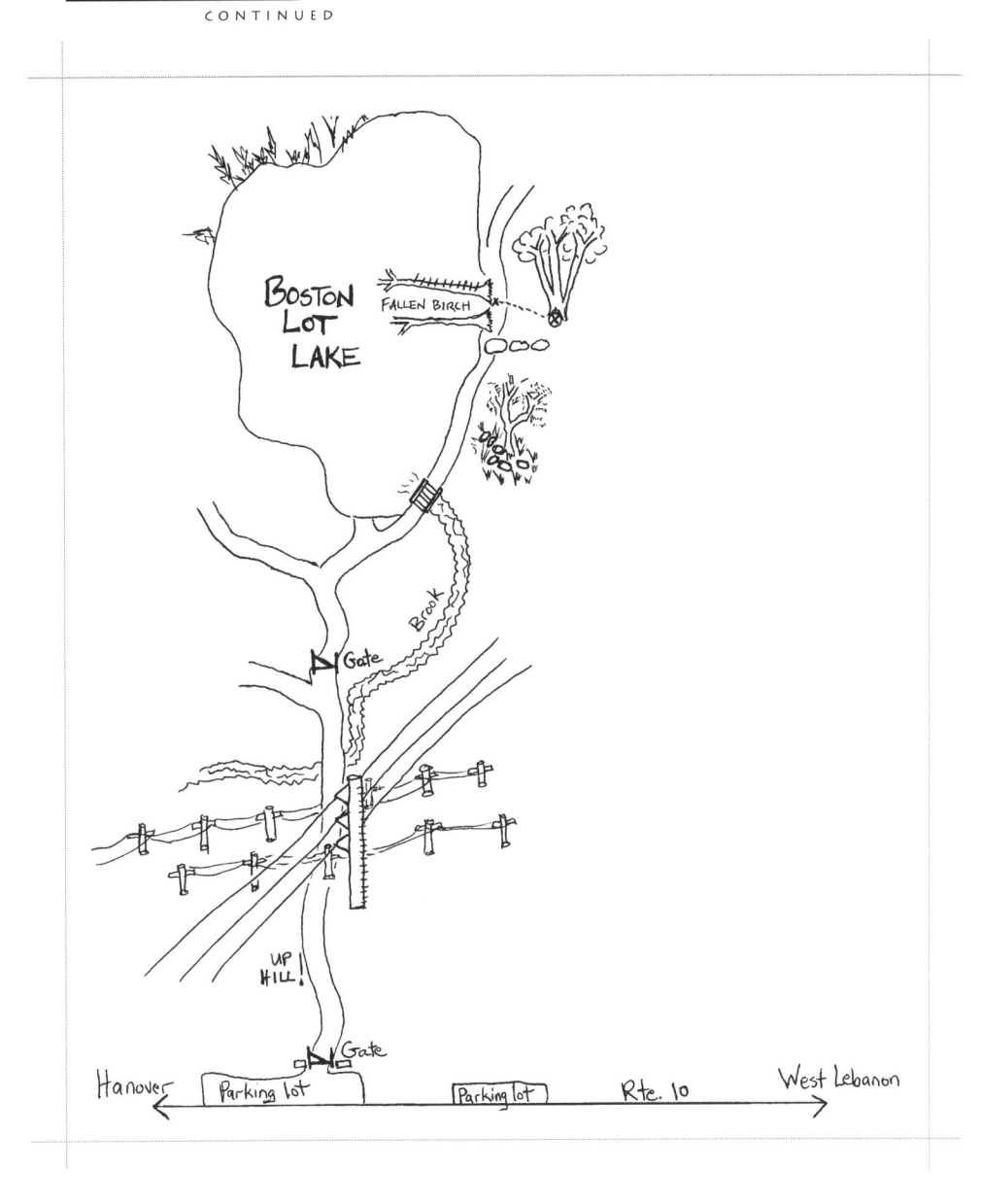

BOSTON LOT LAKE
FALLEN BIRCH
Gate
Brook
UP HILL!
Gate
Hanover ← Parking lot   Parking lot   Rte. 10 → West Lebanon

BOSTON LOT QUEST 151

69
DANA HOUSE QUEST

WEST LEBANON NH

To get there:
Take Route 10 south out of Hanover for about 5 miles. Bear left through the junction of 12A and take the next right onto Elm Street. Dana House will be immediately on your left.

Go to the banks of Dana House
 where the Blak Top sign is at.
Then go straight past the tree
 with a ring of rocks.
Stop at the sign with a date.
From there visit a spot
that you can see at the front of the house.
It's a rectangle and could let you inside.
(You can peek,
but there's not much to see.)
Go twelve paces west and take a rest.
Look around for a big letter T.
(If you walked up the stem
A door you would find.)
So walk to that T and slap your knee.
When you get to the base of the T,
Turn your back to that T.
Walk twenty-three paces and freeze.
Turn to the south and try to decide
The hiding place where the treasure resides.

*'If you walked up the stem
 a door you would find'*

WEST LEBANON NH
CONTINUED

DANA HOUSE QUEST 153

THE FALL CIDER QUEST

**WHEREVER YOU WISH
VT/NH**

To get there:
Wander around the place you live. Travel on foot—or by car. We're sure you'll find some apple trees, and won't have to look that far!

Perhaps it will be a wild tree . . .
   Or maybe it is your neighbors'.
   If the latter seems to be the case
   Knock and offer them this favor:
   If some apples they'll let you pick
   A gallon of cider in return is the trick!

Then pick and pick and pick and pick
   With friends and family.
   Fill up laundry baskets, bags
   And linger beneath the tree.
   The "drops" on the ground
   Well, pick them up too . . .
   Worms and all—
   They're good for you.

When you're tired
   And your trunk is full
   Let your mind and fingers do the walking
   Dial some numbers—
   Don't give up—
   Until to a cider-miller you are talking.

There used to be a cider mill
   Perhaps every three or four miles;
   And when you find one that can help
   Your troops will all have smiles.

Before you go
   Make sure you have
   Lots of clean empty containers:
   Milk jugs, ball jars,
   All will work,
   You'll just need funnel and strainer.

WHEREVER YOU WISH
VT/NH
CONTINUED

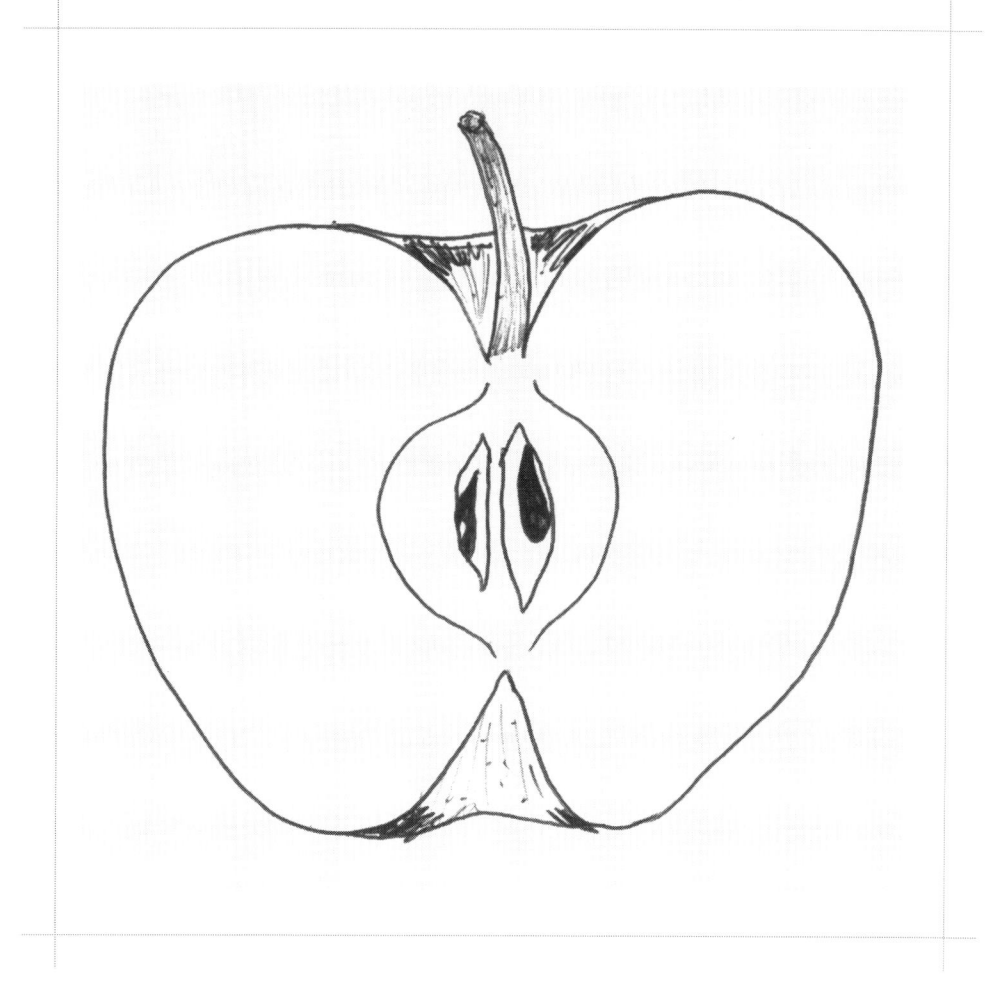

Turn the crank,
    Watch the apples crush!
And amber liquid flow.
    Feel the earth
    Smell its rich full scent
    And watch all the faces glow.

Now that you have made some cider
    Please raise a glass up high . . .
    And give some thanks to this special place
    And the treasures that fall from the sky!

Remember to bring a jug to your neighbor!

THE FALL CIDER QUEST

71 BY THE NUMBERS QUEST

WHITE RIVER JUNCTION VT

To get there:

Take Exit 11 off of I-91 and travel north on Route 5 down the hill toward the village of White River Junction. Continue straight through the second set of lights. Route 5 turns left, but you should continue straight on North Main Street to the stop sign. Continue for one block, go left across the railroad tracks and turn right into the parking lot for the Court House and the Train Station. The Quest begins at the Vermont Welcome Center.

Walk straight out the door
   To where the tracks end
   Then follow to the nose
   Of 494, friend.

(494)

Turning around, way up in the sky
   The words Gates Block do fly.
   Beneath them spy a Golden Train—
   Heading there, you're on your way again.

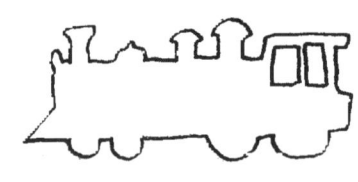

Along your route find five stone blocks
   Then search the park for a square-ish rock
   Placed here in honor of Frederick Briggs
   Who did much for his town—small and big!

Next, as Gates Block on your left does pass
   I ask of you an important task:
   This building has a special number—
   Record it in the space right under.

___ ___ ___ ___

Now follow "The Dot" to Theriault block
   For it has a special number, too.
   Don't give up, look up
   And it will come in view.

___ ___

WHITE RIVER JUNCTION VT
CONTINUED

Look west—you'll see a steeple.
    Stretching up even higher
    Than New England Telephone's wire!
    Taking care—please go to the steeple, good people.

Along your way collect the date for Freeman ___ ___ ___ ___
    And the Gates Library: ___ ___ ___ ___
    Take it slow, there is no need to hurry!

A building on the right—it's made from bricks all red.
    A close look will reveal that here they once baked bread!
The next street is named so well
    And turning left here you can tell
    The Year of the Garden: ___ ___ ___ ___ and
    The Year of the Corner Stone: ___ ___ ___ ___

At the green sign—with a recurring name—
    Make a left turn on your way back to the train.
    A white building you will see
    And on it the number for the Phone Company: ___ ___ ___ ___

Diagonally across is Mr. Miller's
    Inside you'll find lots of thrillers!
    Selling Cadillac's since 1903,
    Even the first up Mt. Washington—Yippee!

Across from here is Artist's Row
    And real cool things, so take it slow.
    Passing eight that look like me:

At the corner you shall see:

There, collect the first number of the trough ___ ___ ___ ___
    Then here's some math to finish you off!

Add up the last digits of the numbers you've collected
    Then diagonally cross the street to the post office headed.

Afront a frame, speckled rock beneath you will turn gray,
    Stop here, and hear the last words I shall say:

"Counting your steps is now what you should do.
    The number? If the sum of your addition is true
    Leads to a door—behind which lies a counter—
    And if you ask there, the treasure you'll encounter."

WHITE RIVER JUNCTION VT

THE JUNCTION QUEST

72

To get there:

Take Exit 11 off I-91 and travel north on Route 5 down the hill toward the village of White River Junction. Continue straight through the second set of lights. Route 5 turns left, but you should continue straight on North Main Street to the stop sign. Continue for one block and turn into the parking lot for the Court House and the Train Station.

Life in White River has changed its ways,
   since the railroad had its glory days.
   With a short walk around the town,
   there's lots of history to be found.

My wheels are not in motion
   though I'm still a sight to see
   Find 494 near the center of town
   and start your Quest with me.

Go left past two old buildings
   the first a seller of restaurant wares
   The second even older building
   a prior purveyor of automotive fare.

Then turn north across Ralph Lehman bridge
   that spans our Class "B" water
   Cleaner today and flowing free
   for fisherman, swimmers, and otters.

Follow the river past a war monument
   and on to a performance site
   Then continue on to a scenic point
   where in 1704 the Iroquois did alite.

Enjoy the confluence, take in the view,
   Then head west from here
   Cross grass onto pavement
   to a garden recently planted; 1991 was the year.

Travel south along a road,
   no need to swim,
   count the ornate light posts
   on your left.

Remember the number,
   you'll need it soon,
   to find the treasure
   at the end of this Quest.

At the last post
   look right to a place

'flowing free for fishermen, swimmers and otters'

WHITE RIVER JUNCTION VT
CONTINUED

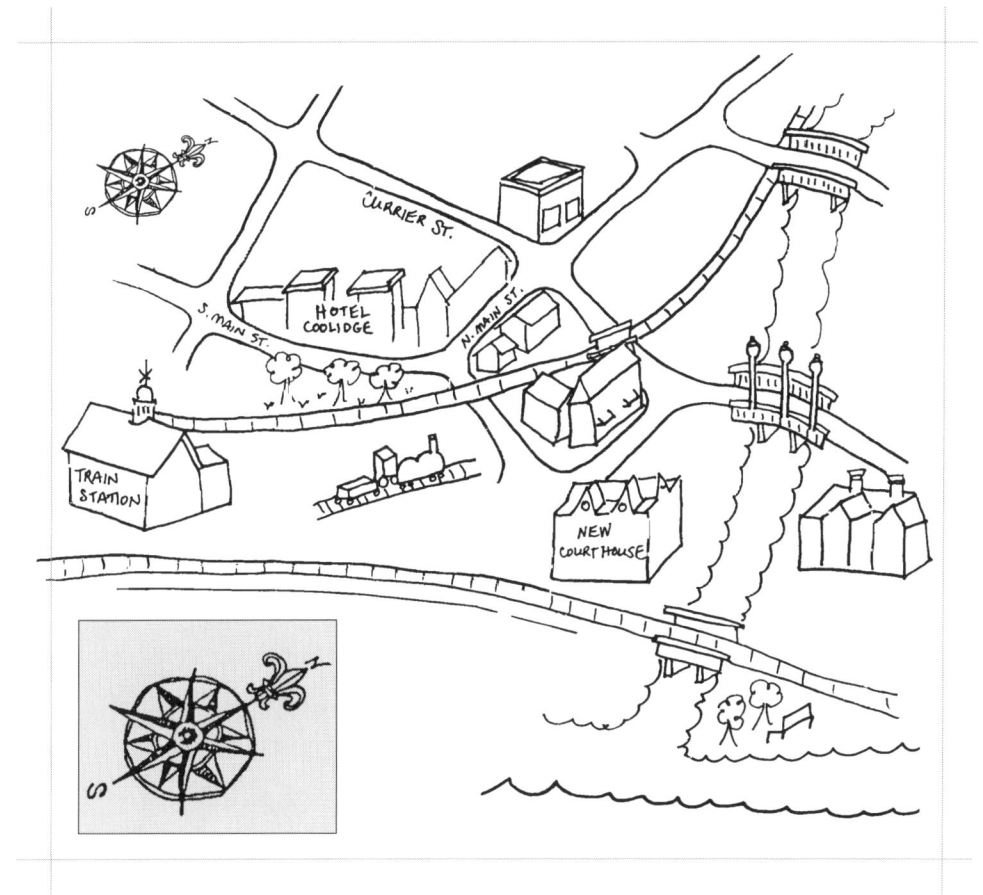

    where red trucks
    once were housed.

A few paces further
    and then on your left
    pass a bakery
    long shut down.

Slip under a trestle walking straight 'til you see
    that there may be some telephones here
    This red brick facade and white brick facade
    have been the home of Ma Bell for years

Heading east from the corner, travel along artist's row,
    our Quest drawing soon to a close
    At the end of the block turn left away from the clock,
    some mathematics to you we pose:

Remember the light posts you counted before,
    subtract 6 from the number you got.
    The answer this leaves equals the doors you must pass
    before reaching our final Quest spot.

Inside this place there's a desk lit by lamps
    and someone seated behind
    This is the person to ask for the box
    that you've worked so hard to find!

THE JUNCTION QUEST

73
LYMAN POINT QUEST

WHITE RIVER JUNCTION VT

To get there:

Take Exit 11 off I-91 and travel north on Route 5 down the hill toward the village of White River Junction. Continue straight through the second set of lights. Route 5 turns left, and you should turn left, cross the bridge and then turn right onto Route 4. The Quest begins at the Municipal Building, on the southeast corner of Maple and Bridge, one block east of the intersection of Routes 4 and 5.

White River's own past tells of people and wars
   And the hills that roll down to alluvial shores
   One hidden gem at the heart of this tale
   Is a point we call Lyman, the site of our grail.

Our Questing begins on a building's front lawn,
   A structure not built from timber once wawn,
   Instead built in 1884 of mortar and brick,
   To be used as a schoolhouse, rooms warm and walls thick.

Soon too small for students, it was doubled in size.
   You can see its dittoed structure if you look with sharp eyes.
   Teaching no longer occurs within these sturdy walls
   Where the town's leaders now work to answer residents' calls.

In front of this building a memorial does stand,
   As a tribute to those who've fought in distant land
   Hartford citizens who responded to their obligation
   And who quite often died defending our nation.

These citizens who fought we give a certain name
   The word's a part of this inscription extolling their fame.
   Take the fifth and the seventh letters of this descriptive word (1, 2)
   And save them for later—you'll need them for sure.

Onward proceed to a horticulturist's delight
   If you are closer to the road, then your instinct is right.
   This small sanctuary honors a grower of plants
   And its presence is enough to make the heart dance!

A poem is tucked amidst these growing things,
   One three-letter word describes a most divine being.
   The third letter of this word is the one that you want (3)
   Before you head off to continue your jaunt.

But there's one more plaque with a clue to lend.
   It is on something made by several groups willing to spend,
   This wooden object begins with a letter you will need to save (4)
   If our final treasure you truly do crave.

A 180-degree turn is quickly in order
   To head across hard ground that grasses do border

WHITE RIVER JUNCTION VT
CONTINUED

Past a large wooden structure for auditory fare
Where musicians perform with their own unique flair.

Up ahead is a sign of White River's industrial past
An above-ground passage for locomotives quite vast.
And at times, like 1964, pedestrians crossed here too
When an ice jam destroyed other bridges—
Leaving nothing else to do.

Under this bridge you must now proceed
And notice the first tree on your left if you please.
It's a non-native ornamental and a bearer of fruit
A kind that is red and that ice cream does suit.

Take the first letter of this fruit's name
And save it once again—that's the gist of this game. (5)
Onward now past a local hardwood tree
And stop at the next, there's much more to see.

This tree produces a treat in the very early spring
That goes well with pancakes and many other things.
Take the last letter of the word that describes this tree (6)
And tuck it away for later—you'll need to use it craftily.

Continue out to the point so you do not miss the view
Of the joining of two rivers and your next important clue.
The river flowing north to south divides New Hampshire and Vermont,
The second letter of its name is the letter that you want. (7)

Hundreds of years back, before Europeans came this way
Native people used to hunt and fish and upon these riverbanks play.
Life revolved around the seasons and the springtime brought them here
When salmon, smelt, and bass swam in waters very clear.

From this point, head to your right along the park's grassy edge
To a cement block tucked against some trees—a big rectangular wedge.
Printed on a manhole cover are two letters for you to see
It's the first one that you want, write it down and you're home free. (8)

Just a few steps further on is a prominent sign board
With a story that describes some of Lyman Point's great lore.
Three native tribes are mentioned—save the first letter of the first, (9)
You'll need the last letter of the second too, to quench your Questing thirst. (10)

Time has come to put it all together, to solve this mystery
Of the location of the treasure box—where, oh where can it be?
Use the blanks provided here to put each letter in its space
Then follow that most ultimate clue to our treasure's hiding place!

___ ___ ___ ___ ___ ___   ___ ___ ___ ___
 4   6   8   9   2   3   1   7   5   10

LYMAN POINT QUEST   161

74. CONSTITUTION HOUSE QUEST

WINDSOR VT

To get there:
From either Exit 8 or 9 off I-91, take Route 5 to Windsor. Turn west onto State Street at the traffic light and within a few hundred feet, park either in the lot for the Episcopal Church on the left at the corner of State Street and Dunham Avenue, or park on State Street.

Start at the place with two columns, four steps,
   and then read—yes, you could.
     Through the door, the plaque is for blood;
     he said "Please donate, if you would."

Walk carefully across State Street to a place where people meet
   Where musicians play music that is oh-so-sweet.

Head north out of this green through a break in the fence.
   A quaint cottage nicknamed "the gingerbread house"
   you will find shortly hence.

Look to your right and you will see
   a building that was once Town Hall.
   today it's used by veterans and soldiers who stood tall.

Go north on Court Street.
   There's a white picket fence on the right—don't kick it.
   Continue forward and you'll see a bit of the year 1786.

Walk about 44 paces—you might think it's a dead-end
   But stay awake—there's even more around the bend.

You will notice a change in the road—be careful not to stumble.
   If you want to finish, please stay humble.

Walk down, down, down, and what do you see?
   Water! As clear and blue as can be.

A boat house once stood
   where feathered animals float near the sand.
   In 1998, a gazebo was built at the point of the land.

Look up high at a peak that touches the sky
   as far as the eye can see.
   What do you think this mountain could be?
   It's a place where people love to ski.

Keep walking, then take a sharp right.
   Upon the ground wood chips lay light.
   Barb and Dave Rhoad fixed the little bridge up right.

WINDSOR VT
CONTINUED

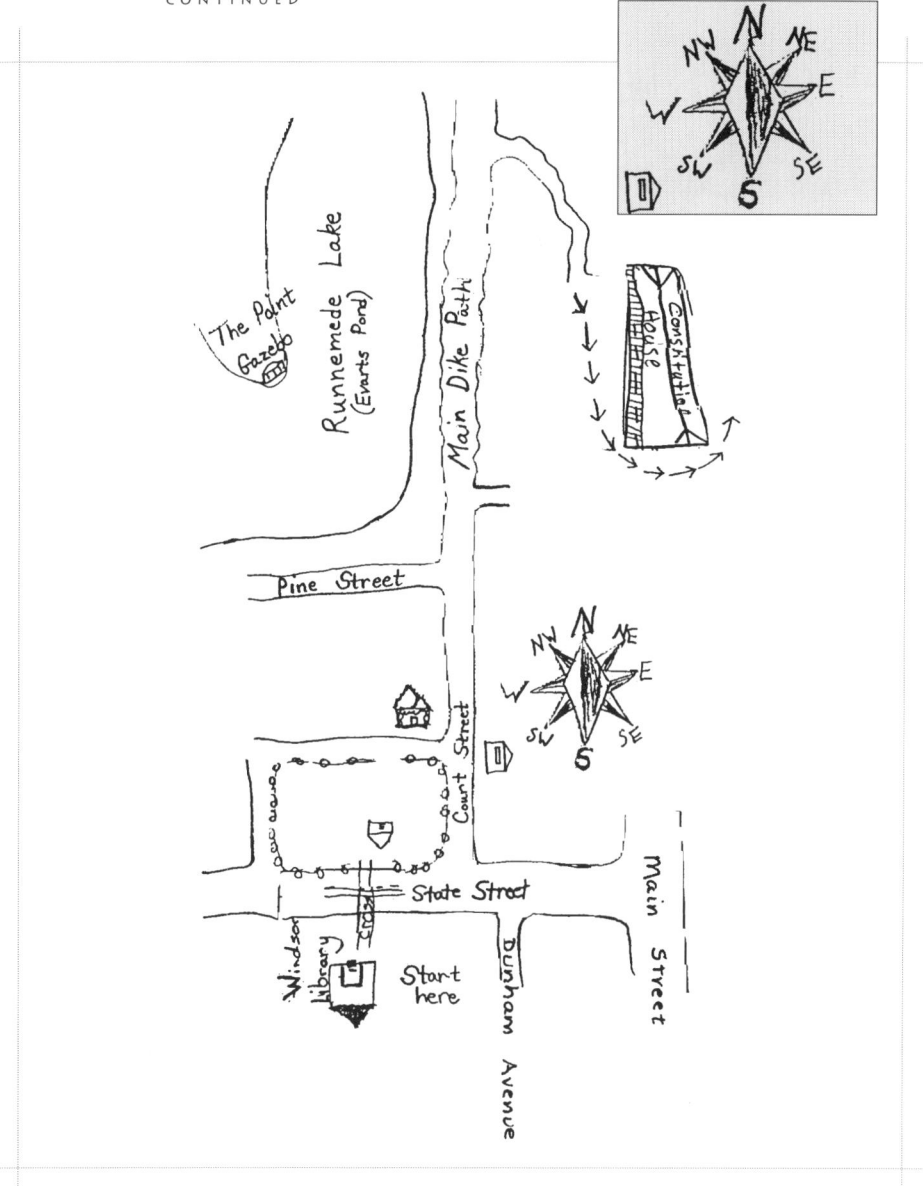

Don't stop now! Keep walking on the path.
  Where there's dirty water, so you can't take a bath.

At the end of the wood chip path, you'll know that you're there.
  You'll be facing the back of an historic house the color of a bear.

Go out in the front, you're still on the hunt.
  Face north and go forth along the wooden porch.

Step down low, where no light shows.
  the Quest box will be below, near where the vines grow.

Open the box, then sign and stamp our book.
  Read some information about the way things used to look.

Take some time to visit the Constitution House after relaxing near a tree.
  Be sure to read the green sign to learn about Windsor's history!

CONSTITUTION HOUSE QUEST 163

HISTORIC WINDSOR QUEST

WINDSOR VT

To get there:
From either Exit 8 or 9 off I-91, take Route 5 to Windsor. Turn west onto State Street at the traffic light and within a few hundred feet, park either in the lot for the Episcopal Church on the left at the corner of State Street and Dunham Avenue, or park on State Street.

Old Benjamin Blood was clearly not poor,
for the library he gifted in 1904.
From the steps of this library you will start your Quest,
when you reach the street do not turn west.

Follow the stones on the hill that make up a wall.
They're next to the church named after St. Paul.
It was built on this site in 1822,
on Judge Hubbard's land we now sit in a pew.

Don't stop at the church, go on down the hill.
Go straight to the lights where cars must stand still.
Without crossing a street you head to the south,
Looking for steps, 55 no doubt.

At the Masonic Hall where men are the rule,
Once stood a building where girls went to school.
Don't take these stairs say the signs on the lawn,
Go south to the graveyard where Captain Smith has gone.

Captain Smith was first to settle here for free.
He brought his family in 1763.
Now continue along before you forget
To see the church stairs without any steps.

Asher Benjamin designed in 1798
The Old South Church with a roof that was slate.
Precision Museum is next on your Quest
Go straight down the street, don't turn right or left.

The Precision Museum is big and it's tall
from textiles to rifles, they have made them all.
Now around the block to the right, you'll continue your Quest
When you see St. Francis Church, don't turn to the west.

Add all the numbers on the doors on the right.
When they total 9-squared (9 x 9) you'll be at the light.
Go on down the hill, 'neath the tracks you must stay
to a bridge that is covered and also two-way.

WINDSOR VT
CONTINUED

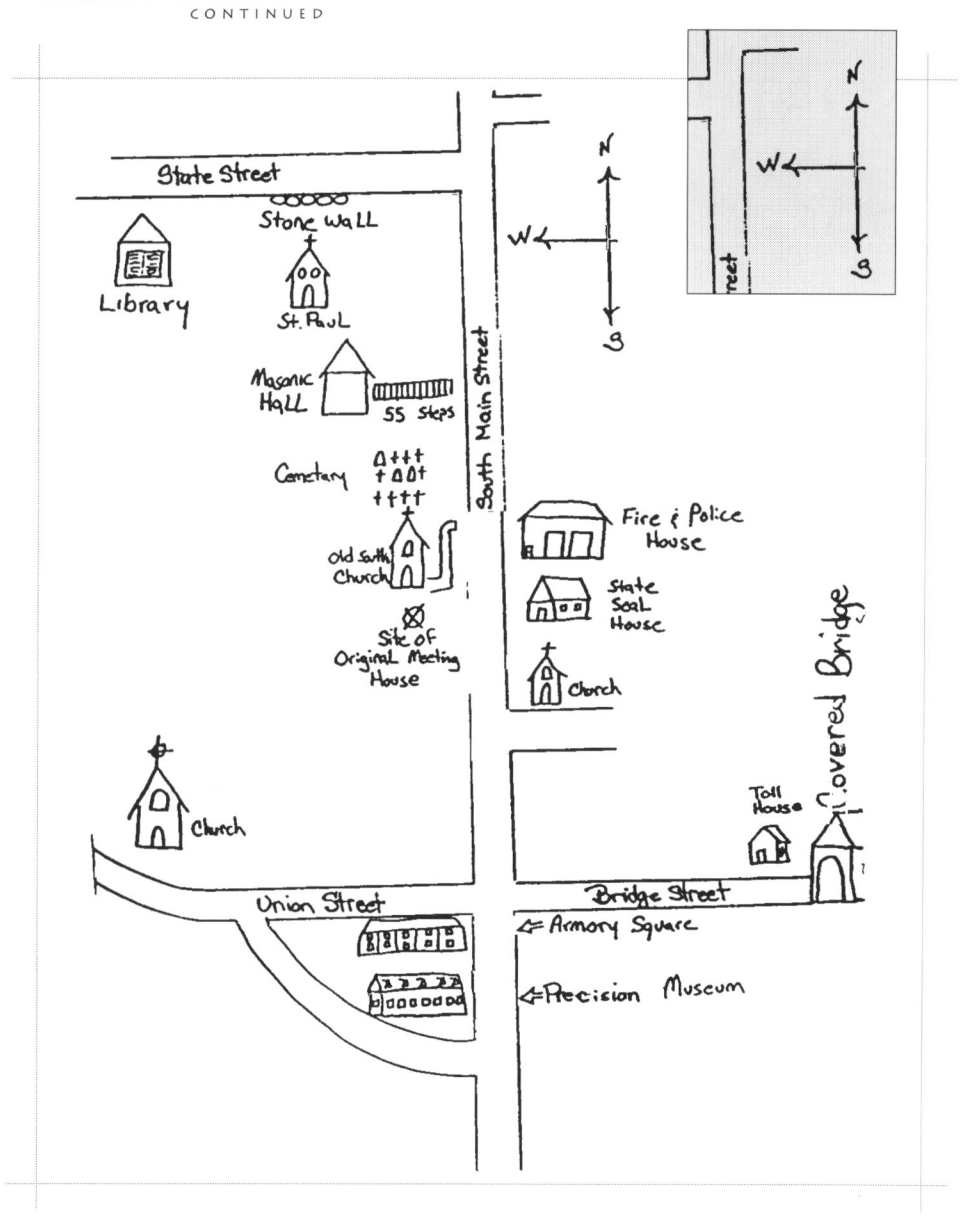

'... on Judge Hubbard's land we now sit in a PEW'

To the left of the bridge where you once paid a fine
There sits the toll house all made of pine.
Now back up the hill with the bridge out of sight
When you get to the Main Street you have to turn right.

Head up on the street and watch as you go
For a church named after Rachael S. Harlowe.
Vermont's State Seal was first pressed by Mr. Dean
In the fourth house on the right. It just has to be seen.

Now at the fire house you'll end your Quest.
In the left door you go, and way back to the desk.
We hope you had fun on this Quest today.
Sign in at the box, and you are on your way.

HISTORIC WINDSOR QUEST 165

NORTH MAIN STREET QUEST 76

WINDSOR VT

To get there:
From either Exit 8 or 9 off I-91, take Route 5 to Windsor. Turn west onto State Street at the traffic light and within a few hundred feet, park either in the lot for the Episcopal Church on the left at the corner of State Street and Dunham Avenue, or park on State Street.

Up on the bandstand, look around,
   Old Town Hall and Library can be found,
   Walk down the hill, find the site
   Of the Old Court House, then left at the light.

Along the way, some shops you'll see,
   All played a part in Windsor's history.
   One hundred years plus—go back in time,
   And you'll understand the rest of our rhyme.

Coming from Boston or Montreal,
   This "house" was the place to have a ball.
   You could get a meal, you could get a room,
   Presidents and guests could arrive soon!

Next is a home of retirees,
   Once the home of railroad executives.
   Dinner for 400 was the norm.
   Guests caught the train for the return trip home.

Walk along and you will find
   The Mansions of Windsor—count them—five,
   Granite fence posts will lead the way
   As you look and dream of yesterday.

(It's not a mansion, but it's pretty as can be,
   The yellow brick road is a favorite to me.)

Move along and you will see
   The birthplace of Vermont history
   Once was just a tavern in 1777
   A signed constitution sealed its place in heaven.

Back up and cross at the crosswalk,
   Look to the right
   House of brick, porch of white.

Keep on walking, find the first steeple,
   Goes to the church that has no people
   In 1846 it was built as a church
   Now you can go in and buy a shirt!

In front of the church, look in the sky,
   A legal eagle you will spy.

WINDSOR VT
CONTINUED

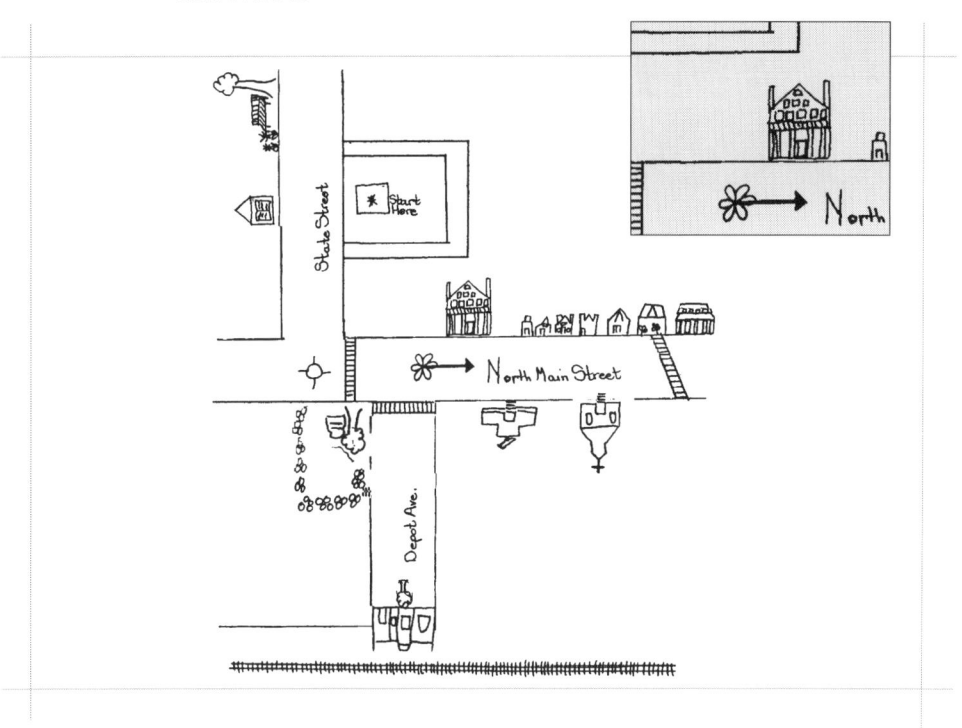

Today this building sends out mail.
yesterday it was Federal Court and jail.

Look around and you will see
    More of Windsor's history.
    Step on a crack and break your back
    Follow the signs to the railroad tracks.

On the corner, take a break in the park.
    Read the message on the history rock.
    On to the Depot and hear the sounds
    1849 brought guests from all around.

Back up to the corner, don't turn right,
    Cross the street—at the light.
    Walk to the bandstand, take a look,
    Cross over to the house of books.

Continue up the road and you will see
    What was once the oldest U.S. prison in history.
    In 1975, it ceased to be.
    Now it is a home for the elderly.
    (Go PAST the Davis House.)

In this "village" you will find
    Benches and flowers to boggle the mind.
    A little wooden box, attached there in a tree
    Tells the rest of our town's history.

Read the stories, stamp your book,
    Walk around and take another look.
    Hope you enjoyed 4-Parker's Quest.
    There are more! Do the rest!

NORTH MAIN STREET QUEST

77
PARADISE PARK QUEST

WINDSOR VT

To get there:

From either Exit 8 or 9 off I-91, take Route 5 to Windsor. Turn west onto State Street at the traffic light and (following signs to the Mt. Ascutney Hospital) travel about .7 miles to County Road. Turn right onto County Road and continue about 1/3 mile to the parking lot for Paradise Park on the right, just before the entrance to the hospital on the left.

Start at Paradise Park entrance off County
  Road at parking lot near green building.
  Proceed on Park Road beyond yellow gate.
  When you come to the *fork,* go to the right.
  Look up to see Shaggy Mane Road sign.

Continue on going over a road bridge—the Kimball Brook flows
    under you.
  Go straight. Soon you will come to a bench on your left.
  Take a rest and look down the bank to see a beautiful waterfall.

Now that your rest is over, continue on the road down an incline to a
    clearing.
  In the clearing, a lean-to will be on your right with a picnic table.
  You can sit and have your lunch and watch and listen
  To the many birds and the little creatures who make Paradise Park
    their home.
  If you brought a ball, this is a great place for a kick-ball game.

'If you brought a ball, this would be a great place for a kick-ball game.'

WINDSOR VT
CONTINUED

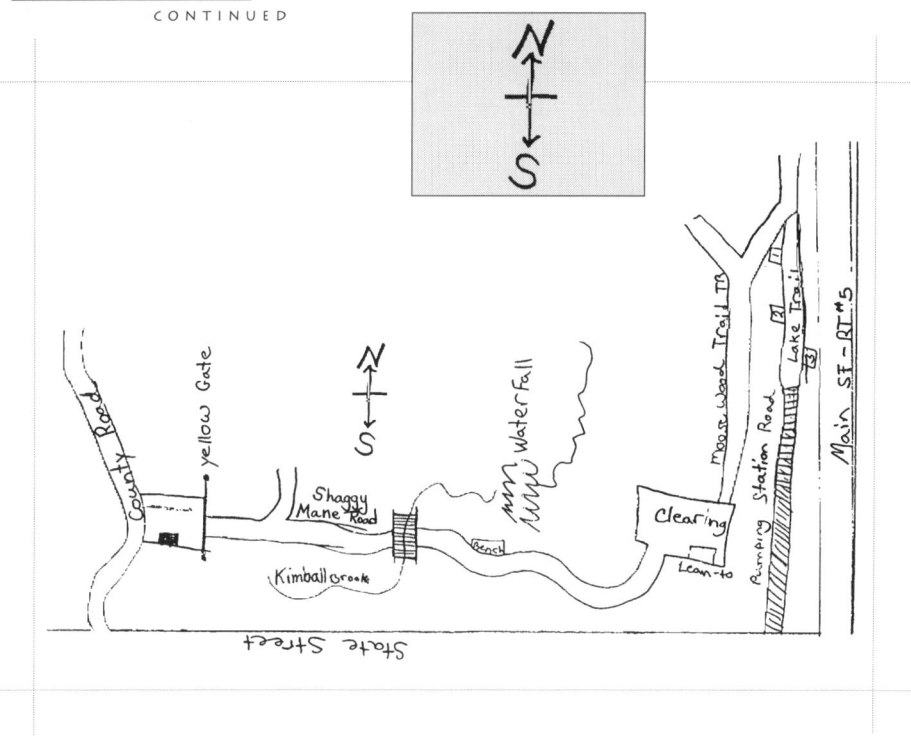

Look up and you might see an osprey.
Look down and your quest you will find.

When you are ready to continue, go to the northeast corner
   of the clearing.
   Go through two gate posts and follow Moosewood Trail.
   Look for Runnemede on your right and in the distance
   You will see the hills of Cornish, New Hampshire.

Soon you will come to another fork and again
   you will take a right down to the Lake Trail—another right!
   On this trail you will see signs of busy beavers from the past.
   Three benches you will pass—make sure you rest on the third.
   Look up and you might see an osprey.
   Look down and your Quest you will find.

Hope you had fun and will have time to explore the rest of the park!

PARADISE PARK QUEST

WOODSTOCK CWM QUEST

78

WOODSTOCK VT

To get there:

Your Quest begins at the Woodstock green. Take Exit 1 from I-89 and follow Route 4 west for about 10 miles to the village of Woodstock and the town green.

Begin in the middle of the village green,
    Off to the left is a stone church to be seen.
    To the right are plenty of places to shop.
    Where you are now it's important to stop!

See the yellow with the black
    Straight ahead and don't look back.

Cars and people can cross together,
    You can do that in all kinds of weather.

The ol' Vermont sugar maker says,
    "Wind from the east, sap runs the least.
    Wind from the west, sap runs the best."
    It's a bad sap day so turn that way.

Beware! Now you pass the living dead,
    Watch out for there's a rolling head.
    Skeletons, vampires, and scary ghosts—
    Look out, for soon you could be toast!

Along the water, go quite a ways
    Stay on the sidewalk that goes both ways.

Look hard to the left in the woods you will see
    Two Adirondack gate houses from the nineteenth century.
    One lower, one higher behind the stone wall,
    They once were the entrances to the mansion so tall.

Honor the contributor where the water flows.
    Hold onto the railing or you'll get wet toes.

Up ahead and on the right
    The clock and bell are quite a sight.
    Please don't worry, please don't cry
    It's where you go to sing and die.

VALLEY QUEST · 2001

WOODSTOCK VT
CONTINUED

Hold onto the railing or you'll get wet toes.   it is not forbidden.

'An eagle flies between two lamps'

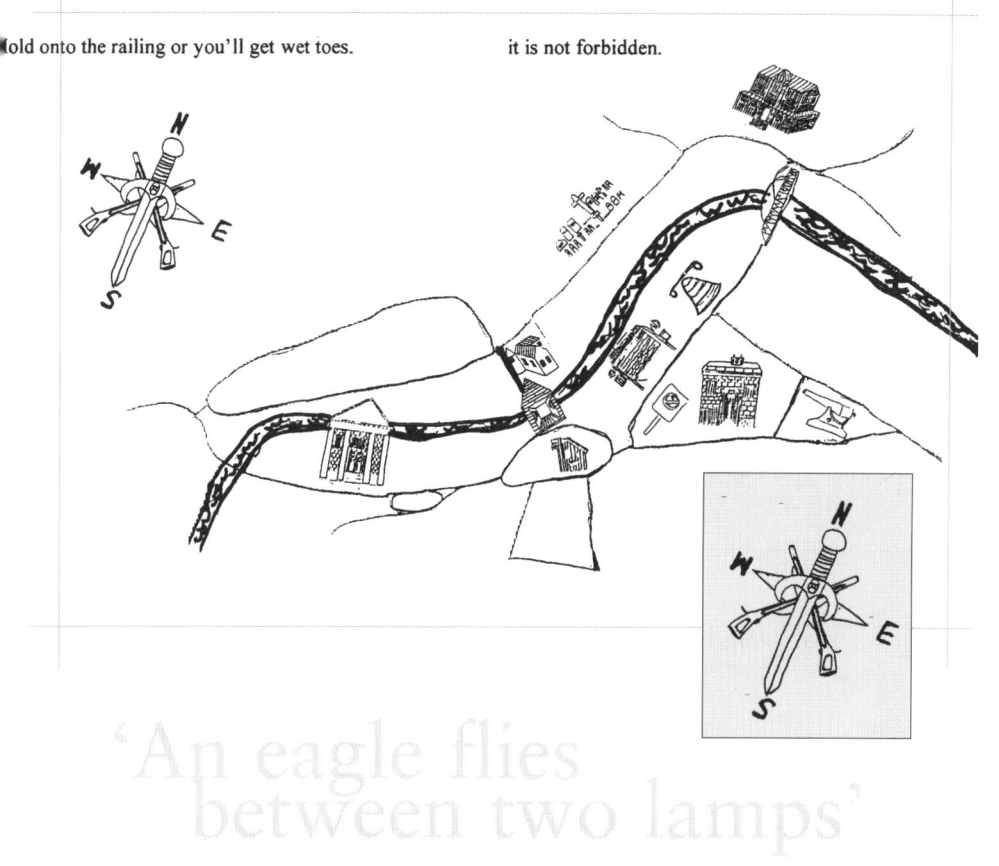

Past flying cows, the "in" and "out" is down the street,
   When buying goods it's where people meet.
   You're outside a store that's been here for awhile
   You are sure to be greeted there with a smile.

On the right is black and white
   The fear of fire has hurt the crier.

"No left turn" is a deceit,
   Ignore the sign and cross the street.

An eagle flies between two lamps
   After awhile he gets lots of cramps.
   Beneath him is the town's zip code—
   See him if you are in the mode.

Look for "Sylvia" right after the dam
   Just keep on going towards the thing that goes BAM.

Hold your horses for Justin Morgan,
   You're getting near, there is no need for fear.

Two maples and an ash
   Behind the site are hidden.
   Look for the three stars
   It is not forbidden.

WOODSTOCK CWM QUEST

WOODSTOCK VT

THE GEORGE, FREDERICK, AND LAURANCE QUEST

To get there:
This Quest begins at the village green in Woodstock.

Please study our map and go to #1.
Then go to each number until you are done.
At each stop collect one or two letters as well,
Fill in the blanks and then see what they spell.

1. Our Quest starts on the south side of the green
   Where a historical marker sign can be seen.
   Woodstock was the site of the very first one
   Find this word on the sign and get set for fun!
   First letter of this word: __ __ __   __ __ __
                                 1

2. Now ladies and gentlemen, girls and boys,
   Go inside this fine building without any noise
   Beside the fireplace on the wall there's a rug
   Find your letter then give your friends a big hug.
   First letter of the second word on the rug: __ __ __
                                                    2

3. Down Bond, last on left, Billing's, #4,
   Look for the tiny sign beside the door.
   Second letter of first word on the sign: __ __ __ __
                                                        3

4. Frederick Gillingham ran this store,
   On the big sign find out who helped him with this chore.
   Second letter of the last word on the sign: __ __ __ __
                                                       4

5. The Rockefellers were married here many years ago
   To the main sign by the driveway you should go.
   First letter after the word "Vermont": __ __ __ __ __ __ __ __
                                              5a

   Go to the left of the building to the Paul Revere Bell,
   Look at the sign on the bell stand and it will tell.
   Second letter of the second word on the sign: __ __ __ __ __ __
                                                       5b

6. Your next clues are inside this visitor center,
   Follow the signs and then you should enter.
   Go to the sign that's straight ahead with great speed

VALLEY QUEST · 2001

WOODSTOCK VT
CONTINUED

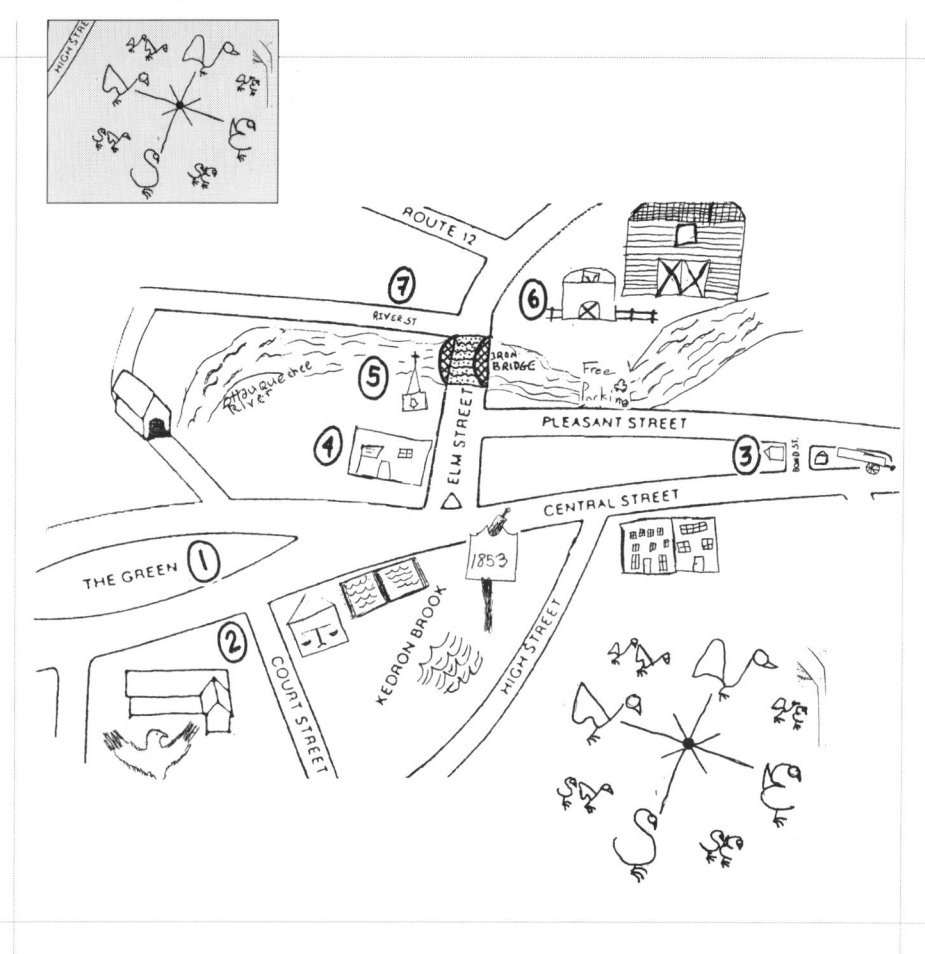

There you will find some letters you need.
First letter on the sign: __ __ __ __ __ __ __ __
6a

Stick with this sign and read it through
You'll learn a lot and have fun, too.
*Fifth letter of the fifth word of the
   last paragraph:* __ __ __ __ __ __ __ __ __ __
6b

Turn to the wall that's toward your right hand
You'll see faces of people that lived on this land.
*Seventh letter of the first word on this sign that starts
   with G:* __ __ __ __ __ __ __ __ __
6c

7   If you want your treasure to meet
    Go back down Elm, then right on River Street.
    Walk along a short way with an eye up to the right
    Until a small open-air hut comes into sight.
    Now look for the thing that the letters do spell
    Stay near the road and your Quest will end well.

__ __ __ __ __ __ __ __ __
6a 2 6b 5a 6c 4 3 1 5b

THE GEORGE, FREDERICK, AND LAURANCE QUEST   173

GPM QUEST

To get there:
Take Exit 1 from I-89 and follow Route 4 west for about 10 miles to the village of Woodstock and the town green. The Quest starts at the Woodstock green.

From the village green . . .

East will be the right direction,
   If you need an answer to a question.

You know you're going the right way,
   If to the south there's a place where books stay.

Then move on to the crosswalks going many ways,
   Take the one to the north and on the correct path you shall stay.

Go the same direction as you did in the start
   And you will see three galleries of art.

Go left around the curve,
   Here the Town Crier you will observe.

Keep your eyes up for a fine clover design,
   Beyond that there is a flying bovine.

Starting from here, look down the third drive,
   What used to have a wagon now is alone.
   Notice the star on the porch of that home.

Keep going, look for a clock, on the porch there's a bell
   Made by a patriot that sure knew how to yell!

A sign for "Free Parking" will be your guide,
   If you cross carefully, you'll save your hide.

Follow the fence to the E
   And cross over a place where fish feast.

Go past seven more homes,
   Follow the crosswalk and westward you'll roam.

Students of history will like what they see,
   Watch out!, that cannon could sting like a bee!

Keep on going, have no fear,
   Your treasure is very near.

WOODSTOCK VT
CONTINUED

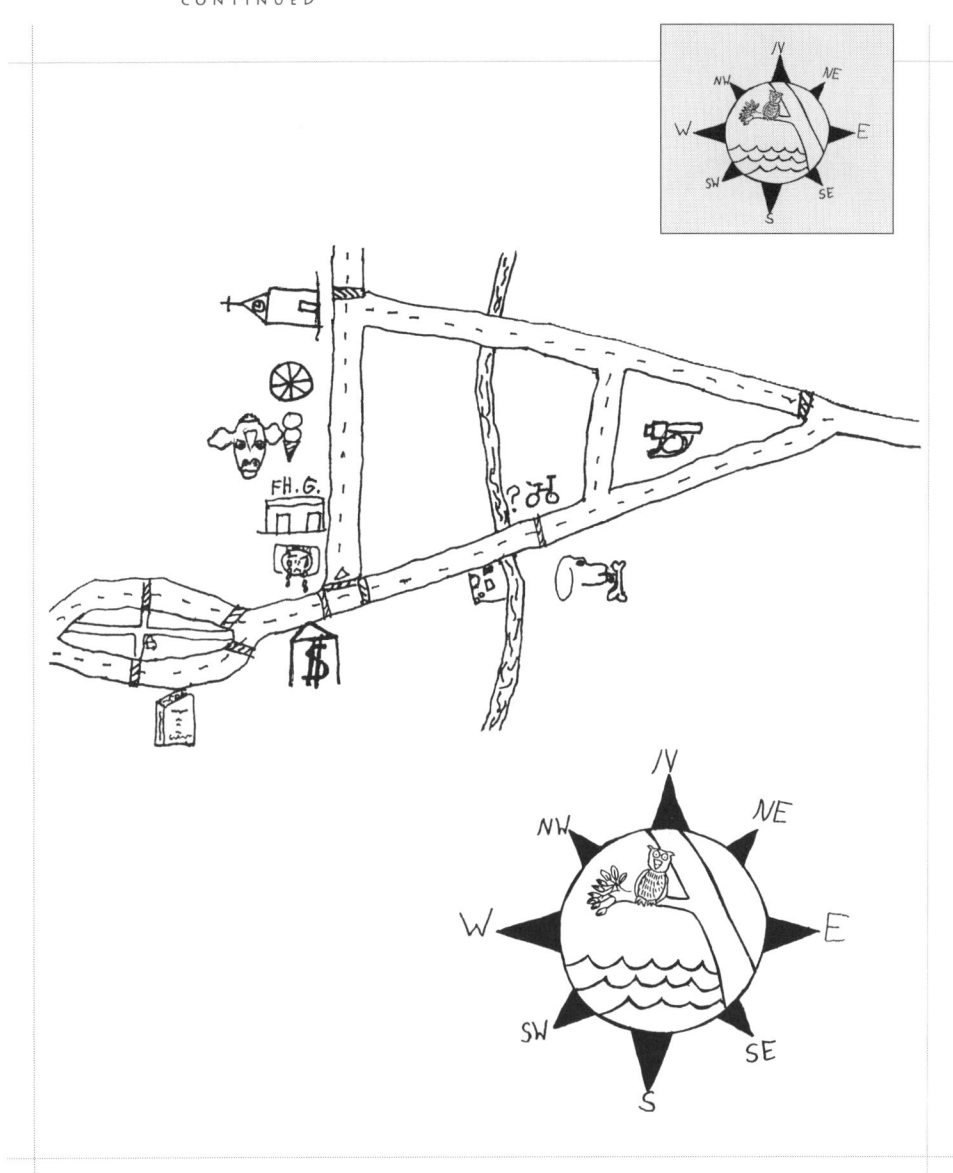

'You made it past the
f l y i n g   b o v i n e s '

"Who is Sylvia?" I'd like to know,
   With her at your back, across the street you will go.

You made it past the flying bovines,
   Now watch out for the flying canine.

This is a place where the river flows,
   Stay a while to cool your toes.

Down thirteen steps, there's a tree with no roots,
   Look under the dates and you'll find our loot!

GPM QUEST 175

MOUNT TOM QUEST

WOODSTOCK VT

To get there:
From the northwest side of the Woodstock green, cross the covered bridge and follow Mountain Avenue around to the park on the right. Take any of the paved paths to the trail going up Mount Tom.

When you reach the final rise,
   Turn around and open your eyes.

Take a rest and pull up your sock,
   The town below is our Woodstock.

If you do not wish to fail,
   Head towards Precipice Trail.

Don't head down this trail but stay up top,
   With each step you are closer to the final stop.

Continue along the path but not too far,
   Look up to see our Cross and Star.

Keep on walking, look to your right and left for the rock wall.
   Mt. Tom is basically flat up here so you will not fall.

The path will soon come to a T,
   Please stay to the left and have a see.

You will now be looking out to the west,
   Killington is the mountain whose height is the best.

Look down and see the Ottauquechee River, which is cool,
   Along Route 4 you can see the Woodstock High School.

As you walk, notice on your left is a post,
   With faces that may remind you of a ghost.

As you walk further, the rock wall will be on your right,
   And the town of Woodstock should come into your sight.

WOODSTOCK VT
CONTINUED

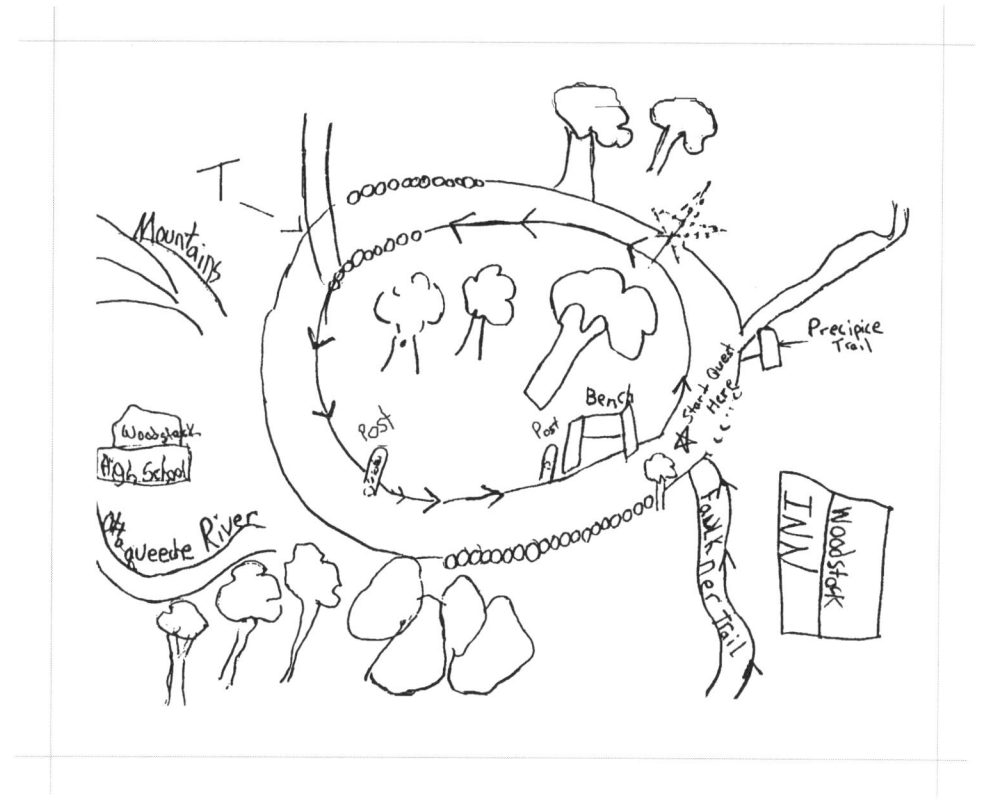

The big white building is the Woodstock Inn,
   The Quest is near complete and you shall win.

The second ghost post will be

behind you . . .

The second ghost post will be behind you,
   Find the Inn and point to it, too.

Follow that line to the edge of the wall,
   Take care, good luck, and do not fall.

Find the treasure under rocks and leaves,
   then be sure to re-hide it, if you please.

MOUNT TOM QUEST

ROOM WITH A VIEW QUEST 82

WOODSTOCK VT

To get there:

Take Exit 1 from I-89 and follow Route 4 west for about 10 miles to the village of Woodstock and the green. This Quest starts at the Woodstock green.

From the Woodstock village green . . .

Go south between twisting crab apples, look ahead way up high,
   go to the eagle high in the sky.

Turn east to white birches, then south again.
   Lilacs will accompany you to the end of the bend.

Left, over the river, follow the curve of the white picket fence,
   Your destination is immense.

At the end of this road stands a lined pole, 73 - 17.
   Turn left up the road here, it's more than it seems.

Eight cedars stand at the gate
   through which lies your final fate.

Hike up over roots on trail well worn to junction sign.
   The forked white pine shows the way to go (an old cement
     post behind).

A narrowing path loops around fallen trees,
   the trail bends 'round rocks pointing skyward among the leaves.

At knobby beech tree with sign, take a right
   to trails that form a triangle within your sight.

Your path takes you up between hemlock and ironwood (with
    peeling bark).
   Then right behind the big white pine (keep an eye out for the red mark).

Go along to a left place to enjoy lunch or brunch,
   then take a right toward the T. S. sign—follow your hunch.

Pass the "private property" sign—
   be courteous and you'll be fine.

WOODSTOCK VT
CONTINUED

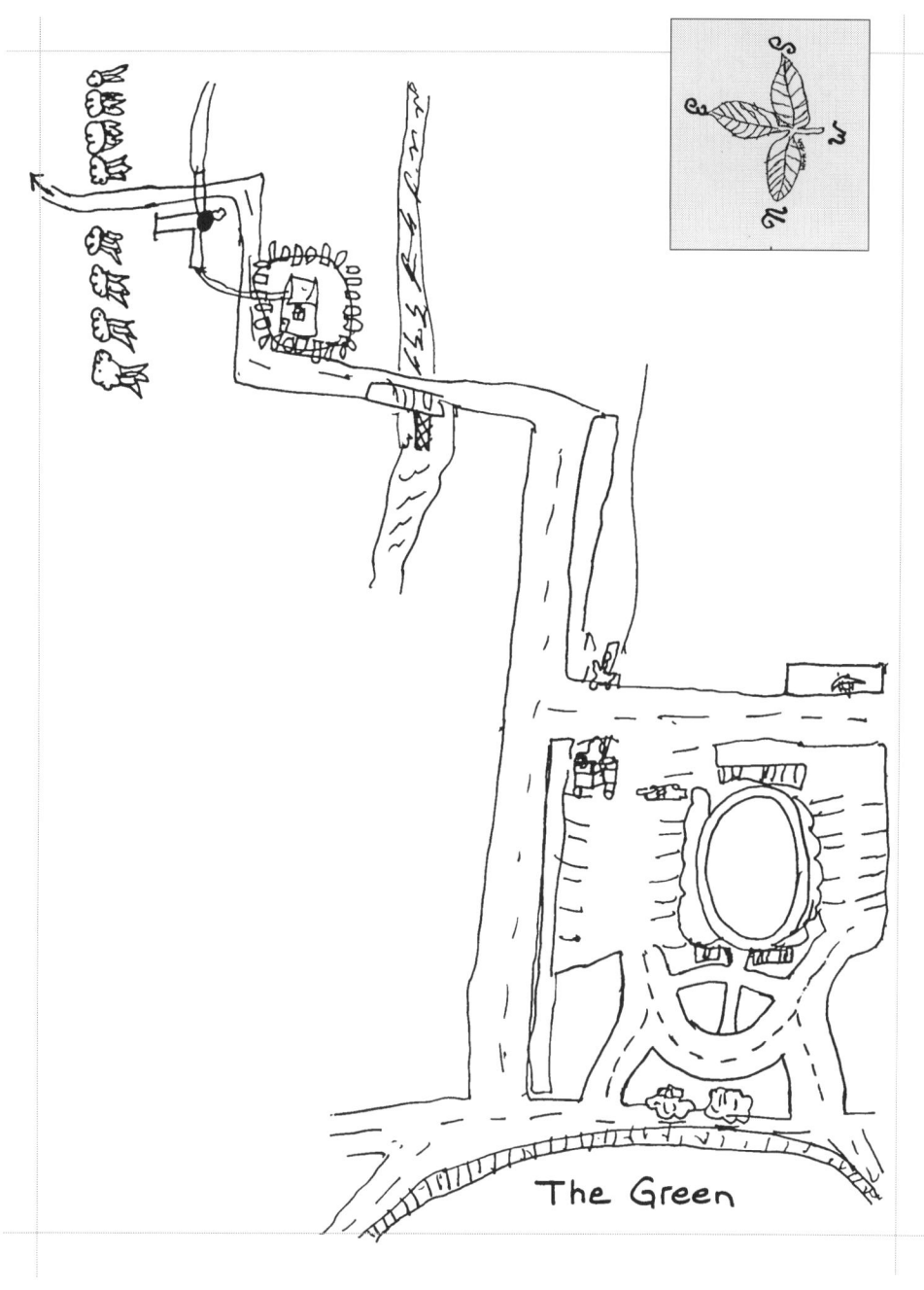

Through red pine plantation and under wires, a red blaze
  shows the way.

Keep on through, then cross clearing to the right, and climb to the sky
  to rest your weary bones away.

Turn opposite the arc of the curved log seat and head up the wooded trail,
  Find blazes on ironwood and oak, and you will not fail.

Somewhere between them lies a maple—with a home in its trunk.
  You will find the secret box if you root around like a skunk.

To return, follow signs to Golf Avenue.

ROOM WITH A VIEW QUEST 179

83
RSC QUEST

WOODSTOCK VT

To get there:

Take Exit 1 from I-89 and follow Route 4 west for about 10 miles to the village of Woodstock and the green. This Quest begins at the Woodstock green.

Go to the bridge that once burned down.
It's located in the center of town.

At the four corners go southwest.
Go round the bend, it's best for your Quest.

Keep to the side of the street with the homes.
If you're on the right track, you'll see one with a dome.

Look to the left where there's an old stone mill.
Then go to the right toward the hill.

Follow the road that is not paved.
In this direction much time can be saved.

At this place you can go hiking.
Lots of kids also use it for biking.

Take the high paved path all the way up around
Until you come down to a stone on which a man's name can be found.

As you continue on, hang a left and follow a stone wall.
Be careful not to trip or fall.

You'll see two posts with the head of a horse.
Now you know you're on the right course.

Keep going around the bend.
Soon your Quest will be at an end.

Four ways to choose, take the road you've not taken.
If you don't, you'll be mistaken.

Go to the place where you see all the stones.
If you dug it up, you would find lots of bones.

WOODSTOCK VT
CONTINUED

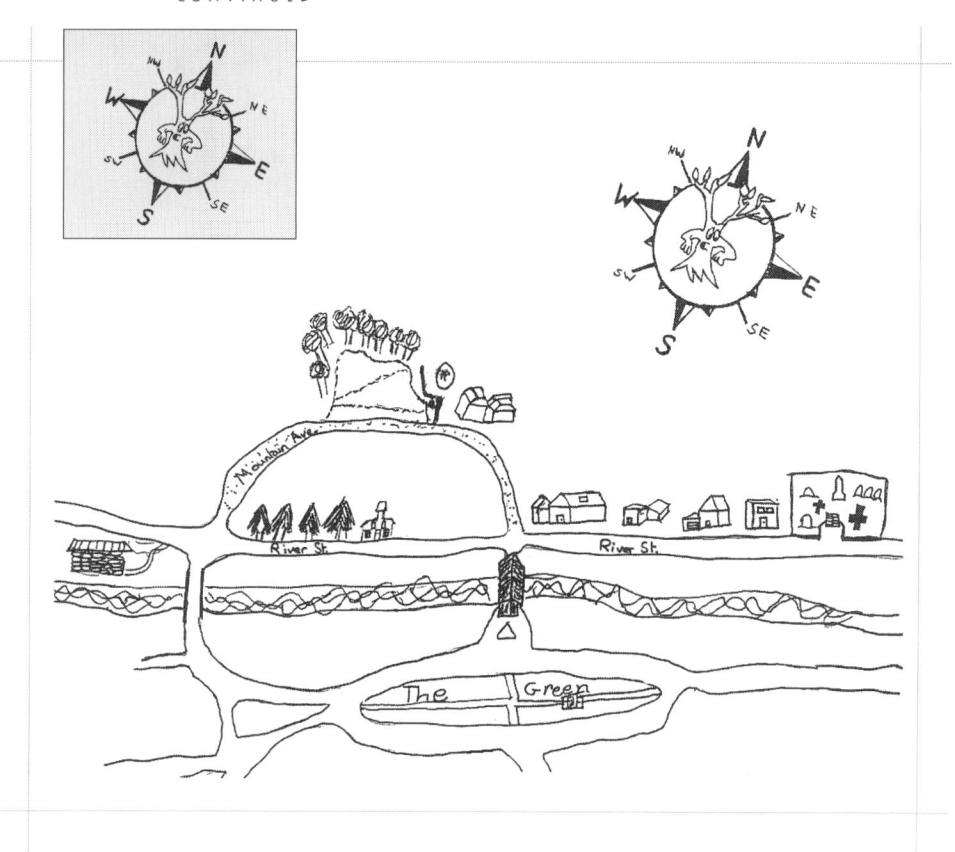

Go down the path if you are willing.
You'll see a stone with the name of Billings.

Walk a little to your left and try to see
The "star" that is hidden in the top of an old tree.

Now do a bit of counting, eight trunks are the key.
A hole is where you want to be.

84
VILLAGE GREEN QUEST A

WOODSTOCK VT

To get there:
Take Exit 1 from I-89 and follow Route 4 west for about 10 miles to the village of Woodstock and the green. Start at the Woodstock green.

Start at the green!

East down Route 4, do not stray,
    Cross two streets, to go stand across from a second floor
        window bay.
    Continue, go east, look for an over-water site, and then take
        the very first right.
    Go up, up, up a high street, go right at the white on a very thin street.
    Pass the old stone mill, clearly not on a hill,
    To the big brick wall standing still.
    Head left down the longer wall, around the curve, pass two windows
        and a door as well.
    Stand and look far at the Paul Revere bell.
    Head back to the road and up stream
    Across the bridge, next to the beam.
    Walk a little bit more, then look far to the "Dead End" sign.
    Pass between the pig and '62, then continue.
    Now go west to see the foot bridge come into view.
    Go over the brook and follow the trail
    Past tennis courts to the hip roof at Vail.
    This yellow slide cannot hide,
    Cross the street to a second yellow slide.
    On your way look with your eye,
    For a golden cross that sits way up high.
    Find WES on the wall,
    Cross South road and do not fall.
    Run for it, run for it,
    North past the cars underground
    And the end of your Quest will soon be found.
    Keep on going curve, curve, curve,
    White brick building tremendous swerve.
    Now look around for an eagle in the sky,
    Careful, 'cause it's not very high.
    Count forty-eight panes on the doors,
    Go straight up and into the very core.
    SLH will meet you and greet you,
    Now just go to the counter and ask,
    For this, for you, is the final task.

WOODSTOCK VT
CONTINUED

VILLAGE GREEN QUEST A   183

WOODSTOCK VT

VILLAGE GREEN QUEST B

85

To get there:

Take Exit 1 from I-89 and follow Route 4 west for about 10 miles to the village of Woodstock and the green. This Quest starts from the Woodstock green.

Across the Green, look for the sign
    Take South Street, it's not hard to find.
To the spot with a cross on the top,
    The most recent date is your *first stop*.
On to the school, a monument you'll see
    Under the eagle, two dates will be.
The eagle's beak on top you see,
    Points to Cross Street, where you should be.
Across the Kedron Brook you'll go
    Take some time to watch it flow.
Around the corner and up the hill
    To the left, don't lose your will.
An eight-sided cone is on the top
    Further along is House 21, your next stop.
Find 13, you're *not* out of luck
    Cross the footbridge, don't get stuck.
In days of old this was a mill
    Go to the left, don't be still.
To the end of the street, look up in the air,
    Find the Inn's weather instruments there.
Around the corner and to the right,
    The Dome of Justice is right in sight.
To the end of this street you will go
    Another right and don't be slow
At this building turn to the right
    A big granite rock is clear in sight.
MDCCCLXXXIII is on the top
    Around the side is where you'll stop.
The birds take shelter in the tree
    In their home is where I'll be!
Open up, take out the square,
    Return me carefully or *beware!*

WOODSTOCK VT
CONTINUED

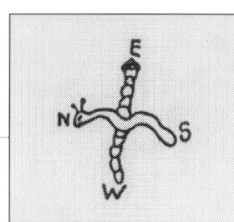

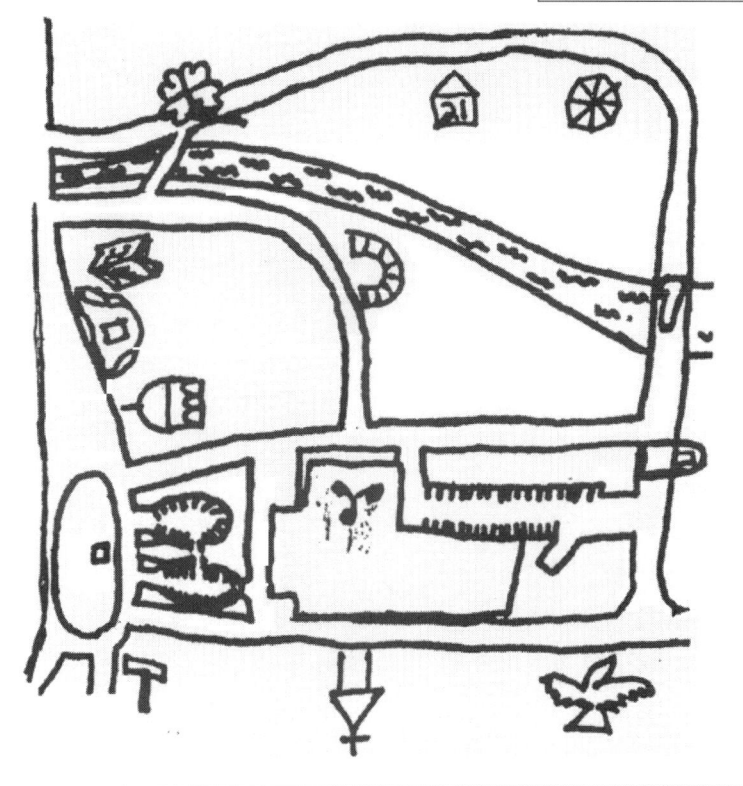

Around the corner

and to the right,

The Dome of Justice

is right in sight.

VILLAGE GREEN QUEST B   185

86
VILLAGE GREEN QUEST C

WOODSTOCK VT

To get there:

Take Exit 1 from I-89 and follow Route 4 west for about 10 miles to the village of Woodstock and the green. This Quest begins at the Woodstock green.

X marks the spot across the road from the Inn,
   then turn north and begin again.

Cross the crosswalk, keep heading north.
   It's a long salt box building where cars drive back and forth.

"Slippery When Wet" the sign will say.
   Walk through this structure and you'll be on your way.

Walk down the sidewalk to a conical roof.
   Turn to your right and there is your proof.

Walk east on the sidewalk to where it ends.
   You'll see a three-arched house with lots of bends.

Cross the street, please don't cry.
   You'll see the place where many have died.

Continue on down to the Billings Park trail.
   Keep on going and you will not fail.

Don't go north, for North Road will end.
   Cross over, keep going up around the bend.

Pass the twin houses, continue on.
   Notice the river down past the lawn.

Continue up the sidewalk along the rail that's green.
   A sign that says "Bike Route" should certainly be seen.

Turn south and face this enormous structure.
   Aren't you amazed at its beautiful architecture?

WOODSTOCK VT
CONTINUED

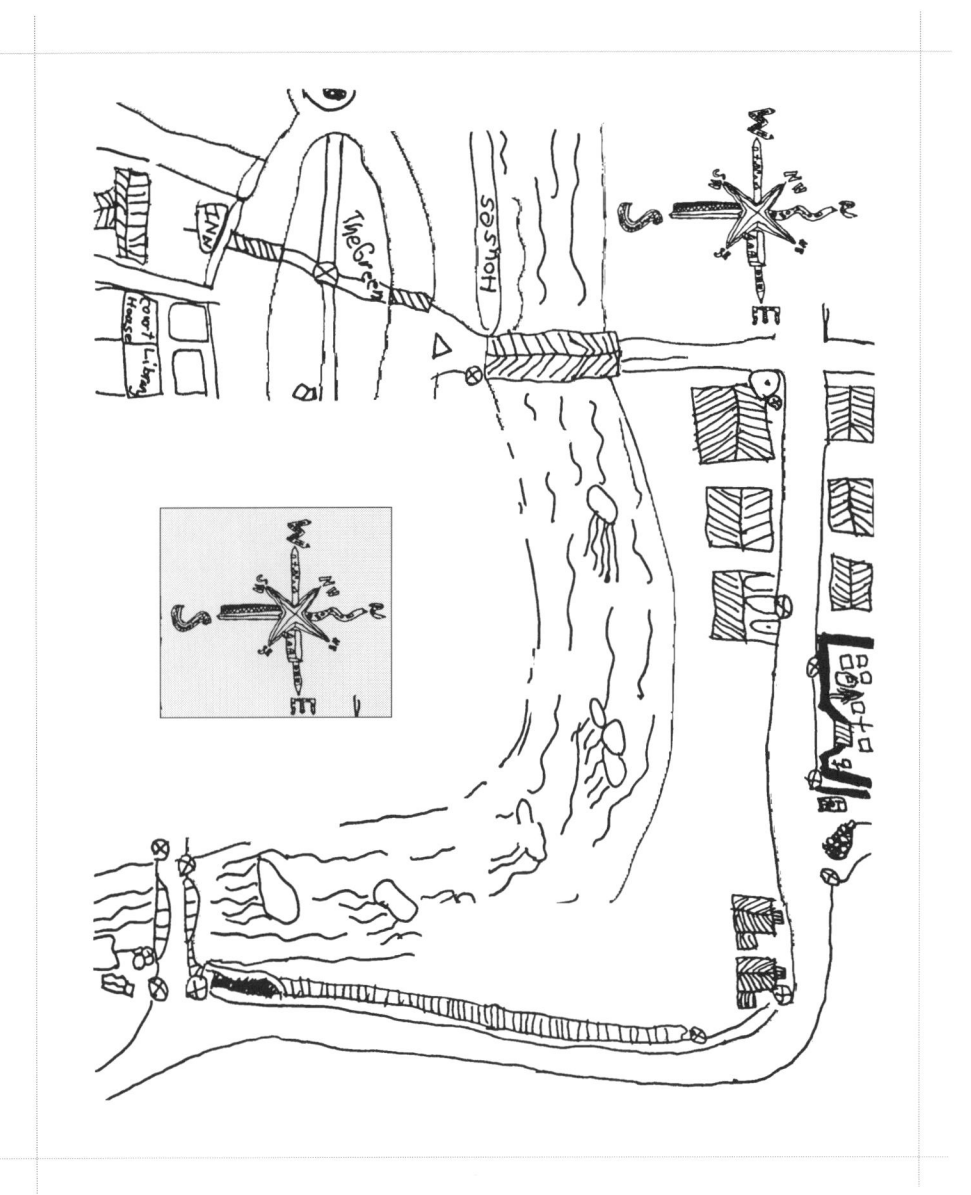

Hold on to the railing as you're going across.
    Give thanks to its contributor Douglas Ross.

Cross over the river to the end of the rail.
    Cross the road and you're on the right trail.

Believe it or not, we ask you once more
    To cross over the river away from the stores.

Three stone steps will be in sight.
    You need to go down them and turn to the right.

Up off the ground a little house will be found.
    Look in it to find something to expand your mind.

VILLAGE GREEN QUEST C

VILLAGE GREEN QUEST D

87

WOODSTOCK VT

To get there:

Take Exit 1 from I-89 and follow Route 4 west for about 10 miles to the village of Woodstock and the green. This Quest begins at the Woodstock green.

Leave the Green heading east
   Look for the store of the Mythical Beast
   Cross the street, take a right
   Looking for windows at a very low height.

Now pass the place where you might get your mail
   Keep on going and you shall not fail.
   Bond Street is left, Lincoln is right
   Keep going straight, your next goal is in sight.

Where cannon balls flew, you'll make a sharp "U"
   Head toward the "Time" that has Mt. Tom behind.
   But, before you head out to the next spot,
   Play it safe and use the crosswalk!

When you pass "1840" below the bird
   The sound of the river can be heard.
   You are on the right path, you can tell
   When you've reached one of Woodstock's five Revere bells.

Head west towards 4, past "1810"
   Go past "1807," then turn in.
   P&P is the place to be
   And behind a treasure you shall see!

Head 'round the back to the open field
   And at the river you'll finally yield:
   And somewhere near a central tree
   You're sure to solve this mystery.

(In case you don't know where it's at, we've enclosed a little map.)

WOODSTOCK VT
CONTINUED

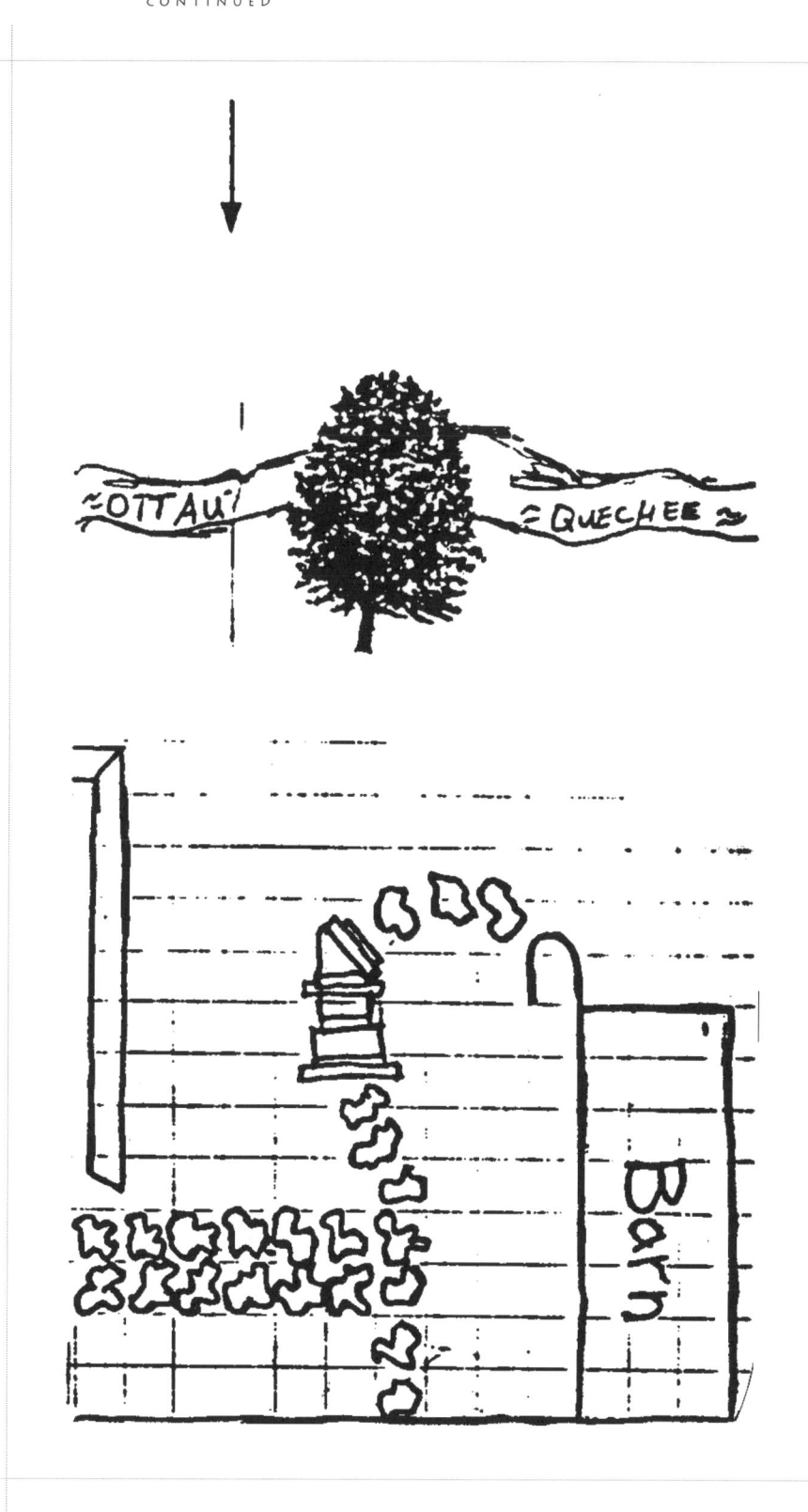

VILLAGE GREEN QUEST D

VILLAGE GREEN QUEST E

WOODSTOCK VT

To get there:

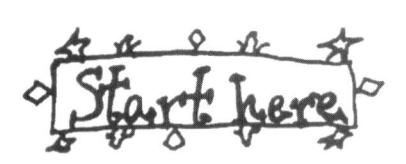

Take Exit 1 from I-89 and follow Route 4 west for about 10 miles to the village of Woodstock and the green. This Quest begins at the Woodstock green.

Start here

Stand at the Info Booth on the green
    Where two nearby mountains can be seen.
    With Mt. Peg on your left—small, green, and round,
    And Mt. Tom on your right—tall, cliffy, and brown,
    Start on down the path, headed straight out of town.

At the very first crosswalk to the right that you see
    cross over and walk left to solve our mystery.

Stay on the sidewalk to the right of Route 4,
    go to a place where you can see movies galore.
    This is also a place for all our town meetings,
    Where neighbors and friends can exchange friendly greetings.
    Number of big columns on the front of this building = ☐
                                                                     A

Stay on Route 4 as it curves out of sight,
    'Til you come to a building that's totally white.
    Don't worry, don't cry, you'll know that you're there,
    When you see this white building point high in the air.
    Number of matching doors on the front of this building = ☐
                                                                     B

Continue on to a place where you can stand on air
    And look over the edge if you want a big scare.
    Listen upstream and to the right for a hint of your glory.
    Number of thin, round poles in each section of the railing = ☐
                                                                                 C

As Route 4 curves to the left, stay by its path,
    Cross "River" then "Mountain," then prepare for some math.
    At the crosswalk up to your left, cross over Route 4,
    You're getting very warm, just a little bit more.

WOODSTOCK VT
CONTINUED

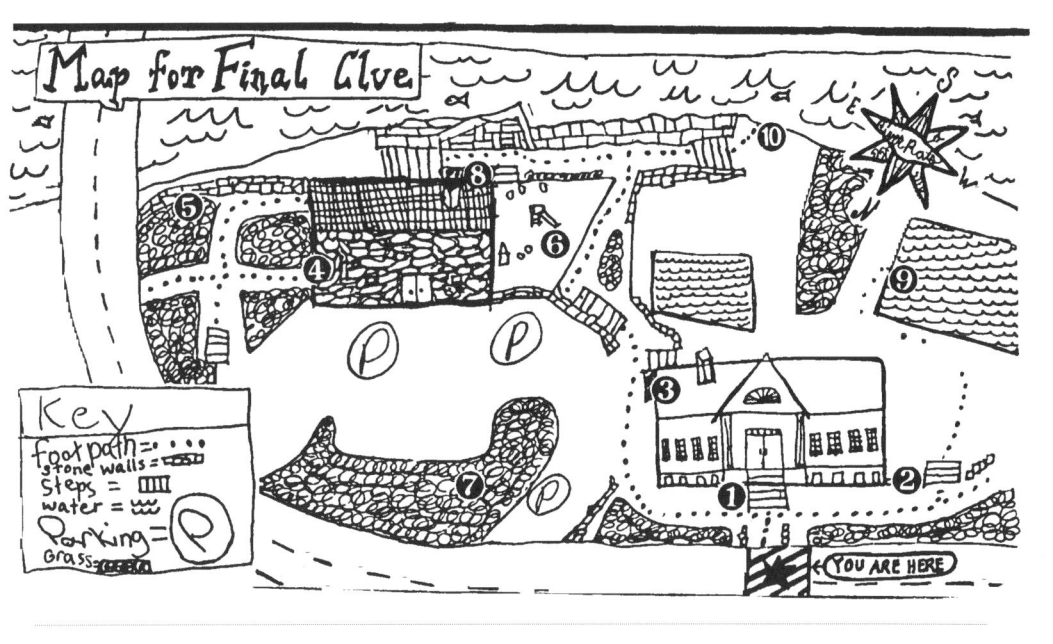

'Look over the edge if you want a big scare.

Listen upstream and to the right for a hint of your glory'

Take your answer for "A" and add it to "B,"
   Together they'll give you an answer that's "D."
   Now subtract "D" from "C," but don't tell a soul,
   Go to this number on your map, you'll be at your goal!

☐ + ☐ = ☐
A   B   D

Then

☐ − ☐ = Magic Number!
C   D

We hope you've enjoyed our Valley Quest,
   If you keep it a secret, we'll think you're the best!

VILLAGE GREEN QUEST E   191

89
VERMONT INSTITUTE OF NATURAL SCIENCE QUEST

WOODSTOCK VT

To get there:
Go around the Woodstock green and turn right onto Church Hill Road. VINS is located up the hill 1¼ miles ahead on the right. You *will need a compass for this Quest.* Please note: VINS will be closed to the public as of 10/31/02. After that date contact VINS at (802) 457-2779 to arrange to do this Quest.

Come follow the clues to our Nature Quest box.
    Enjoy our preserve, notice birds, trees, and rocks.
    And animals too of all shapes and sizes
    As you follow the land through its wallows and rises.

Begin your search at our Natural Trails sign.
    Head toward the pond but not straight in a line.
    There's a left as you pass our picture display
    At VINS we band birds as they go on their way.
    Now follow this path up a slight slippery slope.
    Onward you go and never lose hope!

There's a stone wall alongside you and the pond on your right
    But keep looking left 'til you find a small flight.
    They are wooden stairs that lead to a trail.
    Ignore the "Don't Enter," you won't go to jail.
    Dots mark the way and they shouldn't be red.
    If they are yellow, you've hit the nail on the head!

Follow them up a steep climbing hill
    Winding through forest and shady wood chill.
    Up to the clearing and there in the sun
    A post with a "W," you're close to the fun!
    Follow the path past a hollowed-out tree
    Until you find a post with a "V."

Now use your compass, find 320 degrees.
    Follow that heading past big maple trees.
    Can you see the stone wall that you're headed toward?
    It's there that you'll find your treasure reward!
    There's a gap in the wall that looks like a gate
    You're almost there but you still have to wait.

WOODSTOCK VT
CONTINUED

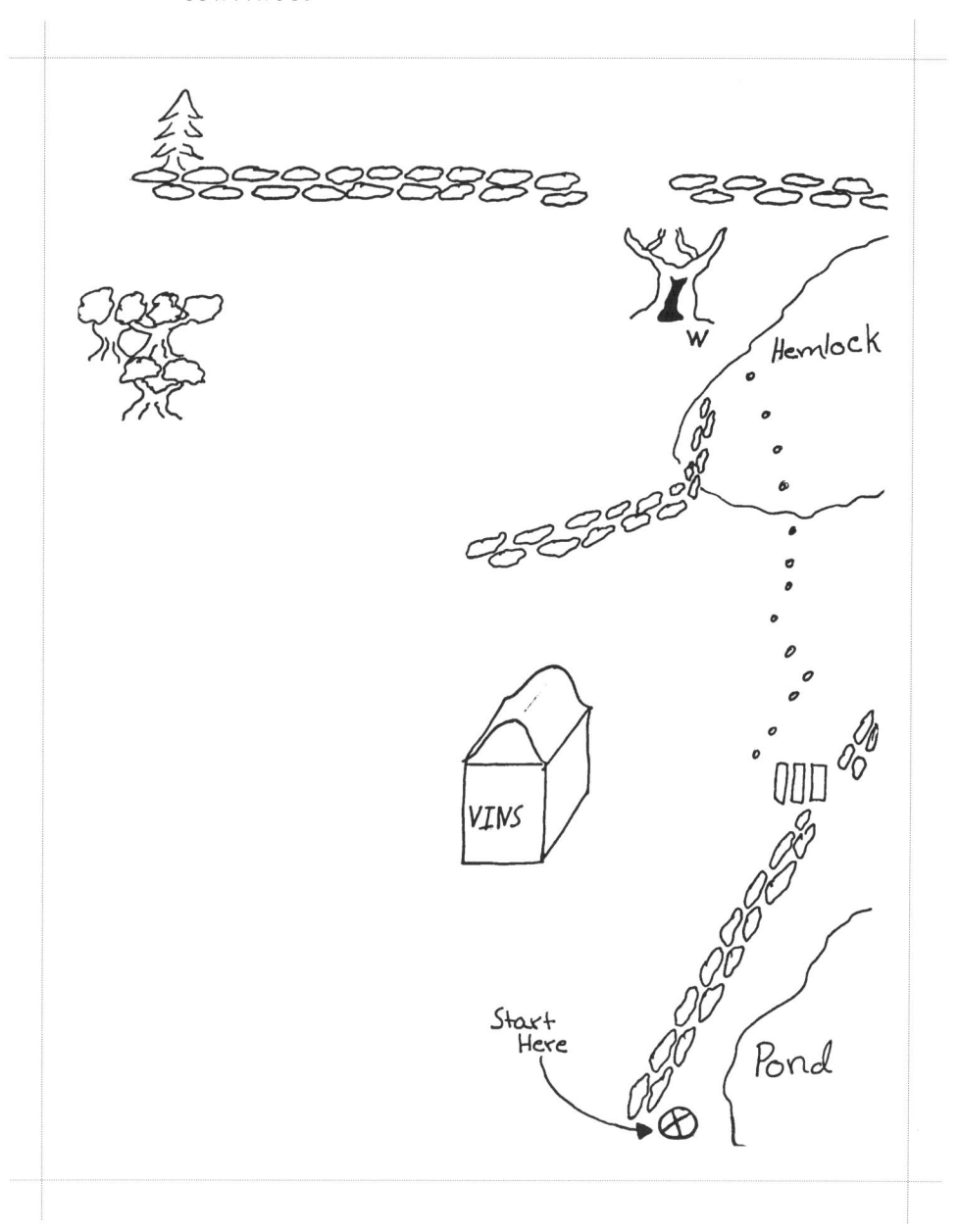

Go through the gap and turn to the left
   To find this treasure you have to be deft!
   Follow the wall and keep your eye bright.
   Look for a rock that's stunning quartz white.
   Now you've done it, so look around
   You're in the spot where the treasure is found!

Onward you go and never lose hope

VERMONT INSTITUTE OF NATURAL SCIENCE QUEST

QUEST DIRECTORY

KEY

SPECIAL FEATURES	WALKING CONDITIONS	PHYSICAL DIFFICULTY	OPTIONAL GEAR	SEASON
A=Architectural	I=Indoor	E=Easy	B=Binoculars	A–N=Apr. 22–Nov. 15
H=Historical	P=Pavement	M=Moderate	Bi=Bicycle	YR=Year-round
N=Natural	T=Trail	D=Difficult	Ca=Canoe	
V=Vista			Co=Compass	
			F=Field Guide	
			S=Swimsuit	

Quest Number, Name, & Location	Estimated Duration	Special Features	Walking Conditions	Physical Difficulty	Optional Gear	Season	Date Created
BELLOWS FALLS, VT							
1 History Quest	1 hr.	A, H	P	M		A–N	2000
CORNISH, NH							
2 Blacksmith Bridge	20 min.	A, H, N	T	M	Co	A–N	2000
3 Blow Me Down Mill	20 min.	H, N	P, T	E	B, Co	A–N	1998
4 Trinity Church	15 min.	H	I, T	E		YR	1998
5 Wyman Sawmill	20 min.	H, N	T	E	Co, F	A–N	2000
CROYDON, NH							
6 Croydon Schoolhouse	10 min.	H	P	E		A–N	1997
7 Croydon's Past	1.5 hrs.	H, N	T	M	F	A–N	1998
8 Four Corner Cemetery	15 min.	H	T	E	B, F	A–N	1997
ENFIELD, NH							
9 Rail Trail	1.5 hrs.	H, N, V	T	M	B, Co	A–N	2000
10 Shaker Village	45 min.	H, N, V	T	M	Co	A–N	1998
FAIRLEE, VT							
11 Fairlee Depot	20 min.	H	P	E		A–N	2000
12 Fairlee Glen Falls	30 min.	N	T	M	F	A–N	2000
13 Miraculous Trees	45 min.	N	P, T	M	B, F	A–N	2000
14 Palisades	1 hr.	H, N, V	T	D	B	A–N	1998
GRAFTON, VT							
15 Grafton Ponds	45 min.	N, V	T	M	B, F	YR	2000
16 The Cave	1 hr.	H, N	T	M	F	A–N	2000
GRANTHAM, NH							
17 Dunbar Hill Cemetery	1.25 hrs.	H	P	M		A–N	1999
HANOVER, NH							
18 Amphitheater	20 min.	H, N	P, T	E		YR	1999
19 Balch Hill	1 hr.	N, V	T	D	B, F	A–N	1998
20 Libraries of Hanover	45 min.	A, H	P	M		YR	2000
21 Mink Brook	1 hr.	N	T	M	B, F	A–N	2000
22 Moose Mountain	2+ hrs.	N, V	T	D	B, Co, F	A–N	2000
23 Velvet Rocks	1.5 hrs.	N, V	T	D	B, F	A–N	1999
HARTFORD, VT							
24 Historical Museum	1.75 hrs.	H	I	E		YR	1999
25 Recycling	30 min.	N	P	E		YR	2000

QUEST NUMBER, NAME, & LOCATION	ESTIMATED DURATION	SPECIAL FEATURES	WALKING CONDITIONS	PHYSICAL DIFFICULTY	OPTIONAL GEAR	SEASON	DATE CREATED
HARTLAND, VT							
26 Three Corners	45 min.	H	P	E		A–N	1999
LEBANON, NH							
27 Colburn Park	45 min.	H	P	E		YR	1998
28 Runnemede School	45 min.	A, H		E		A–N	1998
LYME, NH							
29 Pinnacle Hill	1 hr.	N, V	T	D	B, Co, F	A–N	1997
30 Sheep Quest	1 hr.	H, N	T	D	Co, F	A–N	2000
NEWBURY, NH							
31 Hay Refuge	45 min.	A, H, N	T	M		A–N	1998
NEW LONDON, NH							
32 Sargent/Hayes Farm	1.25 hr.	H, N	T	D	B, F	A–N	2000
33 Wolf Tree	1.25 hr.	H, N, V	T	D	B, F	A–N	2000
NORWICH, VT							
34 Elm Street Loop	45 min.	H	P	M	Co	YR	1998
35 Gile Mountain	1.5 hrs.	N, V	T	D	B, F	A–N	2000
36 Grand Canyon	45 min.	N	T	M	Co, F	A–N	1998
37 Montshire	30 min.	N	T	E		A–N	2000
ORFORD, NH							
38 Boat Landing	25 min.	N	P, T	E	Ca	A–N	1999
39 Brick Quest	30 min.	A, H	P	E		A–N	2000
40 Flat Rock	15 min.	N	T	E	B, Ca, Co, S	A–N	1998
41 Indian Pond	15 min.	N	T	E	B, Ca, Co, S	A–N	1997
PLAINFIELD, NH							
42 French's Ledges	1 hr.	N, V	T	D	B, F	A–N	1997
43 Plainfield Village	45 min.	H	P	E		A–N	1998
QUECHEE, VT							
44 Old Quechee Cemetery	30 min.	H	P	E		A–N	1998
45 Ottauquechee	45 min.	H	P, T	M		A–N	1999
46 Quechee Gorge	50 min.	N	T	M		A–N	1998
47 Quechee Library	20 min.	H	P	E		YR	1998
48 Simon Pearce Waterfall	30 min.	N	P	E		A–N	1998
ROCKINGHAM, VT							
49 Meeting House	25 min.	H	T	E	Co	A–N	2000
SPRINGFIELD, NH							
50 Kidder Brook	1.75 hrs.	H, N	T	D	Co, F	A–N	2000
51 McDaniel's Marsh	15 min.	N	T	E	B, Ca, F, S	A–N	1997
SPRINGFIELD, VT							
52 North Springfield Bog	20 min.	N	T	E	B, Co, F	A–N	1998
53 Springweather A	40 min.	N, V	T	M	B, Co	A–N	1999
54 Springweather B	40 min.	N, V	T	M	Co	A–N	1999
SUNAPEE, NH							
55 Sunapee Harbor	20 min.	N, H	P	M	B, Ca, Co	A–N	1998
THETFORD, VT							
56 Houghton Hill	45 min.	N, V	T	D	B, F	A–N	2000

QUEST NUMBER, NAME, & LOCATION	ESTIMATED DURATION	SPECIAL FEATURES	WALKING CONDITIONS	PHYSICAL DIFFICULTY	OPTIONAL GEAR	SEASON	DATE CREATED
(THETFORD, VT, CONT.)							
57 Lonesome Pine	45 min.	H, N	T	M	B, F	A–N	2000
58 Moving Houses	15 min.	A, H	P	E		A–N	2000
59 Peabody Library	15 min.	H	I	E		YR	2000
60 Thetford Canoe	1.5 hrs.	N		M	B, Ca, S	A–N	1998
61 Union Village	25 min.	N	T	M	B, F, S	A–N	2000
VERSHIRE, VT							
62 Copperfield Town	45 min.	H	P, T	E	Co	A–N	2000
63 Vershire Village	1 hr.	A, H, V	P, T	D	B	A–N	1999
WALPOLE, NH							
64 Fall Mountain	1.5 hrs.	N, V	T	D	B, F	A–N	2000
WARREN, NH							
65 Moosilauke Historical	1 hr.	H, N	T	D	B, F	A–N	2000
WEATHERSFIELD, VT							
66 Crystal Cascade	2 hrs.	N	T	D	B, F	A–N	1999
WEST FAIRLEE, VT							
67 Linny's Loop Bicycle	2 hrs.	H, N	P	D	B, Co, F, S	A–N	2000
WEST LEBANON, NH							
68 Boston Lot	45 min.	N	T	M		A–N	1998
69 Dana House	15 min.	H	P	E		A–N	1998
WHEREVER YOU WISH NH/VT							
70 Fall Cider	All day	H, N	T	M		A–N	2000
WHITE RIVER JUNCTION, VT							
71 By the Numbers	20 min.	A, H	P	M		YR	2000
72 Junction Quest	30 min.	H, N	P, T	M		YR	1999
73 Lyman Point	25 min.	H, N	P, T	M	F	A–N	2000
WINDSOR, VT							
74 Constitution House	1 hr.	H, N	P, T	E		A–N	1999
75 Historic Windsor	1.25 hrs.	H	P	M		A–N	1999
76 North Main Street	1 hr.	A, H	P	E		A–N	1999
77 Paradise Park	1 hr.	N	T	E	B, Co, F	A–N	1999
WOODSTOCK, VT							
78 CWM	30 min.	H	P	M		A–N	2000
79 G, F & L Quest	45 min.	H	P	M		A–N	2000
80 GPM	25 min.	A, H	P	E		A–N	1999
81 Mount Tom	1 hr.	N, V	T	D	B, F	A–N	1997
82 Room with a View	1 hr.	N, V	P, T	D	B, F	A–N	1999
83 RSC	25 min.	A, H	P	E		A–N	1998
84 Village Green A	40 min.	A, H	P	E		YR	1997
85 Village Green B	30 min.	A, H	P	M		A–N	1998
86 Village Green C	30 min.	A, N	P, T	E		YR	1997
87 Village Green D	40 min.	A, H	P	E		A–N	1997
88 Village Green E	40 min.	A, N	P, T	E		A–N	1997
89 VINS	50 min.	N	T	M	B, F	A–N	1997

HOW TO MAKE A QUEST

We invite you to create your own Quest. You may create a Quest in your backyard for your friends and family—or you can create a Quest as an offering to the greater community. We hope you will choose to do the latter, and submit a copy of it to us for possible publication in the next edition of Valley Quest! Here's how to do it!

1. Pick a spot that is a special place for you, perhaps a unique natural or cultural feature of your town.

2. Find out who owns or manages this property and request permission to make a Quest there.

3. Make a few trips to the site to uncover its details, and to begin to think about the best approaches to making a Quest there.

4. Find people in your community who can teach you more about your site—community elders, members of your town historical society or conservation commission. Invite them to take a trip out on the land with you.

5. Take good notes!

6. Decide on your Quest strategy: a detailed map Quest; a map-less Quest; a jumble Quest (collecting words); a pict-o-Quest (no words—only following pictures!). Or any combination. Use your imagination and creativity—it's up to you!

7. Draw rough maps of your site. Also sketch or note the unique features that would make good clues.

8. Make a rough draft of your Quest Map and riddles or accompanying text.

9. Test your Quest with as many different people as you can get to try it out—and make appropriate changes as necessary.

10. Create a written description of what makes the site special. This should come from your research and should only be a few paragraphs long—small enough to be laminated and glued inside the cover of the Quest Box. You can focus on whatever you think visitors to the site will be most interested in. Depending on the site, possible things to write about include: the historical significance of the site to the town; a true story about something that once

happened at the site; the natural history of the site—trees to look for, special rocks, plantings, etc.; why people in your town love this site so much; fun or interesting things to do; amazing-but-true trivia facts about the site (height of steeple, age of building, number of orchid species, number of granite blocks and where they came from, etc.).

11. Polish final Quest Map and clues.

12. Design a logo for the stamp for the site and carve it into a plastic eraser or make a stamp out of rubber and wood.

13. Get a waterproof box to use as a Quest Box. Waterproof the introduction to the site and attach it securely to the inside cover of the box. Label the outside of the box with a water-proofed copy of the Valley Quest label. Place in the box: a log book; pencil/pen; stamp; ink pad; pencil sharpener.

14. Hide the box

15. Make sure you have someone adopt the box for long-term monitoring, and supply Valley Quest staff with their name and phone number.

16. Fill out the Valley Quest Submission Form that follows, and send your Quest in for possible publication in the next edition of Valley Quest!

NEW QUEST SUBMISSION FORM

Thank you so much for taking the time, energy, and creativity to create a Valley Quest Treasure Hunt! We appreciate your persistence, as well as your offering of generosity toward our community. Quests offer a unique way to share special places and special stories with those we may never meet, may never know.

In order to make sure everything is complete—and also ensure that your Quest is included in the next edition of the Valley Quest Map Book—we ask you to please take a moment to review the following checklist, answer a few questions, and return this form to:

>Valley Quest Coordinator
>Vital Communities
>104 Railroad Row
>White River Junction, VT 05001
>802-291-9100 / E-mail: info@vitalcommunities.org

CHECKLIST:

___Original Map Art

___Clues (that have been tested, to make sure they work! On disk please, or by E-mail)

___Compass rose, indicating North (if necessary)

___Precise directions to the Quest's starting point

___Landowner permission (if required):
   Name _____ Phone _____

___Estimation of time required to complete Quest (round trip): _____

___Degree of difficulty: ___Easy   ___Moderate   ___Difficult

___Special features (check all that apply):   ___Architectural   ___Historical   ___Natural   ___Vista

___Walking conditions: ___Indoor   ___Pavement   ___Trail
   Other _____

___Optional Gear: ___Canoe   ___Compass   ___Bike   ___Binoculars
   Other _____

___Season (please check one)   ___April–November   ___Year-round

___Treasure Box complete: ___Box   ___Stamp   ___Stamp Pad   ___Sign-in book   ___Other

___Treasure Box placed out there: ___Yes   ___No

___Quest Box Monitor: Name _____
Address _____
Phone _____ E-mail _____

___"Cheater's directions," i.e., the exact location of box for prompt monitoring—or helping frustrated callers find their treasure:

ACKNOWLEDGMENTS

"The journey of a thousand miles begins with a single step." Valley Quest has been made possible through the time, generosity, commitment, and steps taken by so many wonderful people and organizations.

This book is possible because of the generosity and support of: The Anne Slade Frey Charitable Trust, the Byrne Foundation, Connecticut River Joint Commissions Partner Program, The Donley Foundation, Friendship Fund, Furthermore Fund, Globe Fund, A. D. Henderson Foundation, the Kitchel McLaughlin Family Fund, the League of Women Voters Education Fund, The Lilla Fund, Lyme Foundation, Mascoma Savings Bank Foundation, the National Park Service Rivers, Trails and Conservation Assistance Program, Newfound Foundation, New Hampshire Charitable Foundation, Ellis L. Phillips Foundation, The Robins Foundation, The Spirit in Community Fund, Stettenheim Foundation, Sudbury Foundation, the U.S. Environmental Protection Agency, the Upper Valley Community Foundation, the Vermont Community Foundation, and the Windham Foundation—as well as the contributions of hundreds of individuals, families, and businesses.

There would be no Quests without the hard work, good fun, and contribution of students, teachers, school staff, and community members from thirty-one towns across two states. Thank you, to each and every one of you, named or un-named: Mary Grove and the students at the Compass School in Westminster; Ros Seidel and the students in her Cornish Elementary School Valley Quest Exploratory; Linda Fuerst and her 4th graders; Judy Hatch's 1st–3rd grade class; the homeschooling family of Dale Shields, John Auble, and their kids Cecilia, Nathan, and Devin; Mary Ellen Burrit's Girl Scout troop; Rebecca Bailey and the Fairlee school 3rd and 4th graders; Linny Levin's 5th and 6th grade class; Joyce Berube's Girl Scout troop; Nan Parsons' 4th and 5th grade; Lynn Ujlaky's 2nd and 4th grade reading buddies; Cathy MacDonald and Pam Graham's Girl Scout troop; participants in the Howe Library Centennial Celebration; Ginger Wallis, Linny Levin, and Jay Davis; Marjorie Rose and Betsy Davis's Hanover Brownie troop; Mitsu Chobanian's Girl Scout troop; Pat Stark; Victoria Davis; Jill Janas and Marilyn Mock's 5th grade; students at the Runnemede School; Lynn Bischoff's 4th grade; Steven Dayno and Sara Goodman's 4th grade classes in Lyme; Maggie Stier and Loa Winter; Meredith Bird Miller; T. J. Grossman, Ryan McCabe, and Elaine Warshell; Amy Vanderkooi; Sue Kling's 2nd grade classes; Gary Barton's 4th grade students; Betsy Rybeck Lynd's 2nd grade class; Mindy (Longacre) Taber's 3rd grade class; Amy Kinder's 5th grade; Sarah Rhoades and Ellen Bantin's 5th grade class; Cathie Ely's 5th grade; Philip Major's class at Kearsarge Regional Elementary School; Steve Pruyne; Marita Johnson's 7th grade; students of Marita Johnson and Mike Frank; Bill Shepard; Joe Deffner's 7th grade students; children of the Peabody Library After School Program; Kristin Brown and Stuart Close; Barbara Griffin's 2nd and 3rd grade class; Becky French's 5th grade class; Sue Kirincich and Chuck Wooster; Wendy Smith; Ted Levin; Phyllis Wolford's 5th grade; Rickey Poor's 1st grade; Marty Layman-Mendonca; Karen Hull's 4th grade; Tim Ives' 4th grade; Linda Parker's 4th grade; Barbara Rhoad; John Souter's many students in Woodstock; Jamie MacDonald; Ms. Bahlenhorst's 4th grade; Kathy Sehnal's 4th graders; Shirley Burrough's 4th graders; Richard Burrough's 6th grade; Cindy Siegler's 3rd grade; Jill Holran's 3rd grades; and the 1997 Student Naturalist Program at VINS!

We appreciate the support and dedication of our Valley Quest box monitors: Hannah Humpal, Emily Miller, Jen Smith, Mary Ellen Burrit, Elizabeth and Joyce Berube, Nan Parsons, Pam Graham, Mitsu Chobanian, Pat Stark, Linda Becker, Janet Sweezey, Michael Jenkins, Sarah Cram, Loa Winter, T. J. Grossman, Sue Kling, Wendy Johnson, Mindy Taber, Kate Schall, Delia Clark, Marita Johnson, Mike Frank, Meredith Bird Miller, Kristin Brown, Stuart Close, Wendy Smith, Barbara Rhoad, Karen Hull, Tim Ives, Linda Parker, Rosemary and James McGinty, Tyson, Bruce, and Meg Seely, Mary and Talia Roy, Sally Miller, Betty Walker, Heather Behrens, Sheila Swett, and Sarah Schwaegler.

Many thanks to the Valley Quest Council: Carola Lea, Ted Levin, Sylvia Provost, Deborah Stanley, and Diana Wright.

A VERY BIG THANK YOU to Delia Clark, Sue Kirincich, Linny Levin, Betty Porter, Sylvia Provost, David Sobel, John Souter, Maggie Steir, and Ginger Wallis—for lighting, carrying, and passing along the Valley Quest torch.

The editor wishes to extend his personal thanks for the encouragement and assistance of: Jim Sheridan, Gary Barton, Sheila Moran, Teddy Reichert, Carl Schmidt, Doug Tifft, the Orford Historical Society, Roxanne Barbeau, Peter Blodgett, Olivia Chapman, Joseph Deffner, Uri Harel, Charles Latham, Jr., Ted Levin, the Marshall family, Bill Shepard, Ginger Wallis, the Thetford Historical Society, David Briggs, Byron Hathorn, Alice Adams, Rebecca Bailey, Jay Barrett, Hester Gardner, Dick Hodge, Russ Smith, Noelle Vitt, Georgette Wolf-Ludwig, the Fairlee Historical Society, Richard Ewald, Mary Grove, Ros Seidel, Mitsu Chobanian, John Souter, Marge Brittner, Nick Brunette, Lila DeCoste, Sabra Ewing, Barb Griffin, Kathy Hooke, Naomi LaBarr, Ernie Parker, Alfred Balch, Charles Balch, Don Cooke, Steve Dayno, Ken Elder, Sara Goodman, Bob Green, Carola Lea, Don Metz, Dorf Sears, Mike Smith, Mark Steyn, the Lyme Historians, Lyme Timber Company, the staff in the Lyme Town Office, Meredith Bird Miller, Paul Sawyer, Andy Williams, Deb Williams, Paul Bruhn, Lisa Cashdan, Judy Hayward, Kate Read, Jim Schley, Glenn Britton, Roberto Rodriguez, Chris Hill, Sharon Francis, Helene Tingle, Carol Barleon, Mark Kutolowski, Mary Wilson, Binx Selby, Linda Fong, Len Cadwallader, Lisa Johnson, Lizann Peyton, Jennifer Schiffman, Heather Trillium, and my friends at Living Education.

Much gratitude to our good friends at GDT for their generous assistance and map-making expertise: Don Cooke, Chris Mabey, and Rich Beier.

Thank you, Rachael Cohen, for your assistance in proofreading and editing this manuscript.

Thanks (and a bear hug) to Ted Levin, for your magnificent cover photography.

And to Suzanne Church, Design Master: Thanks so much, great fun, and "You rock!"

Thank you, Delia, and Vital Communities, for the work of a lifetime.

For 2nd printing revisions a big "thank you" to: Simon Brooks, Dale Shields and John Auble, Monique Cleland, Karen and Russ Davis, Liz and Paul Sunde, David Kotz and David Glueck.

Last and most: Much love and gratitude to my partners on the big Quest: Stacey, Kayla, and Emma.

happy questing!

STAMP HERE

QUEST: DATE:	QUEST: DATE:	QUEST: DATE:
QUEST: DATE:	QUEST: DATE:	QUEST: DATE:
QUEST: DATE:	QUEST: DATE:	QUEST: DATE:
QUEST: DATE:	QUEST: DATE:	QUEST: DATE: